NEW ASIAN CUISINE

Fabulous Recipes from Celebrity Chefs

Wendy Chan & Grace Niwa

Commentaries by Joyce Jue ■ Edited by Andrea Rademan

First edition, January 2006

ISBN: 0-9772370-0-1
ISBN: 9-780977-237005

■

Created and produced by
Savory Productions, Inc.
1375 Broadway, #405
New York, NY 10018
www.savoryproductions.com

Published by
International Food, Wine & Travel Writers Association
1142 South Diamond Bar Boulevard, #177
Diamond Bar, CA 91765-2203
www.ITWTWA.org

■

NOTE: This book is not a publication of the USDA (United States Department of Agriculture.)
The new Food Pyramid, the MyPyramid dietary guidelines and the MyPyramid symbol are public information. Materials are available on www.mypyramid.gov. The USDA does not endorse any products, services or organizations. For more information, please visit www.mypyramid.gov.

Front Cover: Photo by Ray Grefe, featuring "Origami Salmon" by Chef Chris Yeo, Straits Restaurant, San Jose, CA

Cover and book design: Jessica Ellis of Jellisdesign

Printed in the United States of America

AN APPRECIATION

DAVID SHAW
(1943-2005)

David Shaw's joyous appetite sprang from a heart and mind as grand as a twenty-course Asian banquet. In the more playful of his two *Los Angeles Times* columns, "Matters of Taste," he combined the eye of a Pulitzer Prize-winning reporter with his gusto for the world's table and an appreciation of its gifts: sustenance, camaraderie, journey, sanctuary, pleasure.

A frequent traveler, he planned his trips first on where he would dine and only second on what he might see en route. "What matters is not so much what you eat — or don't eat," he wrote, "but that you approach the experience with an open mind, a sense of adventure and anticipation, and a genuine eagerness to try something new."

He did that over the Asian dinners he shared with— and wrote about— our multi-ethnic dining group. He was as interested in the people as in the food, and he enriched each experience with his graciousness and enthusiasm. There will always be a place for him at our table.

Andrea Rademan

ACKNOWLEDGEMENTS

Wendy Chan & Grace Niwa
Savory Productions, Inc.

As strong advocates for Asian cuisine, professionally and personally, we decided to create a book to spark more interest in Asian food and beverages on all levels. Thankfully, we found many zealous individuals sharing this vision along the way who helped not only make this project happen, but also expanded it to one that is international in scope and scale.

Our concept was simple. We wanted to include a collection of recipes from leading professional chefs— allowing home cooks to prepare wonderful Asian food at home — when not dining out. We decided to enrich the book with information allowing readers to understand how Asian food fits into the new USDA dietary guideline. Therefore, you will find recipes that include a healthier interpretation of classic dishes and contemporary creations rich in Eastern sensibilities.

Do you ever wonder if you could prepare that exquisite Black Cod in Miso dish you enjoyed at Nobu Matsuhisa's restaurant? Could you make the fabulous Crab-Crusted Ahi Tuna served at Yi Cuisine? Or Wolfgang Puck's famous Chicken Salad Chinois? *New Asian Cuisine* shares these well-known recipes with you and takes the extra steps to provide helpful information for aspiring chefs to find the ingredients they would need. We have compiled a complete list of Asian grocery stores and online stores around the U.S., as well as a directory of our chefs' restaurant locations on **www.newasiancuisine.com**. This website will be kept current as a helpful source of updated information for our readers.

After buying and reading this book, we hope you will feel hungry for healthy and delicious Asian cuisine and come away with the knowledge of choosing food and menu items wisely. We also hope you will have the chance to visit our talented participating chefs' restaurants. For this reason, we have provided a passport journal at the back of the book for you to document your enjoyable dining experiences.

We are very grateful to a large number of individuals whose support was essential in making this book a success. We want to thank Professor Michael Pardus, who helped us unconditionally from the very beginning. He not only acted as our culinary consultant, sounding board and recipe editor, but also developed the Asian food pyramid. We appreciate the contribution of Asian food writer Joyce Jue who provided her valuable Asian culinary and cultural background, adding depth and texture to the book with her commentaries. We are grateful to Andrea Rademan, our editor, who tirelessly outreached to top chefs from around the world and in the U.S., guiding us to produce a book with a wider appeal, way beyond what we originally imagined. We are indebted to Lillian Africano, president of the International Food, Wine & Travel Writers Association, who did not hesitate to publish our book, believed in us and supported us every step of the way.

This book would not have been produced without the diligence and devotion of our entire team of highly motivated individuals, including Jessica Ellis, our distinguished designer; Julie Sellew, our multi-tasking assistant with the "can-do" spirit; and Gary Cheong and Chau Lam, our relentless chef coordinators who ventured deep into the kitchens of many of these contributing chefs to get what we needed. We are thankful to the public relations teams behind many of our star chefs who have offered assistance every step of the way answering our endless questions about ingredients and measurements. We also want to thank Linda Ayares and her team at M. Silver & Associates who extended their expertise and encouragement. We are very proud of our web team, designer Wen K. Huang and Rumee Singh, our researcher, newsletter editor and web whiz.

A special thank you goes to K.Y. Chow, proprietor and owner of GM Printing, New York, who was undaunted with all the challenges we gave him and proudly supported our mission. The guidance and support from Nancy Smoller of Book Clearing House proved to be an important source of confidence that we were on the right track.

Our circle of supporters really expands to countless contributors which include Jason Young and David Ramirez of Pearl Image, Susan Brady, Hanna Lee, Carl Chu, Jannis Swerman, Keith Williamson, Eric Seeger (who graciously allowed our editor to focus on this book, preempting his project), John Krich, Troy Thompson, Dianora Ginn, Susan Jorgensen, Chinese food expert Jacqueline Newman, and South East Asian Cuisine expert Carol Selva Rajah.

A very special thanks to our corporate sponsors— **Haw-Di-I Foods Co., Ltd.** (Bull Head)**, H Mart, Hong Kong Tourism Board, Nestle USA, House of Spices India, Kai Tzr Soju Inc., Korea aT Center, New York, Pearl River Bridge Soy Sauce, Phillips Foods, Inc., Pucci Foods, Roxy Trading, South East Produce, Ltd. (USA), Twin Marquis Inc., Vasinee Food Corp., W. Y. International, Inc.** and **Zespri International** — who gave us the financial support we needed to get off the ground and enabled us to present amazing value to our readers. They believed in the mission of promoting Asian food and beverages across the board and believed in our ability to produce this book.

Most importantly, we want to thank all the chefs who have generously given us their recipes and patiently responded to our endless questions in trying to make steps easier for readers to understand and follow. Chefs Chris Yeo and Khai Duong, founding members of Asian Chefs Association; Martin Yan, a core supporter of the project, provided us with the means to reach many of the top Asian chefs in America. Special thanks to Anthony Bourdain, Masaharu Morimoto and Jean-Georges Vongerichten— who agreed to review and endorse our book. We have both found the experience of this project a remarkable journey— during which we found joy in doing what we love and with people we respect. Lastly, we would like to dedicate this book to both our families who are our backbone and foundation and are always in support of what we do. We give special thanks to David, Veronica and Kelly of the Chan family and Paul Niwa.

CONTENTS

FOREWORD

Several years ago I was asked to teach an overview course in Asian cuisine. As a Caucasian chef, born and raised in the US and trained in the European tradition, it was a scary assignment. I was just familiar enough with the techniques and ingredients of Asia to be one step ahead of my American students, but there was so much to know and, heck, I couldn't even read the labels on the packaging. But the exotic appeal got under my skin, and the unfamiliar fueled a new passion. I felt like a twenty-year-old cook again, exhilarated with each new "discovery."

As I learned, of course, cooking is cooking the world over: fire is fire; boiling is boiling; and frying is frying— it's the way you apply them that makes the difference. Techniques vary only slightly from region to region and even unfamiliar ingredients have similar tastes— sweet, sour, salty, pungent, or spicy. What sets culinary cultures apart is the approach of the cooks and the diners.

Western food has grown to depend on richness and opulence for its appeal. Big steaks, rich sauces, and masses of fried foods have become the touchstone of western dining. A skilled western cook stuffs the guest; a satisfied diner is one who can't move at the end of a meal. Contrast this with the Asian propensity to use meat as a garnish, a flavoring ingredient in dishes that consist mainly of grains, vegetables, herbs, and spices. A skilled eastern cook is mindful of the health of the diner; a happy diner is content at the end of a meal, balanced— not over-stuffed.

Cooking flavorful and healthfully balanced meals need not be a formidable task. This book contains recipes that are true to, or inspired by, ancient cuisines, but simple enough for the modern home cook to prepare. Once you have experimented with a recipe, try adapting the techniques to other ingredients from the same region— odds are that you will end up with something which is not only delicious and healthful but "authentic" as well.

Applying the USDA Food Pyramid guidelines to New Asian cuisine is easy. What has been challenging is to bring a note of authenticity to each food group by recognizing the distinct and varied ingredients from across a large, diverse region. The cooking of Japan is as distinct from that of Thailand as Boston baked beans are from New Orleans jambalaya.

The recipes in this book are an example of how modern chefs are adapting the foods of their homelands to the global sensibilities of today's diners. Where appropriate, the recipes are marked with the food pyramid symbol, suggesting these make smart choices if you are planning your meals to follow the guideline. All of us who worked on this book hope that it will inspire you to explore and experiment, not with "healthy cooking" in mind per se, but with exhilaration and passion for balance and bold, satisfying flavors.

Michael Pardus
New Paltz, New York

NEW ASIAN CUISINE

AN INTRODUCTION

For Asian food aficionados, your time has arrived and so has the cookbook you have been waiting for— ***New Asian Cuisine: Fabulous Recipes from Celebrity Chefs.*** This book started as a grassroots project to promote and recognize the vast scope of Asian cuisine and how it fits easily into a healthy lifestyle. Asian food and celebrity chefs now share center stage. Headliners and marquee billings for mainstream food magazines and television shows as well as industry journals for culinary professionals, frequently feature Asian cuisine. It is the talk on the town. Much like knowing and being up on wines, Asian cuisine is 'in' and a frequent topic of conversation while in the midst of professional shop talk, networking affairs, and around the water cooler. ***Food & Wine's*** "Everyone Loves Asian" dedicated an entire magazine to Asian noodles, curries, spicy salads, dumplings, restaurants and celebrity chefs. Asian food awareness is all the rage and has been growing at a fever pitch for some time.

The Asian version of the USDA's new food pyramid was created with the help of Professor Michael Pardus, Certified Hospitality Educator (CHE) at The Culinary Institute of America. The Asian Food Pyramid translates the food groups into Asian ingredients and is a recent depiction and explanation of the historically healthful eating habits of the people of rural Asia. It is a diet built on nutrient-rich plant-based foods combined with smaller amounts of animal based products. ***New Asian Cuisine*** will help you incorporate the qualities of the Asian Food Pyramid into your own eating style. Recipes that follow these guidelines in the book are labeled with the pyramid logo.

New Asian Cuisine is not a dieter's cookbook. The recipes adhere to the principles of the Eastern eating philosophy of maintaining balanced lifestyle and the renewal of an "instinct" for moderation. Asians have been eating lots of grains, seeds, legumes, vegetables, and fruits and small amounts of poultry and red meat for centuries as a habit resulting almost entirely from culture and customs acquired mostly at home and early in life.

While the rich history and a steady eye toward healthful cooking are the central elements driving recipes in this book, some recipes tilt that healthful scale a tad presenting an opportunity for a dish perfect for entertainment or festive occasions. The recommendation of the pyramid is to enjoy an occasional feast while paying close attention to finding a balance between food and physical activity, and maintaining that balance for a healthy and happy lifestyle.

ABOUT OUR CHEFS

New Asian Cuisine began with a group of talented Asian chefs who had already started the process of elevating Asian cuisine to the top rungs of the international culinary ladder as well as non-Asian chefs who have been inspired by Asian cooking and its nuances. ***New Asian Cuisine*** grew rapidly with a flood of international chefs and food personalities from Japan to Australia all wanting to contribute to the common cause. The final list of chefs who are showcased have generously donated their recipes and was the result of those who quickly embraced this concept. It was not by design that many other talented chefs are not included in this book or overlooked. We could have filled another volume but we just literally ran out of space and time.

Now, there is no need to leave the comforts of your own kitchen to sample the exciting Asian recipes we have gathered from celebrity chefs around the globe. Asian or Asia-influenced, acclaimed in their own locales or worldwide, these men and women are feeding and fueling the current fascination with Asian cuisine that has captivated the appetites of people everywhere. Their recipes— many of them healthful by tradition, all of them delectable by design— are based on an understanding of and appreciation for Asian cuisine. Our chefs are passionate about great food, a passion they share with you in the pages of this book. Many of the chefs chose to send their favorite home-style dishes— recipes from their childhood that reach deep into their cultural roots. They also refashioned many traditional Asian dishes, often employing Western culinary techniques and ingredients and always adding a heavy dose of creativity, to turn out refined, innovative, contemporary plates that are guaranteed to appeal to nearly everyone.

A central message you will see often in the recipes is the connection between the past and the present. *Chef Susanna Foo*, who is known for her sophisticated and unique dishes says, "Everything I cook is based on what I remember from my childhood." *Chef Ming Tsai* of Blue Ginger relates that, like all Asian cooks, he learned from an early age not to waste any food, although his blissful recipes don't betray such basic motivations. *Anita Lo*, chef and owner of Annisa in New York City, says her steamed pompano "is based on my mother's recipe, so I feature it on Mother's Day."

American food enthusiasts will recognize names such as *Nobu Matsuhisa*, *Martin Yan* and *Wolfgang Puck* but unless you live in Mumbai, you may not have watched *Sanjeev Kapoor*, the Indian TV counterpart to *Emeril Lagasse*; if you're not from Adelaide, Australia, you probably haven't tasted the true fusion dishes of *Cheong Liew*. Did you know that the Landis Taipei Hotel in Taiwan is the only place you can indulge in the gourmet delights of *Chef Tseng Hsiu Pao*? And that it requires a visit to Wooreega Restaurant in Seoul, South Korea, to appreciate the delicacies of *Ms. An Jung-Hyun*, a favorite chef of Seoul's dining scene.

We hope you will be delighted by the culinary contributions of the chefs that shared one collective vision to present to the international culinary community a new way of thinking about Asian cuisine— that it is refined, innovative and au courant— and packed with healthy paybacks.

BON APPÉTIT!

ASIAN FOOD PYRAMID

HELPING YOU MAKE HEALTHY LIFESTYLE CHOICES

The Traditional Healthy Asian Diet Pyramid stresses the superior nutrients of a plant-based diet and promotes a lifestyle of moderation in eating combined with regular exercise. It is based on the collaborative efforts of Oldways Preservation & Exchange Trust, the Harvard School of Public Health, and the Cornell-China-Oxford Project on Nutrition, Health and Environment at Cornell University.

The traditional Asian diet is high in fiber, vitamins, minerals, and antioxidants and low in saturated and other fats. This healthful dietary profile contrasts dramatically with the typical high fat eating pattern found in much of the West, and accounts for the relatively low incidence in Asia of many of the chronic conditions that afflict Western populations. The primary difference between the diets of the East and the West is that the Asian diet draws its protein from the consumption of rice and other grains, legumes, nuts, seeds, and fish— in other words, plant and aquatic sources— rather than from meat, poultry, and dairy.

The new dietary guidelines at MyPyramid.gov details how often— daily, weekly, or monthly — the foods in the various categories may be eaten according to one's personal needs. An interactive nutritional educational tool allows individuals to customize food portions and selections based on age, weight and physical activity. Being your own advocate for your healthcare requires an understanding of food labels and terminology, such as the differences between saturated, polyunsaturated, monounsaturated fats, as well as trans fats and to know how many grams of fat may be ingested daily. Select olive, peanut or canola oils (monounsaturated fats) instead of butter (saturated fat) or hydrogenated vegetables, such as margarines and shortenings, which are trans-fats.

Dairy products are not a traditional food in Asia, with the exception of India and remote regions of western China. Creators of the pyramid encourage followers to eat only small amounts of milk, cheese, and other dairy products, preferably low fat or non fat. Common Western thinking promotes a substantial consumption of high-calcium dairy products for good health and to fight against osteoporosis. T. Colin Campbell, Cornell professor of nutritional biochemistry and director of the Cornell-China-Oxford Project, insists otherwise, pointing out that Western countries show significantly higher rates of osteoporosis than Asian countries, where most of the calcium in the diet is derived from plants. Calcium intake is indeed lower in Asian countries, but the daily vigorous activity of many rural Asians is thought to be a factor in the reduction of bone loss, and thus may account for the lower rates of osteoporosis.

MyPyramid is broken down into the following categories:

VARIETY— Represented by six vertical color bands (the narrow yellow band represents oils) which portray the six new food groups.

PROPORTIONALITY— Shown by different bandwidths to suggest the quantity of foods recommended from each group.

PERSONALIZATION— Represented by the figure on the steps. Using the MyPyramid approach, each person selects food groups and frequency of consumption based on individual needs and preferences.

ACTIVITY— Represented by the person climbing the steps, symbolizing the importance of physical activity.

MODERATION— Represented by the tapered shape of each food group, the wider base signifying foods with little or no solid fats or added sugars, which may be selected more often. The narrower top indicates foods containing added sugars and solid fats. The more active you are, the more of these foods can fit into your diet.

Finally, the pyramid stresses the importance of daily physical activity, recognizing that a sound diet and regular exercise are equal players in a well-balanced lifestyle. In the West, regular exercise often means a gym membership. But in rural Asia, that activity is typically long, hard workdays, most often spent laboring in the fields. Even in urban Asia, many people commonly walk or bike to their destinations, rather than jump into an automobile, so that keeping fit is an integral habit of daily life.

Knowledge is power. Published wellness magazines by health care organizations stress getting smart about your own health care. Practice moderation in the amounts eaten and your choice of foods. Make a habit of reading food labels and understanding them. The modern lifestyle is all about choices.

ABOUT THE FOOD PYRAMID LOGO

Recipes with the Food Pyramid logo in this book depict a "smart choice" and typically, are ones with a total fat content of lower than 35%. Many recipes without the logo, on the other hand, can be very healthful, but on their own as a meal, may not satisfy that simple criteria. If you plan to follow the dietary guideline from the USDA Food Pyramid, you may want to plan your meals carefully, pay attention to portion size, as well as balancing your intake of other food groups.
Since the government guideline is designed to be individualized (variables include age, sex and activity level) and is based on the consumption of different food groups on a daily, weekly or monthly basis, no single recipe holds the solution to an overall healthy diet.

According to the 2005 Dietary Guidelines for Americans, a healthy diet is one that:

- Emphasizes fruits, vegetables, whole grains, and fat free or low fat milk and milk products;
- Includes lean meats, poultry, fish, beans, eggs, and nuts; and
- Is low in saturated fats, trans fats, cholesterol, salt (sodium), and added sugars

The American Dietetic Association recommends a "healthy" diet be approximately 30% fat, 50-60% carbohydrates and 10-20% protein per day. Average daily food consumption in terms of calories is 2,000 for an active female and 2,400 for an active male.
For more information about the Dietary Guidelines for Americans, 2005, and on how to adopt a consistent healthier lifestyle, please visit **www.mypyramid.gov.**

MyPyramid.gov

STEPS TO A HEALTHIER YOU

GRAINS	VEGETABLES	FRUITS	MILK	MEAT & BEANS

GRAINS Make half your grains whole	Eat at least 3 ounces of whole grain cereals, breads, crackers, rice or pasta every day 1 ounce is about 1 slice of bread, about 1 cup of breakfast cereal, or 1/2 cup of cooked rice, cereal, or pasta
VEGETABLES Vary your veggies	Eat more dark-green veggies like broccoli, spinach, and other dark leafy greens Eat more orange vegetables like carrots and sweet potatoes Eat more dry kidney beans and peas like pinto beans, kidney beans, and lentils
FRUITS Focus on fruits	Eat a variety of fruit Choose fresh, frozen, canned, or dried fruit Go easy on fruit juices
MILK Get your calcium-rich foods	Go low fat or fat free when you choose milk, yogurt, and other milk products If you don't or can't consume milk, choose lactose-free products or other calcium sources such as fortified foods and beverages
MEAT & BEANS Go lean with protein	Choose low fat or lean meats and poultry Bake it, broil it, or grill it Vary your protein routine— choose more fish, beans, peas, nuts and seeds

Find your balance between food and physical activity

- Be sure to stay within your daily calorie needs.
- Be physically active for at least 30 minutes most days of the week.
- About 60 minutes a day of physical activity may be needed to prevent weight gain.
- For sustaining weight loss, at least 60 to 90 minutes a day of physical activity may be required.
- Children and teenagers should be physically active for 60 minutes every day, or most days.

NOTE: PLANT-BASED BEVERAGES Except for tea, beverages such as sake, wine, beer, soju and other alcoholic drinks should only be consumed in moderation.

For a 2,000-calorie a day diet, you need the amounts listed for each food group. To find the amounts that are right for you, go to MyPyramid.gov.

GRAINS – **180 grams / 6 ounces per day**
White Rice, Brown Rice, Barley, Black Sticky Rice, White Sticky Rice, Wheat grains or noodles, Millet, Sorghum, Sago (not a grain, but used as a staple starch), Corn, Cracked Wheat, Barley, Buckwheat, Wheat Bread, Oats, Rice— black glutinous, Jasmine Rice, Rice Noodles, Rice Paper, Sticky Rice

VEGETABLES – **1680 ml by volume / 2$^{1/2}$ cups per day**
Water Lily Plant, Water Spinach, Bok Choy, Mustard Greens, Napa Cabbage, Gai Lan— Chinese Broccoli, Lettuces, Ong Choy, Kai Choy, Spinach Green and Red, Cabbage, Drumstick leaf, Methi leaf, Amaranth, Green Cabbage, Broccoli, Shiso, Fiddlehead and Dried Fern Stems, Choi Sum, Pea Shoots, Morning Glory, Chinese Kale, Coriander Leaf, Thai Basil Leaf, Thai Morning Glory Leaf, Table Salad Herbs, Ong Cai— Water Spinach, Pumpkin, Maize, Sweet Potato, Carrots, Onion, Winter Squashes, Summer Squashes, Red Bell Pepper, Beets, Tomato, Cauliflower, Paprika Peppers, Chrysanthemum Petals, Bamboo Shoots, Red Chili Peppers, Hard Squashes, Soft Summer Squashes

FRUITS – **480 ml by volume / 2 cups per day**
Mango, Pineapple, Banana, Papaya, Lychee, Pomelo, Tamarind, Star Fruit, Apple, Pear, Peach, Watermelon, Persimmon, Plum, Jackfruit, Mangosteen, Orange, Guava, Indian Plum, Durian, Salak, Mandarin, Grape, Asian Pear, Melons, Peach, Soursop, Rose Apple, Lychee, Rambutan, Green Guava

MILK – **720 ml by volume / 3 cups per day (2 cups for kids 2-8)**
Sweet Condensed Milk, Milk Powder, Whole Milk, Butter, Goat's Milk Cheese, Sour Cream, American Style Cheeses, Yogurt, Farm Cheese, Yakult (fermented milk beverage), Cheeses

MEAT & BEANS – **165 grams / 5$^{1/2}$ oz. per day**
Pork, Chicken, River Catfish, Chickpeas and chickpea flour, Peanuts, Sesame seeds, Chickpea Curd (similar to tofu), Beef, Duck, Elephant Fish, Mud Fish, Mung Beans, Red Beans, Lamb, Carp, Flounder, Soy Bean/Fermented Soy bean, Quail, Bangus (milk fish), Tuna, Mackeral, Onaga, Opah, Filipino long beans, Goat, Duck eggs, Hilsa, Tengra, Dal (wide variety of Legumes), Pappads (lentil cracker), Sheep, Crab, Snapper, Salt/dried fish, Tempeh, Adzuki beans, Cuttlefish, Croaker, Shrimp, Soy Beans/Tofu, Lentils, Tilapia, Kidney beans, Sataw beans, Baramundi (fish), Basa fish

Know the limits on fats, sugars, and salt (sodium)

- Make most of your fat sources from fish, nuts, and vegetable oils.
- Limit solid fats like butter, stick margarine, shortening, and lard, as well as foods that contain these fats.
- Check the Nutrition Facts label to keep saturated fats, trans fats and sodium low.
- Choose food and beverages low in added sugars. Added sugars contribute calories with few, if any, nutrients.

■COOKING OILS

Peanut oil, Corn oil, Soybean oil, Macadamia nut oil, Ghee, Coconut oil, Palm oil, Sesame oil, Palm oil, Lard/pork fat

■SUGAR/SWEETS/SWEETENERS

Palm and cane sugars, Molasses, White sugar, Jaggery, Honey, Barley syrup, Brown sugar

ASIAN FOOD

HEALTHY & NUTRITIOUS

Most Westerners first encounter Asian food in restaurants where many of the oily and fatty dishes offered are meant to cater to non-Asian palates. Not surprisingly, these dishes have left a lingering negative impression. Fortunately, more and more Asian restaurateurs are offering sophisticated menus. However, the most authentic Asian food has always been prepared at home, rather than in restaurants. Most dishes are always packed with more vegetables than meat. The oven is still not a standard appliance in Asian kitchens. Asian food is frequently steamed, simmered, wok fried or braised on top of the stove, all of which are popular and healthly methods.

Here are just two examples of everyday dishes that provide flavor and reported medicinal value. The Vietnamese tonic-like rice noodle soup known as *pho* is home cooking at its best. The soup is eaten with a generous side plate of healthy fresh aromatic herbs, bean sprouts and a squeeze of lime. Southeast Asian slow-cooked curries are laced with rhizomes such as ginger, galangal, turmeric, and lesser ginger, pounded together with chilies, lemon grass, and dried Indian spices, to simmer together with small portions of meat and lots of vegetables. In the kitchen, these typical Indian spices— cinnamon, turmeric, cumin, chilies, and ginger— add zest and flavor to the dishes but they are also loaded with numerous vitamins, nutrients and medicinal benefits, purporting to have anti-clotting action, have antioxidant ability, prevent growth of cancer cells, are effective for digestion and nausea, have anti-inflammatory action, and reduce blood sugar levels in diabetes.

Grilling, which calls for little if any added fat, is yet another popular and healthy preparation method especially for whole fish and seafood and for the meat and poultry kebabs of Southeast Asia known as satay. All these dishes share the daily menu with large portions of rice, noodles, or other grains, and all of them respect the basic principles expressed in the Asian Food Pyramid.

Much of the current interest in the Asian diet has grown out of studies that show that many chronic conditions such as heart disease, certain cancers, osteoporosis, obesity, and diabetes are far less common in Asia than in much of the West. These findings have prompted many of the same researchers and others to look closely at the traditional Asian diet to learn what sets it apart from the everyday diet of most westerners.

Nowadays, Asian food is gaining momentum as something worthy to emulate, whether you are preparing an authentic multi-entrée dinner or simply adding Asian touches to your Western repertory. This significant and important change is due in large part to the hard work and extraordinary talent of the many chefs cooking today.

One cannot talk about healthy Asian food without devoting some attention to the important legume— the *soybean*. This "miracle bean" started as an important food source in China some five thousand years ago. Ironically, the United States is one of the world's largest producing country of the soybean, yet most Americans are still not familiar with it. Soy products only made their way to the western pantries and kitchens not too long ago— and often are seen as a health product than a delicious dish.

The soybean is unquestionably the most important legume of the Asian diet. It has nearly two times the protein content of other legumes and five times that of corn, and its amino acid balance is nearly that of meat. It boasts ecological advantages as well: the amount of acreage needed to raise cows, pigs, and chickens for human consumption and to cultivate the grain needed to feed them is many times greater than the land needed to grow soybeans to yield the same amount of protein. This amazing bean is a staple of the Asian diet. Soybeans turn up in dozens of forms, as many of the recipes in this book illustrate.

Soy sauce, perhaps the best-known soybean product, is widely used in China, Japan and Korea, and to a lesser degree in Southeast Asia. This ubiquitous table seasoning sauce that has come to symbolize Asian food may be humble, but it is packed with antioxidants, and definitely plays an important role in the global food culture. One has to be knowledgeable in knowing how to select a good bottle of soy sauce— as the market is flooded with different brands, and even counterfeits. One way is to choose a reliable brand, look for one that is naturally, not chemically produced, and free from preservatives.

There are two main types of soy sauce— the light and the dark. A superior quality light one has a bright, light red-brown color, and after shaking the bottle, the light yellow foam will remain for a long time. The flavor should be light and fresh tasting, with the aroma of soybean paste. It is an excellent way to enhance the taste of the food without overpowering the main ingredients. This light soy sauce is often used as table seasoning as well as in marinating and cooking. The better dark soy sauce is richer, and sometimes flavored with mushroom, and has a viscosity that makes the sauce stick against the surface of the glass bottle wall. A good bottle should not have sediment at the bottom. The dark soy sauce is often used for cooking, and in dishes that require more color without making it salty. When the sauce is manufactured in a natural way, it will also be naturally low in sodium.

Miso, Japanese style fermented soybean paste, is added to soups, marinades, and salad dressings. There are many other fermented soybean products that play a vital role in cooking Asian dishes, The mild whole and puréed brown soybean sauces, variously labeled yellow bean, brown bean, bean paste, and other names, are used in braised and stir fried meat, seafood, and vegetable dishes in China, Singapore, Thailand, Malaysia, Korea, and elsewhere. When chilies, sometimes along with other seasonings, are added to these bean sauces, the label changes to hot chili bean sauce, hot bean paste, or a similar name, condiments popular in China (particularly in Sichuan and Hunan) and in Korea. Salted and fermented black soybeans, sometimes flavored with tiny shards of dried citrus peel and ginger, form the basis for a sauce that is a fixture of the southern Chinese pantry. The beans are typically combined with garlic and ginger and steamed, braised, or stir fried with meats, seafood, poultry, and/or vegetables.

Soybeans are much more than a base for fermented condiments. The backbone of the Asian vegetarian diets, soybeans can be boiled or steamed and eaten fresh, or they can be turned into crunchy, salty snack foods. Soy nuts are now frequently served on airplanes, replacing peanuts and mixed nuts. Highly nutritious soybean milk, made by soaking yellow soybeans for many hours and then pureeing them with water, is drunk in China, Japan, Korea, and in parts of Southeast Asia. A popular breakfast drink and also a common pick-me-up in the afternoon and evening, *soy milk* has a mellow aroma, full flavor, and mild sweetness. It is also a healthful, inexpensive alternative to cow's milk: it contains 51 percent more protein, 16 percent less carbohydrates, 12 percent fewer calories, and 24 percent less fat (48 percent less saturated fat). Soy milk is also recommended for those who are lactose intolerant.

When soy milk is combined with a coagulant (gypsum), the curds separate from the whey and are pressed into molds to produce fresh soybean curd, or *tofu*. These custard-like blocks are eaten fresh, stir fried, braised, deep fried, stuffed, and best of all, steamed. They are also the basis for many other soy products, such as dried bean curd skins or strips and pressed bean curd slabs (used as a meat substitute in vegetarian dishes). In Indonesia, *tempeh*, dense fermented cakes made by combining whole soybeans with rice, millet, or another grain, is a daily source of protein, fiber, vitamins, and nutrients.

Soybean oil, a popular Asian cooking fat, is yet another important product of the miracle bean. Because it contains 61 percent polyunsaturated fat and 24 percent monounsaturated fat, it helps to reduce total cholesterol and lower LDL (low-density lipoprotein, or "bad" cholesterol) levels, thus reducing the risk of heart disease. Soybean oil should never be consumed in excess, however, as it can also reduce the levels of HDL (high-density lipoproteins that draw cholesterol away from arteries). The oil also contains linolenic acid, an omega-3 fatty acid that is another critical component in the fight against heart disease. As mentioned earlier, soybean and other vegetable oils, which occupy their own band on the pyramid, are traditionally consumed in small amounts on a daily basis in Asia, making soybean oil's healthy profile a perfect fit for quantity and healthy food values for the food pyramid.

People in the West are now more conscious of the health benefits of consuming tofu than in the past, but the extraordinary value of the soybean and its many creative spin-offs is still not fully appreciated. In *The Book of Tofu*, authors William Shurtleff and Akiko Aoyagi insist that tofu will soon be regarded as one of Asia's greatest contributions to mankind: a major step in the direct utilization of the earth's bounty of protein. They also believe that the soybean holds the answer to solving a global crisis: the profound shortage of protein in the daily diet of too many people around the world.

EATING, ASIAN STYLE

What is *New Asian Cuisine*? It's traditional Asian cuisine with a modern sensibility that's based on the gastronomy of Asian cooking. And it's not only the food itself but also the customs and traditions of these countries. Meals are eaten family style so everyone gets to try a variety of different things.

In Asia, daily life revolves around cooking and eating. In the large outdoor food markets you find in many Asian cities, diners use their chopsticks to pick through the skeletons of steamed fish in search of every last delectable bite. They wrestle with crab shells to capture the tiniest morsels of flesh, lapping up the last drop of sauce to luxuriate in one final surge of gastronomic ecstasy.

In China, people often stop at sidewalk stands on their way to work. They buy fresh crullers, which they dip into bowls of *jook* (rice congee soup) or warm soy milk, much as Americans do with donuts and coffee. Later on, they might cool off with a piece of melon or slices of mango. Tea and late night snacks is just the thing to fill the gap between lunch and dinner or dinner and bed.

In Malaysia, you might have some *rujuk* (spicy vegetable salad), *satay* (skewers of grilled meat or chicken) or a bowl of *laksa* (curry noodles). In India, it might be a glass of salty *lassi*. in Singapore, it could be *kuih* (rice flour cake); and in Vietnam, it might be *banh mi thit* (a sandwich of cold cuts, pickled cucumbers, carrots and radishes) or just a handful of melon seeds, or deep bowls of Vietnamese *pho* (a tonic-like rice noodle soup) which are accompanied by generous side plates of fresh aromatic herbs, bean sprouts, and lime.

Affluence is bringing a rapidly-changing Asia with Western-style fast food restaurants and eating habits. Many Asians show off their new wealth by increasing the consumption of saturated fats in the form of meat, poultry, and dairy products in their daily diets. As the urban Asian diet becomes more westernized, the population is experiencing an increase in the rate of heart disease, certain cancers, and diabetes, the same chronic diseases that strike people in the West in such high numbers. There is no better time for all of us, Asian and non-Asian alike, to adapt the traditional principles of Asian dining and use them to forge a healthier future.

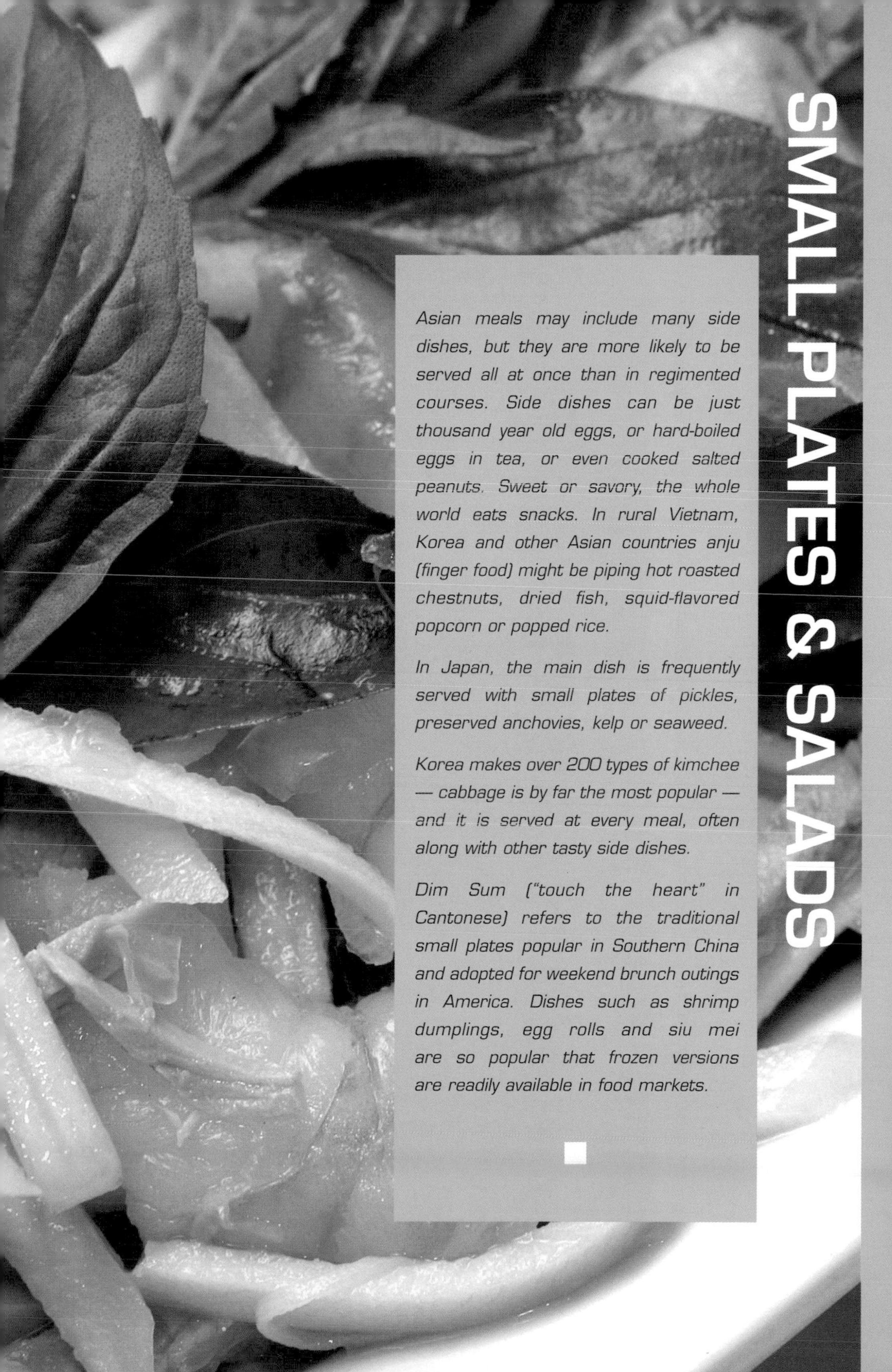

SMALL PLATES & SALADS

Asian meals may include many side dishes, but they are more likely to be served all at once than in regimented courses. Side dishes can be just thousand year old eggs, or hard-boiled eggs in tea, or even cooked salted peanuts. Sweet or savory, the whole world eats snacks. In rural Vietnam, Korea and other Asian countries anju (finger food) might be piping hot roasted chestnuts, dried fish, squid-flavored popcorn or popped rice.

In Japan, the main dish is frequently served with small plates of pickles, preserved anchovies, kelp or seaweed.

Korea makes over 200 types of kimchee — cabbage is by far the most popular — and it is served at every meal, often along with other tasty side dishes.

Dim Sum ("touch the heart" in Cantonese) refers to the traditional small plates popular in Southern China and adopted for weekend brunch outings in America. Dishes such as shrimp dumplings, egg rolls and siu mei are so popular that frozen versions are readily available in food markets.

ASIAN WRAP

Ritsuo Tsuchida • Blowfish Sushi to Die For • San Francisco, CA*

Wrap
3 ounces maguro (tuna)
2 ounces tobiko (flying fish eggs)
2 pieces shiso leaf
1/2 tomato, seeds removed
1 ounce Japanese cucumber
1 sheet oboro nori

Salsa
1 tablespoon chopped tomato
1 tablespoon chopped yellow onion
1 tablespoon diced avocado
1 teaspoon chopped cilantro
1/2 teaspoon fresh lime juice
1/4 teaspoon kosher salt

Sansho Mashed Potato
1 medium Yukon gold potato
1/3 cup cream
1 tablespoon Japanese mayo
pinch of kosher salt
1 teaspoon sansho pepper

Coconut Tempura Batter
1/4 cup coconut milk
1/2 cup flour
1/4 cup water

Sauce
1/2 cup rice vinegar
1/2 cup white soy sauce
1/4 cup water
2 ounces bonito flakes
1 teaspoon yuzu citrus juice

Shiso Infused Oil
20 pieces shiso leaves
1/2 cup grapeseed oil
oil for frying
1/3 cup of salad oil
2 tablespoons sesame oil

Heat oven at 425° F.
Sauce: Mix the rice vinegar, white soy sauce, water and the yuzu citrus juice. Mix well and add bonito flakes. Refrigerate for 6 hours and strain.
Sansho Mashed Potato: Brush salad oil on the Yukon gold potatoes and bake in the oven for 25 minutes. Mash the potatoes and add cream, Japanese mayo, salt and sansho pepper. Keep warm.
Coconut Tempura Batter: Mix coconut milk, flour and water in a bowl. Keep cold with ice water.
Salsa: Mix all ingredients in a bowl and refrigerate.
Shiso Infused Oil: Blend shiso leaves and grapeseed oil in a blender and strain.
Wrap maguro, tobiko, shiso, sliced tomatoes, sliced Japanese cucumber with the oboro nori sheet. Dip roll into the coconut tempura batter and deep fry until crispy for 20 seconds (don't overcook, must be rare inside). Slice the roll into 5 pieces. Spread mashed potato on the plate and arrange the 5 pieces on top. Pour the sauce into a glass container and place on the side of the dish.

Serves 2

PHOTO: Ray Grefe

*Please see page 260 for a complete list of restaurant locations.

CRAB MEAT MARTINI ORIENTAL RATATOUILLE AND DIJON-LIME DRESSING

Philippe Chin • CuiZine • Aiken, SC*

8 ounces lump crab meat
1 large tomato
1 small zucchini
1 small yellow squash
1/2 small eggplant
1 small onion
1 green bell pepper
1 red bell pepper
3 garlic cloves, chopped
2 tablespoons olive oil
1 tablespoon oyster sauce
1 tablespoon cilantro, chopped
2 tablespoons mayonnaise
1 tablespoon Dijon mustard
juice of 1 lime
2 cups mixed greens
1 cup green papaya, shredded
6 endive leaves, cut lengthwise for garnish

Dice all the vegetables into 1/4 inch pieces. In a large sauté pan, heat olive oil in high heat. Sauté onions and peppers for 3 minutes. Add garlic and the rest of the vegetables and cook for another 5 minutes. Chill. Add cilantro and oyster sauce. Season with salt and pepper. In a mixing bowl, toss crab meat with lime juice, mustard and mayonnaise. Set aside. In a large martini glass, garnish with endive leaves, ratatouille and top with crap meat. Put chopped mixed greens and shredded papaya over crab meat and serve.

Serves 2-4

*Please see page 260 for a complete list of restaurant locations.

CRISPY PRAWN COCKTAIL WITH PINEAPPLE, MANGO AND MINT SALSA

Simpson Wong • Jefferson Grill • New York, NY*

12 large prawns, shelled and deveined
1 cup flour
1 teaspoon togarashi pepper (optional)
5 ounces soda water
3 cups oil for frying
salt and pepper to taste

Salsa
1/2 cup mango, diced
1/2 cup pineapple, diced
1/8 cup chiffonade mint
1/2 cup lime juice
1/2 cup sugar
1/4 cup fish sauce
2 bird's eye chilies, finely chopped and seeds removed

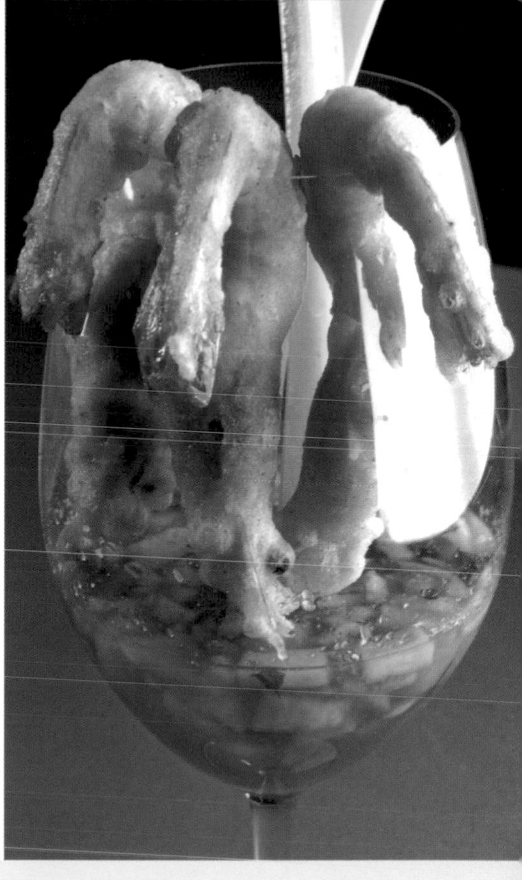

Dissolve sugar in lime juice and fish sauce. Add and mix all the remaining ingredients for the salsa. Pour into four glasses. Set aside to chill. In a pot, heat oil to 300° F. Meanwhile, mix flour, togarashi pepper, and soda water. Season the mixture with salt and pepper. Stir mixture until you get a medium consistency. Dip prawns in the batter mixture. Gently lower each prawn into hot oil. Fry for 2 to 3 minutes or until golden brown. Place prawns in the glass containing the salsa. Serve immediately.

Serves 4

*Please see page 260 for a complete list of restaurant locations.

PHOTO: This page, Martin Jansche

CRUNCHY INDIAN SNACK WITH FRESH TOMATOES AND ONION *(BHEL PURI)*

Suvir Saran & Hemant Mathur • Dévi • New York, NY

1/2 package (400 grams) bhel puri mix
1/2 red onion, chopped
1 tomato, chopped
1 1/2 tablespoons green chutney (see recipe below)
2 tablespoons tamarind chutney (see recipe below)
1 boiled potato, peeled and chopped (optional)

Green Chutney (Haree Chutney)
Makes 1 1/2 cups

1 1/2 cups firmly packed fresh cilantro, chopped
1/2 cup firmly packed fresh mint leaves
2 or 3 fresh hot green chilies, stemmed
2 inch piece fresh ginger, peeled and cut into chunks
1/2 red onion, quartered
juice of 2 lemons
1 tablespoon sugar
1/2 teaspoon salt
1/4 cup water

Tamarind Chutney (Imlee Kee Chutney)
Makes about 1 1/4 cups

1 tablespoon canola oil
1 teaspoon cumin seeds
1 teaspoon ground ginger
1/2 teaspoon cayenne pepper
1/2 teaspoon fennel seeds
1/2 teaspoon Asafoetida (optional)
1/2 teaspoon garam masala
2 cups water
1 1/4 cups sugar
3 tablespoons tamarind concentrate

Green Chutney: Combine all of the ingredients in a blender and process to a puree. This won't blend easily; you'll need to stop and start the blending and stir the ingredients often to get the mixture to catch. You can add a bit more water to facilitate the process, but the flavor of the chutney will be milder. Refrigerate and eat within 4 to 5 days.

Tamarind Chutney: Combine the oil and spices in a medium saucepan over medium-high heat and cook, stirring, for 1 minute. Add the water, sugar and tamarind concentrate. Bring to a boil, turn the heat down, and simmer until it turns chocolaty brown and is thick enough to coat the back of the spoon, 20 to 30

This is the quintessential Bombay street food dish. Chowpati Beach is the busiest beach in Bombay and hundreds of vendors walk it with their amazing array of foods. Both Indian kids and adults love this snack. It's based on a packaged snack food called bhel mix (a combination of puffed rice and chickpea noodles) that is stirred with chopped onion and tomato, and then flavored with coriander and tamarind chutneys. If you have boiled potatoes on hand, chop

minutes. (While still warm, it will look like a thin chocolate sauce and it will thicken a bit as it cools.) Store in the refrigerator in a tightly closed container up to 2 weeks.

Bhel Puri: Fold everything together in a large bowl and serve immediately (the bhel mix will get soggy if you wait).

Serves 3-4

PHOTO: Ben Fink

ONE UP AND THROW THAT IN TOO. BHEL MIX IS AVAILABLE AT INDIAN SUPERMARKETS AND SOME SPECIALTY FOOD STORES. THIS SALAD IS DELIGHTFUL FOR ITS MIXTURE IS SOFT, WET AND CRISP AND SO MUST BE EATEN IMMEDIATELY BEFORE THE CRISP BHEL MIX TURNS SOGGY. —*SUVIR SARAN & HEMANT MATHUR*

CURED SALMON WITH YUZU SORBET AND GRANNY SMITH APPLE CLOUD

Mario Lohninger • Cocoon Club • Frankfurt, Germany

10 ounces salmon fillets
1/2 cup sugar
1 1/2 cup salt
1 cup rice vinegar
1 cup water

Yuzu Sorbet
3 ounces yuzu juice
4 1/2 ounces lime juice
1 1/2 ounce seltzer water
1 1/2 ounce simple syrup
(simple syrup— 3 tablespoons sugar
and 3 tablespoons of water,
cook together to dissolve
sugar and cool)

Granny Smith Apple Cloud
2 cups Granny Smith apple juice
1 pinch vitamin C (approximately
1/16th teaspoon of ascorbic acid
— crushed Vitamin C tablet)
1 teaspoon lemon juice
3 sheets gelatin or 1 1/2 teaspoon
gelatin powder
pinch of salt

Plate and Finish
4 teaspoons trout roe
1 tablespoon extra virgin olive oil
1 teaspoon freshly grated horseradish
1 pinch of fleur de sel

Cover the de-boned salmon fillet (skin on) for about 60-80 minutes, depending how intense you want to have the salmon cured. Wash the salmon with 1 cup of water and the rice vinegar for about 5 minutes. Let dry and rest in refrigerator. If you do not wish to bother with this preparation of the salmon, you may purchase 4 slices of good quality Graved Lax or Smoked Salmon from a specialty store.

Yuzu Sorbet: Mix everything together. Whisk the mixture to blend and pour into the canister of an ice cream maker. Freeze according to the manufacturer's directions.

Granny Smith Apple Cloud: Add vitamin C (or citric acid powder) and the lemon juice to the apple juice to prevent oxidation. Soften the sheets of gelatin or gelatin powder in cold water, once soft, transfer and melt in a small pot with a little bit of warm apple juice. Mix the melted gelatin into the rest of the apple juice and season with salt. Fill it into an espuma bottle (whip cream maker) and chill on ice.

Plate & Finish: Plate the dish in a small glass (the size of a coffee cup). First, put in a slice of the cured salmon without the skin. Put a coffee spoon of trout roe on the side of the salmon and on the other side put a coffee spoon size of the apple cloud. Put a little quenelle of the yuzu sorbet on the salmon. Top with a bit of olive oil, freshly grated horseradish and fleur de sel. Serve right away.

Serves 4

PHOTO: Thomas Schauer

FRIED TOFU WITH ALMONDS

Mari Fujii • Fushiki-An • Kamakura, Japan

2 blocks firm tofu (about 1 3⁄4 pounds)
1 teaspoon salt
dash of white pepper
3/8 cup all-purpose flour
1/5 cup water
5/8 cup sliced almonds
vegetable oil, for deep frying
salt, for serving
1/2 lemon, cut into wedges

Wrap the tofu in a paper towel, cover with a plate and refrigerate for 30 minutes to remove excess moisture. Cut each block of tofu into 6 pieces and sprinkle with salt and pepper. To make the batter, mix the flour and water. The batter should be slightly lumpy. Coat the tofu pieces first with batter, then with almond slices. Heat the vegetable oil to 315° F, add the tofu pieces and deep fry until golden brown. Arrange on a serving plate with salt or lemon wedges.

Serves 4

Tofu is a light and simple ingredient that can be cooked in many ways for a variety of flavors. Deep fried tofu is particularly delicious. In this dish, the tofu is encrusted with almond slices before frying. The outside is crispy and aromatic, while the inside is soft and moist. This dish tastes best served hot with a sprinkling of lemon juice.
—*Mari Fujii*

MINCED SHRIMP ON BELGIAN ENDIVES

Hsiu-Pao Tseng • Tien Hsiang Lo at Landis Taipei Hotel • Taipei, Taiwan

6 ounces shrimp meat, cleaned and dried with a paper towel
8 Belgian endive leaves
2 tablespoons peas, cooked
2 teaspoons of pine nuts, lightly pan roasted on medium heat until nuts are about to turn brown
2 medium strawberries, finely diced
2 tablespoons mango, finely diced
2 tablespoons olive oil

Seasoning
1/2 egg whites
1/2 teaspoon cornstarch
1/2 teaspoon salt
1 tablespoon olive oil
pinch of white pepper
1 teaspoon cooking wine

Wash and dry endives, then set two each in a martini glass. Mince the shrimp and mix with seasoning. Heat olive oil in a wok or saucepan. Add shrimp and stir fry until just cooked and sit on paper towel to drain. Put shrimps, cooked peas, diced fruits in a mixing bowl and mix well. Divide evenly into 4 martini glasses. Sprinkle pine nuts on top and serve immediately.

Serves 4

PHOTOS: Left, Koji Iwamoto; This page, Landis Taipei Hotel

ORGANIC SHETLAND COD LIVER PONZU

Shin Tsujimura • Nobu Next Door • New York, NY

1 lobe organic Shetland cod liver, 8-12 ounces
1 teaspoon salt
6 ounces sake in a bowl for marinating
scallions, finely diced

Momiji Oroshi
1 pound daikon root, peeled and coarsely chopped
1/3 cup water
1/4 teaspoon togarashi pepper
1/4 teaspoon hot paprika

Ponzu
4 tablespoons soy sauce
8 tablespoons rice vinegar
2 tablespoons fresh lemon juice
3/4 inch square kombu (dried seaweed)

Momiji Oroshi: Puree daikon in water in blender. Pour pureed mixture into a cheesecloth or fine sieve to drain for 1/2 hour. Place in a non-reactive stainless steel or glass bowl. Whisk in the togarashi and paprika. Cover and refrigerate until needed, but should be made fresh each day.
Ponzu: Heat the kombu over a gas flame or under a broiler (grill), then put into a bowl with all other ingredients. Leave overnight or longer in the refrigerator.
Organic Cod Liver: Boil 2 quarts of water with 1 teaspoon salt in a small but deep pan. Turn off the heat. Cut the organic Shetland cod liver into 2 inch cubes. Marinate in sake for 1 minute, then dip into hot water for 30 seconds. Plate and garnish with scallions and momiji oroshi. Drizzle the Ponzu over the top.

Serves 8

Johnson Shetland Organic Cod is a unique new culinary product. The first commercially and only organically certified cod in the world is making its way into the best restaurants across America. Wild cod liver is largely unusable as they are bottom feeders and therefore subject to parasites whereas organically farmed cod are not. Ponzu is ideal to use on fish and shellfish dishes, or as a marinade. —*Shin Tsujimura*

PRAWNS IN EGG NETS *(ROTI JALA UDANG)*

Carol Selva Rajah • Chef, South East Asian Cuisine • Sydney, Australia

1 pound prawns, shelled and deveined with tails left on
1/2 cup coriander leaves
1/2 cup mint leaves
1 teaspoon black peppercorns
2 cloves garlic, peeled
2 ounces cooking oil
2 tablespoons fish sauce or to taste
1/2 teaspoon sugar or to taste
2 kaffir lime leaves, veins removed and finely julienned
5 eggs, beaten

Garnish
4 ounces mint leaves
3 to 4 red serrano chilies, seeded and finely sliced
3 to 4 pickled garlic heads, sliced
6 kalamansi or Tahitian limes, cut into wedges

Chop coriander and mint leaves, blend with peppercorns and garlic into a fine paste. Heat 1 tablespoon oil in a hot pan and sauté paste until aromatic. Add prawns and stir to mix. Quickly, add fish sauce, sugar and kaffir lime leaves. Stir until prawns are pink, not overcooked and the mixture coats the prawns. Keep warm and set aside. To make nets, you have to use your fingers to do this well (a little bit of practice will help). Lightly grease pan with a piece of absorbent paper dipped in oil and heat until hot but not smoking. Curl up hand and dip fingers into bowl of beaten egg. Scoop up egg and drop, spreading it in a rotary fashion over pan. Continue doing this until you have a web like net, the size of a dinner plate. Ensure that the edges are reinforced with more egg so the net can be lifted out quickly with a spatula. Continue making more nets until the eggs are used up. Do not remove too early or your egg will not come up as well. Transfer each net to a flat plate and place 4 to 5 mint leaves in the center. Top with 1 tablespoon prawn mixture, a few chili strips and pickled garlic slices. Fold net over the prawn and serve with a couple wedges of kalamasi.

Serves 8

PHOTO: This page,

SASHIMI OF NZ BREAM WITH GINGER AND MINT ORANGE AND SHISO DRESSED TUNA TATAKI

Chris Behre • Cinch • Santa Monica, CA

1/2 pound NZ bream
1/2 pound fresh tuna, whole loin piece, not sliced
4-5 mint leaves, sliced thinly
3 ounces bean shoots
small bunch arugula leaves or other salad leaf
ground pepper
white sesame seeds

Ginger and Mirin Dressing
3 ounces sushi vinegar
2 teaspoons mirin
2 teaspoons soy sauce
1 1/2 ounce olive oil
3 ounces grapeseed oil
1 teaspoon grated ginger (add after dressing is mixed)

Orange Shiso Dressing
1 small orange zest and half the juice
2 teaspoons Au shiso sauce
1 teaspoon soy sauce
3 ounces grapeseed oil
1 teaspoon mirin

Roll length of tuna in ground pepper, brush off excess, then sear evenly in a lightly oiled hot pan 2-3 seconds each side, then chill. Slice bream on an angle in thin strips and marinate in small amounts of ginger dressing 2-3 minutes. Slice chilled seared tuna in 1/4 inch slices and marinate in orange dressing 2-3 minutes. Mix marinated bream with mint strips and place on arugula leaves. Sprinkle with white sesame seeds and dress with more marinade. Place 3-4 slices of marinated tuna tataki on bean shoots, bream strips and salad greens. Dress with more marinade and serve.

Serves 4

SATAYS WITH PEANUT SAUCE

Hisham Johari • Red 8 at Wynn Las Vegas • Las Vegas, NV

Satays
4 pieces chicken thigh or flank steak

Marinade
2 stalks lemon grass, chopped
1 whole red onion, finely chopped
1 cup corn oil
4 tablespoons ginger, chopped
4 tablespoons turmeric powder
2 tablespoons cumin powder
1 teaspoon coarse black pepper
1 teaspoon salt
3 tablespoons sugar

Peanut Sauce for Dipping
2 cups roasted peanuts, roughly chopped
1/2 cup coconut milk
6 tablespoons granulated sugar
1 tablespoon salt
1 teaspoon turmeric powder
1/2 cup water
3 tablespoons red chilies, pounded
3 tablespoons corn oil
1 teaspoon shrimp paste
1 whole white onion, chopped
1 stalk lemon grass, finely chopped

Satays: Soak bamboo skewers overnight in water before use. Marinate chicken or beef for 3 hours in a mixing bowl with satay ingredients. Grill using charcoal for better flavor. Serve with peanut dipping sauce.

Peanut Sauce: Heat oil in pan. Add chopped onions, shrimp paste, turmeric powder, lemon grass and pounded chilies. Stir all ingredients until fragrant. Add in coconut milk and water and bring to a boil. Put in sugar, salt and peanuts. Stir constantly and reduce to moderate heat. Simmer until sauce thickens.

Serves 4

PHOTOS: Left, Martin Herbst; This page, Bill Milne/Milne Studios

SAUTÉED OYSTER MUSHROOMS WITH SCALLIONS AND ONIONS

Sue Lee • Korean Chef •
New York, NY

8 ounces oyster mushrooms, shredded by hand after boiling for 5 seconds
7 ounces onions, thinly shredded
5 ounces scallions, cut into 3 inch lengths
2 cups mixed green salad
1 teaspoon sesame seeds, toasted

Sauce
1/2 cup Asian pear, diced small
1/2 cup orange, diced small
3 tablespoons onions, diced small
3 tablespoons ginger, puréed
1/2 tablespoon sesame oil
1/4 cup water
2 tablespoons brown sugar
6 tablespoons soy sauce
1 tablespoon sake
1/4 piece lemon for juice
1 tablespoon potato starch

Bring diced pears, oranges, onions and sauce ingredients together in a mixing bowl and mix thoroughly. Then, mix in the mushrooms, onions and scallions. Over medium heat, sauté the mixed ingredients quickly for about 2 minutes. Spread the mixed green salad on the plate, then top with the sautéed ingredients. Sprinkle with a teaspoon of toasted sesame seeds before serving.

Serves 2

SPICY KIMCHI MUSHROOM PANCAKES

Sue Lee • Korean Chef •
New York, NY

2 pounds of Napa cabbage kimchi
(can be bought ready made from a Korean grocery store)
4 stalks of spring onions
1/4 pound oyster mushrooms
1 tablespoon garlic, grounded
2 teaspoons salt
1 pound wheat flour
1 1/4 cup water
cooking oil

Dice the kimchi, oyster mushrooms and spring onions into small pieces. In a big bowl, mix the flour with water, garlic and salt until the batter is evenly blended. Add the kimchi, spring onions and mushrooms to the batter and mix well. Scoop a full ladle of the batter and fry the pancakes in a heated frying pan with cooking oil, making sure that both sides are cooked evenly until light brown. The pancakes should be about 5 inches in diameter.

Makes 10 pancakes

TARTAR OF TUNA, HAMACHI AND SALMON WITH TARO ROOT CHIPS

Takashi Yagihashi • Okada at Wynn Las Vegas • Las Vegas, NV

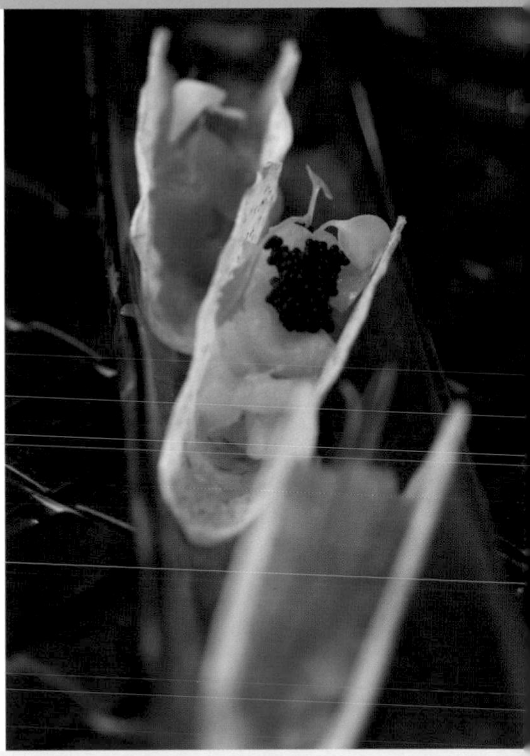

6 ounces tuna loin (sashimi grade), small dices
6 ounces hamachi (sashimi grade),small dices
6 ounces salmon (sashimi grade), small dices
2 teaspoons red onions, small dices
2 teaspoons chives, small dices
1 1/2 teaspoon tobiko caviar (flying fish roe)
2 teaspoons soy sauce
2 teaspoons chili oil
18 pieces baby red shiso leaves
pinch of sesame seeds (optional)

Taro Root Chips
1 quart vegetable oil
18 pieces taro root, sliced paper thin into
4 inch diameter discs
salt to taste

Tartar: Place tuna, hamachi and salmon in three different mixing bowls. Cover with plastic wrap and store in refrigerator until needed. In a medium mixing bowl, place onions, chives, tobiko, soy sauce and chili oil. Stir together until well mixed. Divide onion-caviar mixture evenly among tuna, hamachi and salmon. Fold each gently until all are well mixed. Place plastic wrap over each and store in refrigerator for later use. Note: This is a raw fish recipe and should be eaten that day.

Taro Root Chips: Preheat oil in a large pot to 350° F. Fry taro root into individual chips. Remove from fryer and drain on paper towel and immediately season with salt. Store covered in a dry place.

Assembly: Place approximately 1 ounce of each of the tartars onto the taro root chips, then add baby red shiso leaves to each. Sprinkle sesame seeds on each tartar chip and arrange one of each type of tartar on plates. Serve immediately.

Serves 6

PHOTO: Bill Milne/Milne Studios

TRI-COLOR WHEAT PANCAKES *(SAM-SAEK MIL SSAM)*

An Jung-Hyun • Woorega • Seoul, Korea

Pancakes
1 cup all purpose flour, well sifted for softer texture
1/2 teaspoon salt
1 1/2 cup water
1 teaspoon sesame oil
1/4 teaspoon green tea powder
1/4 cup dried shrimp, finely ground in a coffee grinder
1/4 cup dried Shiitake mushrooms, finely ground in a coffee grinder

Fillers
3 ounces ground beef
1/2 small onion, finely chopped
1/4 zucchini, finely chopped
2 tablespoons vegetable oil

Dipping Sauce (may vary to suit your taste)
1 tablespoon soy sauce
pinch of sugar
pinch of salt
1 teaspoon vinegar
1 teaspoon sesame oil
1/4 teaspoon pureed garlic (optional)

Mix the pancake mix together to form dough and split into three parts. Add green tea powder to one of the three parts and mix well. Add ground dried shrimp to the second part and mix well. Add ground black mushrooms to the third part and mix well. Split each colored dough into 3 parts and roll flat to make thin, round pancakes. Using a little vegetable oil, pan fry each pancake until cooked and set aside. Mix all the filler ingredients and pan fry in vegetable oil until cooked. Place a small amount of filler in each pancake and roll like an egg roll. Place different colored rolls on a plate and serve with dipping sauce.

Serves 2-3

UME POPCORN

Troy N. Thompson • Jer-ne Restaurant and Bar at The Ritz-Carlton • Marina del Rey, CA

olive oil
popcorn
ume powder, to taste
(1 pound umeboshi plums, see recipe below)

Ume Powder: Take the seeds out of the umeboshi plums and place them in a food dehydrator for 12 hours or until dry and brittle (it's best to do overnight). Let them cool down and pulse them in the coffee grinder and then sift them through the screen of the sifter. Place the powder in an airtight container.

Popcorn: Put the olive oil in a pot. Use enough to cover the bottom of the pot to a depth of half the diameter of a kernel of corn, give or take. Try not to use too much olive oil. Put the pot on the stove. The burner should be turned to its hottest setting. Put a few kernels of popcorn in the pot. Put the lid on. Wait for all kernels to pop. Remove the lid. Pour in enough popcorn to cover the bottom of the pot evenly. Don't use much more than that. Put the lid back on. The popcorn should start popping fairly briskly shortly after that. The popcorn will continue to pop briskly for a few minutes, then will slow down. At this point, dump the popcorn into the bowl before it starts to burn. Once the popcorn is in the bowl, add ume powder to taste. Do not add salt because the ume has enough salt in it.

YOU CAN ADD SOME MELTED BUTTER IF YOU WANT. YOU WILL BE SURPRISED HOW WELL BUTTER, OLIVE OIL AND POPCORN GOES WITH THE UME TASTE. USE THE UME POWDER ON MANY OTHER RECIPES AS WELL. UMEBOSHI MAY BE PURCHASED DRIED OR IN PASTE FORM IN MOST ASIAN MARKETS SHOULD YOU NOT HAVE THEM FRESH OR OWN A FOOD DEHYDRATOR. —*TROY N. THOMPSON*

YOUNG MOUNTAIN LAMB SATAY

Nathan Uy • Wild Ginger • Seattle, WA

Lamb
1 pound lamb sirloin, trim fat and cut into 1 inch cubes
2 garlic cloves, finely chopped
2 small shallots, finely chopped
1 tablespoon Indonesian sweet soy sauce (Kecap Manis)
2 teaspoons black pepper
8 wooden skewers
1/2 tablespoon grapeseed or canola oil

Peanut Sauce
2 tablespoons peanut or vegetable oil
2 slices medium shallots
2 slices small red onion
1/4 teaspoon cumin
1/2 teaspoon ground coriander
1/2 teaspoon dried red chili flakes
3 candlenuts, crushed
1/4 cup coconut milk
1/4 cup coconut cream
2 teaspoons brown sugar
1 teaspoon salt, to taste
1/4 cup roasted peanuts, pounded

Rice Cakes
1/2 cup Jasmine rice
1/2 cup sticky rice
(may substitute coconut milk for 1/2 of the cooking liquid)

Cucumber and Ginger Pickles
1 pound small pickling cucumbers, sliced
2 tablespoons distilled white vinegar
2 tablespoons sugar
2 teaspoons coarse salt
4 slices fresh ginger, peeled
4 shallots, peeled and quartered

Lamb: Mix garlic, shallots, soy sauce and black pepper in a medium size bowl. Add lamb and coat with marinade. Cover and refrigerate for at least 2 hours. While lamb is marinating, soak wooden skewers in water. Put 4 pieces of marinated lamb on each skewer and grill, 2 minutes on each side, over charcoal or gas. Serve with peanut sauce, rice cakes and pickled cucumber slices.

Peanut Sauce: Heat oil in wok or shallow pan and fry shallots and red onions until light brown. Add cumin, coriander and chili flakes and cook over medium heat until fragrant (about 30 seconds). Add candlenuts and cook for 1 minute. Add coconut milk, coconut cream and brown sugar and simmer for 5 minutes over medium heat,

"SATAY" IS AN INDONESIAN WORD MEANING SKEWERED AND GRILLED. ONE OF THE MOST MEMORABLE EXPERIENCES OF A TRIP TO ASIA IS ENJOYING FOODS FROM SIDEWALK HAWKER STALLS. ENJOY ONE OR TWO FOR A SNACK OR MAKE A MEAL WITH A VARIETY OF SKEWERS. —*NATHAN UY*

stirring occasionally. Remove from heat. Transfer cooked ingredients to blender or food processor. Add crushed peanuts and salt. Blend until smooth.

Rice Cakes: Cook rice in rice cooker or on stovetop. Spread cooked rice onto square or oblong sheet pan with 1 inch high sides. Cover with wax paper or plastic wrap and use a rolling pin to compress rice. Cut into 1-1/2 inch squares.

Cucumber & Ginger Pickles: Combine sliced cucumbers with 1 teaspoon salt. Let sit for 1 hour. Rinse cucumbers with fresh water and drain well. Combine remaining salt, vinegar, sugar and 5 tablespoons of hot water. Stir to dissolve. Pour over cucumbers and toss with shallots and ginger. Serve after 1 hour.

Serves 4

PHOTO: Diane Padys

BANANA BLOSSOM AND ARTICHOKE SALAD WITH CHILI JAM DRESSING

Ian Chalermkittichai • Kittichai • New York, NY

7 ounces banana blossoms, cut into 1 inch pieces and soaked in lemon water
7 ounces artichokes, sliced thinly and soaked in lemon water
3 ounces roasted chili paste in soy bean oil
3 ounces tamarind base (see recipe below)
3 ounces coconut cream
fish sauce to taste
lime juice to taste
1 1/2 ounces roasted coconut flakes
3 ounces rough, chopped cashew nuts
1 1/2 ounces crispy fried shallots

Tamarind Base
2 1/2 ounces palm sugar
3 ounces tamarind concentrate (in liquid form)

Blossom Salad: Poach banana blossoms and artichokes in coconut milk and water (equal parts). Poach for 20 minutes. Cool, drain and set aside. Save a couple of large petals of banana blossoms and cut the rest into 1 inch pieces for presentation.

Tamarind Base: Dissolve palm sugar in tamarind concentrate over medium heat in saucepan.

Chili Jam Dressing: Add roasted chili paste, coconut cream, lime juice and fish sauce to saucepan with tamarind base. Mix well. To serve, pour dressing over blossom salad. Top with coconut flakes, chopped cashew nuts and crispy fried shallots.

Serves 4

CHICKEN SALAD CHINOIS

Wolfgang Puck • Spago • Beverly Hills, CA*

Chinese Mustard Vinaigrette

1 egg yolk
2 teaspoons dry Chinese mustard (may substitute with standard dry mustard powder)
1/4 cup rice wine vinegar
1 teaspoon soy sauce
2 tablespoons light sesame oil
2 to 3 tablespoons peanut oil
salt
freshly ground pepper

Chicken Salad

one 3 pound chicken (its cavity filled with celery, carrots, onions, garlic, bay leaves, thyme, salt and pepper)
2 ounces unsalted butter, melted
2 small heads or 1 medium head Napa cabbage
1 cup romaine lettuce, cut into 1/4 inch julienne strips
8 to 10 snow peas, cut into 1/4 inch julienne strips
1 teaspoon black sesame seeds

Place all the vinaigrette ingredients in a blender and blend until smooth. Season to taste. Set aside. Preheat the oven to 425° F. Place the chicken on a rack in a roasting pan and baste it with some of the butter. Roast for about 1 1/2 hours, or until just done. (The meat near the joints should still be slightly pink). Baste every 15 to 20 minutes with the butter and the drippings. Select 4 to 8 nice leaves from the Napa cabbage and reserve them. Slice the remaining cabbage into 1/4 inch julienne strips. Shred the meat from the breasts and thighs of the chicken. Combine the chicken, cabbage, romaine and snow peas in a bowl and toss with enough vinaigrette to coat the salad nicely. Arrange the reserved Napa cabbage leaves around the edge of a large serving plate. Mount the salad in the center and sprinkle with sesame seeds.

Serves 3-4 (or more for smaller portions)

*Recipe courtesy of Wolfgang Puck, *The Wolfgang Puck Cookbook*, 1986
*Please see page 260 for a complete list of restaurant locations.

PHOTOS: Left, Martin Jansche; This page, Ron Manville

FRENCH BEAN AND APPLE SALAD WITH CRÉME FRAICHE, TOASTED CUMIN AND CARPACCIO OF TOMATO

Vikram Garg • IndeBleu • Washington, DC

French Bean Apple Salad
4 ounces french beans
1 Granny Smith apple
2 ounces low fat crème fraiche
salt to taste
crushed black pepper to taste
1/4 teaspoon shallots
4 ounces assorted lettuce

Carpaccio of Tomato
2 vine ripe tomatoes

Carpaccio Dressing
1/4 teaspoon basil, shredded
1/4 teaspoon tarragon, shredded
1/4 teaspoon shallots, minced
2 ounces balsamic vinegar
2 ounces olive oil
1/4 teaspoon sugar
crushed black pepper to taste
salt to taste

Garnish
1/4 teaspoon toasted cumin
1/8 teaspoon crystal sea salt
1 ounce parmesan shaving

French Bean Apple Salad: String french beans and cut 2 inches long. Cook until soft in salted water and refresh. Peel apple and cut similar size to beans. Toss with lemon juice. Combine crème fraiche, salt, crushed pepper and finely chopped shallots to make a dressing. Dress apple and beans with the dressing. Clean assorted lettuce and keep chilled.

Carpaccio: Choose firm vine ripe tomatoes and slice paper thin.

Carpaccio Dressing: Shred basil and tarragon and chop shallots. Combine with balsamic vinegar, salt, sugar and crushed pepper. Whisk in olive oil.

Garnish: Broil cumin seeds in a pan until golden brown. Remove and roughly crush.

Plating: Place lettuce on plate. Put French bean and apple salad over bed of lettuce. Spread tomato carpaccio over salad. Garnish with crushed cumin seeds. Finish with freshly shaved parmesan and crystal sea salt.

Serves 4

FRESH BURMESE GINGER SALAD

Toni Robertson • Silks at Mandarin Oriental Hotel • San Francisco, CA

3 ounces fresh young ginger, peeled and shredded
1/2 cup lime juice
3 tablespoons crispy fried garlic slices
3 tablespoons toasted chick pea flour
3 tablespoons roasted peanuts
2 tablespoons toasted sesame seeds
1 cup green papaya, peeled and shredded
1 cup green cabbage, thinly shredded
1/2 cup carrots, peeled and thinly shredded
1/2 cup green tomatoes, diced small
1/2 cup yellow split peas, soaked in water for 6 hours, drained well and fried in hot oil for 1 minute
3 tablespoons dried shrimp powder
2 tablespoons fish sauce
1 teaspoon corn oil
lemon slices, for garnish
lime slices, for garnish
cilantro, for garnish

Place the young ginger in a small bowl and cover with lime juice, marinating for at least 3 days in the refrigerator. Firmly squeeze out the juice from the ginger pulp, and discard the lime juice. Mix the ginger together with the other ingredients, including the toasted chick pea flour, toasted sesame seeds, and fried yellow split peas. Place the salad in a small bowl and garnish with fresh lime and lemon slices and cilantro. Serve at room temperature.

Serves 4-6

PHOTO: Ray Grefe

THIS IS AN EXTRAORDINARILY SIMPLE SALAD THAT PROVIDES A QUICK AND HEALTHY MEAL. THE UNUSUAL FLAVORS AND TEXTURES OF THIS DISH ARE A REFLECTION OF THE SIMPLE AND UNPRETENTIOUS CHARACTER OF BURMESE CUISINE. THE KEY INGREDIENT, GINGER IS WELL KNOWN AS A DIGESTIVE AID. —*TONI ROBERTSON*

GREEN MANGO SALAD *(NYUOM SVAY)*

Longteine & Nadsa de Monteiro • Elephant Walk • Boston, MA*

4 medium green mangos, finely julienned
1/2 lb lean pork (fresh ham or tenderloin), cooked and finely julienned
16 medium size shrimp
1 large shallot, very thinly sliced
1 cup loosely packed fresh mint leaves
1 cup loosely packed fresh Asian basil leaves
1/2 small red bell pepper, thinly sliced
1/3 cup peanuts, roasted and coarsely ground
1/3 cup salad dressing (see recipe below)

Salad Dressing
1/4 cup water
1/2 cup sugar
1 garlic clove, minced
1 small shallot, minced
2 tablespoons fresh lime juice
2 teaspoons table salt

Finely julienne the green mango and reserve. Cook the shrimp and let cool. Peel off tail and slice in half, lengthwise. Finely julienne the red bell peppers about 1/4 inch thick and 2 inches long. Pluck the basil and mint leaves and reserve. Toast whole blanched peanuts in a 320° F oven for about 8 minutes or until golden brown. Let the peanuts cool completely. Coarsely chop the roasted peanuts in a mini chopper or food processor. Set aside a handful for garnish, mix in the ground peanuts. Peel and finely slice the shallots as thin as possible. In large bowl, toss all the ingredients together with the julienned pork and shrimp. Add the dressing and toss. Sprinkle with the remaining peanuts and serve immediately.
Salad Dressing: In small pan, heat up water until hot but not boiling. Remove from heat and add all the ingredients. Stir to mix well and dissolve sugar completely. Cool down completely before using.

Serves 4

*Please see page 260 for a complete list of restaurant locations.

Green mangos are grown not just in Asian countries with tropical climate, but also in Florida, Mexico and Haiti. These mangos have deep green skin with very firm flesh. Once peeled, the flesh is easily julienned or shredded. This salad is tart and sweet with freshness of the mint and Asian basil to enliven everything. If so desired, add fresh bird's eye chilies for a spicy kick. —*Longteine & Nadsa De Monteiro*

GREEN PAPAYA SALAD

(SOM TAM MARAKOR)

Taweewat Hurapan • Hurapan Kitchen • New York, NY

3 ounces green papaya, shredded
1/2 ounce fish sauce
1/2 ounce lime juice
1/2 ounce palm sugar
1 ounce roasted unsalted peanuts, ground
1/2 teaspoon garlic and chili, chopped
10 pieces Thai long beans, cut 1 inch length
5 pieces whole grape tomatoes or cherry tomatoes

Shred the green papaya in a food processor, pulsing and do not puree. Mix fish sauce, lime juice and palm sugar well, if necessary, over low heat to make dressing. Mix shredded papaya, Thai long beans, grape tomatoes in a bowl. Add dressing and place on plates. Top with ground peanuts and serve.

Serves 2

PHOTOS: Left, Robert Perry; This page, Martin Januschе

GRILLED PRAWNS SPICY SALAD WITH AROMATIC THAI HERBS

(PLAA GHOONG)

Vichit Mukura • Baan Rim Naam at The Oriental • Bangkok, Thailand

10 ounces prawns, shelled with tail on, grilled
2 teaspoons lemon grass, thinly sliced
1/2 teaspoon kaffir lime leaves, shredded
4 tablespoons shallots, sliced
2 teaspoons spring onions, sliced
2 teaspoons Siamese coriander (phag chee lorm), chopped
3 1/2 tablespoons fish sauce
3 1/2 tablespoons lime juice
2 tablespoons sugar syrup (sugar syrup is 1 part water and 1 part sugar)

Prig Yam
2 tablespoons big red chilies
1 teaspoon big yellow chilies
1 teaspoon coriander roots
1 tablespoon small garlic clove
1 1/2 teaspoons pickled garlic
1/2 teaspoon pickled garlic juice

Prig Laab (Chili Paste)
2 teaspoons dried big red chilies, grilled
1 tablespoon small garlic, grilled
1 tablespoon shallots, grilled
1 1/2 teaspoons› galangal roots, grilled and shredded coarsely
1/2 teaspoon shrimp paste, wrapped in banana leaf and grilled

Prig Yam: In a blender, mix the red chilies, the yellow chilies, the coriander roots, the garlic and the pickled garlic together until they become a smooth paste. Add the pickled garlic juice and mix well with the paste.
Prig Laab (Chili Paste): In a blender, mix the chilies, garlic, shallots and the galangal root together until pasty. Add the shrimp paste and mix well.
Dressing: Mix prig yam and prig laab, fish sauce, lime juice and sugar syrup together until dissolved.
To Serve: Add the grilled prawns, lemon grass, shredded kaffir lime leaves, sliced shallots, sliced spring onion, chopped Siamese coriander into a mixing bowl. Mix well, then add dressing. Toss well and serve.

Serves 2-3

MyPyramid.gov

LEAF LETTUCE SALAD *(SANGCHU KOTJORI)*

Hi Soo Shin Hepinstall • Author & Food Consultant • Silver Spring, MD

12 ounces leaf lettuce, torn into bite size pieces
20 wild sesame leaves, julienned (or shiso leaves)
20 crown daisy leaves, cut into bite size pieces
1 Asian pear, about 12 ounces, peeled and cut into matchsticks

Dressing (yaknyomjang)
1 clove garlic, crushed and finely chopped
1 tablespoon salted shrimp
1 tablespoon sesame oil
1 tablespoon rice wine or dry vermouth
2 tablespoons rice or distilled white vinegar
1 teaspoon Korean hot red pepper flakes
2 tablespoons freshly squeezed lemon juice, or if in season, yuja*
1/2 tablespoon dark soy sauce
2 walnut halves, coarsely chopped
1 tablespoon toasted sesame seeds
1 regular green onion, white and pale green part only, finely minced
pinch of freshly ground black pepper
1 tablespoon olive oil

Garnish
1 Korean hot green pepper, halved, cut into mini-dices
1 Korean hot red pepper, cut into mini-dices
2 tablespoons toasted pine nuts

Prepare the greens several hours ahead of time. Wash and dry. Cut each according to the directions. Wrap in a paper towel and place in a plastic bag. Chill in the refrigerator. In a large bowl, add garlic, salted shrimp, sesame oil and mix. Let mellow for a few seconds and then add the rest of the ingredients, except olive oil. Mix well. Just before serving, add the pear to the vegetables and toss very lightly. Drizzle the olive oil and toss a few times. Divide into individual bowls and sprinkle the garnish on top. Serve immediately.

Serves 4

PHOTO: This page, Larry G. Hepinstall

*Yuja is similar to Japanese Yuzu, which can be purchased bottled in Asian markets.
Adapted from Hi Soo Shin Hepinstall's *Growing Up In A Korean Kitchen: A Cookbook*, Berkeley: Ten Speed Press, 2001

THIS SALAD IS AN ANCIENT KOREAN RECIPE FOR PREPARING FRESH BABY FINGER SIZE LEAF LETTUCE. THE CLASSIC RECIPE FOR THE DRESSING WAS SIMPLY A DELICIOUS MIXTURE OF GREEN ONIONS, GARLIC, HOT PEPPERS AND GRAIN SYRUP IN SOY SAUCE, DANJANG (FERMENTED SOYBEAN PASTE) OR KOCH'UJANG (RED HOT PEPPER PASTE). THIS IS A CHILDHOOD FAMILY RECIPE, EXCEPT FOR THE OLIVE OIL. —*HI SOO SHIN HEPINSTALL*

LOBSTER AND PICKLED LOTUS ROOT SALAD

Cedric Tovar • Peacock Alley, Waldorf=Astoria Hotel • New York, NY

four 1 1/2 pound Maine lobsters
1 bunch scallions
1/4 pound peppercress
4 heirloom tomatoes
2 ounces of sea beans
1 pound of lotus root
1 gallon of water
1 lemon
6 pieces of star anise
2 tablespoons of black peppercorn
4 bay leaves
salt

Pickling Liquid
1 cup white wine
1/2 cup white wine vinegar
3 pieces star anise
10 whole cloves
2 tablespoons coriander seeds
2 tablespoons black peppercorns
1 tablespoon dill seeds
1/4 bunch dill

Orange Nuoc Mam Vinaigrette
4 oranges
1/2 bunch cilantro
1 tablespoon of sesame oil
2 ounces extra virgin olive oil
2 tablespoons fish sauce (nuoc mam)

A day in advance, pickle the lotus root. Combine all the pickling liquid ingredients in a stainless steel pot and bring to a boil. Simmer for 15 minutes. Peel and slice the lotus root into 1/6 inch slices. Put the lotus root slices into the pot with the liquid. Boil for two minutes. Cool at room temperature, leaving the lotus root in the liquid. Keep refrigerated. On the day you plan to serve, set a pot of boiling water with lemon juice, bay leaves, lemon and orange zest, peppercorns, anise seed and salt. Add the lobsters and cook for 5 minutes. Remove from cooking liquid and cool at room temperature. Crack the lobster shell and remove all meat delicately including the claws. Don't forget the good meat located in the knuckles. Keep refrigerated. To make the orange nuoc mam vinaigrette, squeeze 4 oranges and

THIS DISH IS THE EAST WEST DISH PAR EXCELLENCE. LOBSTER FROM THE COLD WATERS OF CANADA AND THE LOTUS ROOT, TYPICAL AQUATIC RHIZOME FROM THE CENTER AND TROPICAL EAST. THE VIETNAMESE INFLUENCE, WITH THE ADDITION OF FISH SAUCE (NUOC MAM), CAME WHEN I EXPERIMENTED WITH TUNA TARTAR AND GREEN APPLE. I TRIED TO FIND THE RIGHT BALANCE WITH THE SWEETNESS OF THE APPLES. IN THIS CASE, I FOUND THE COMBINATION OF NUOC MAM, ORANGE JUICE AND LOBSTER IDEAL. THIS RECIPE CAN BE ADAPTED WITH ANY KIND OF SHELLFISH, ESPECIALLY WATER PRAWNS. —*CEDRIC TOVAR*

reduce the juice by half. Cool the liquid down and emulsify with the sesame oil, fish sauce, virgin olive oil, and finally add the chopped cilantro and a pinch of black pepper. Blanch the scallions and the sea beans in salted water for 30 seconds. Shock in ice water to stop the cooking. In a bowl, combine the lobster tail, sea beans, heirloom tomatoes, and scallions. Season with sea salt, black pepper, and olive oil. Place each lobster tail and claw on a bed of lotus root. Garnish with peppercress and pour the orange nuoc mam vinaigrette over each salad. You can also garnish with chive flowers when in season.

Serves 4

PHOTO: Brett Mensh

NORTHEAST STYLE BEEF SALAD WITH SNAKE BEANS

Ian Chalermkittichai • Kittichai • New York, NY

1 1/4 pound steak

Marinade

1/2 cup oyster sauce
1/2 cup puree cilantro root
5 cloves garlic, finely chopped
1 teaspoon ground white pepper
1 tablespoon Golden Mountain seasoning sauce

Dressing

3/4 tablespoon palm sugar
1 1/2 tablespoons tamarind concentrate
4 tablespoons fish sauce
4 tablespoons lime juice

Salad

1/2 cup mint leaves, finely sliced
1/2 cup sawtooth coriander
1/2 cup thinly sliced shallots
1-2 teaspoons dried roasted chili flakes to taste
5 tablespoons ground aromatic sweet rice (see ingredients and preparation below)
7 ounces snake beans, cut into 2 inch lengths, quickly blanched in heavily salted water
1 medium white cabbage, cut into big wedges

Steak & Marinade: Mix all the ingredients for the marinade in a bowl, add the beef, and marinate for at least 2 hours. Light or preheat the grill to high, and grill the beef directly over the coals until medium rare. Allow to rest for 10 minutes before slicing.

Salad & Dressing: Add palm sugar and tamarind to a small bowl and heat in a saucepan, half filled with water, until warm and mixed. Add the remaining salad ingredients to a medium bowl and stir in the tamarind mixture. Toss the sliced beef with the salad ingredients and check the seasoning. The flavor should be salty, sour and spicy. Serve the salad with a wedge of raw white cabbage.

Sweet Rice: Preheat oven to 375° F. Spread the rice on a cookie sheet. Roast for an hour or until dark brown, stirring occasionally to stop the grains around the edge from becoming too brown. Reduce oven temperature to 200° F. Spread the lemon grass, shallots, garlic, kaffir leaves and galangal on a sheet pan and dry in the oven for about 2 hours or until crispy. Check occasionally to make sure the garlic does not burn. Mix the aromatics with the browned dried rice and grind to a powder in a coffee grinder. Sprinkle over salad and serve.

Serves 4

SALAD OF HONSHIMEJI AND KOREAN BUCKWHEAT NOODLES IN BROTH

Anita Lo • Annisa • New York, NY

1/2 pound fresh Korean buckwheat noodles (naengmyun), blanched and shocked (may substitute with Japanese soba)
1 teaspoon oil
2 cups buckwheat sprouts (may substitute with daikon sprouts or beansprouts)
1/3 cup shredded blanched large cap stems (see recipe below)
2 tablespoons green scallions, julienne cut
1 tablespoon mushroom soy
1 teaspoon lemon juice
salt and pepper to taste
1/2 cup Honshimeji mushrooms, large caps separated from the stems and reserved, smaller ones kept separate and whole

Broth
3 cups chilled blanching liquid from the Honshimeji
1/4 cup mushroom soy
2 tablespoons lemon juice

Tempura (optional)
3/4 cup flour
1/4 cup cornstarch
1 pinch baking soda
1 egg yolk
iced seltzer
salt and pepper

Garnish
Button mushroom caps, deep fried in tempura
4 quail egg yolks

Bring 1 quart of water to a boil. Add a pinch of salt. Add the smaller whole Honshimeji mushrooms. Simmer and cook for about 3 minutes until done. Fish out with a strainer and set aside. Repeat with the large mushroom stems, keeping them separate. Mix the broth with the mushroom soy and lemon juice, then taste and adjust seasonings and chill. Just before serving, make the tempura batter. Mix the dry ingredients together and the wet in a separate bowl. Mix the wet and dry together using chopsticks, just until lumpy. Coat the mushroom caps in the batter and deep fry at 350° F until golden and crispy. Drain on a clean paper towel. Keep warm. Shred the blanched mushroom stems and mix with blanched noodles, oil, sprouts, and scallions. Season to taste with the mushroom soy, lemon, salt and pepper. Divide the noodles into 4 portions. Twirl each portion into a nest using a fork and top with a quail egg yolk. Surround with 4-5 ounces of broth, a few blanched whole mushrooms and a few tempura mushroom caps.

MyPyramid.gov

Serves 1

PHOTOS: Martin Jansche

SEAWEED SALAD

Jason Ha & Sean Ahn • Zip Fusion Sushi • Los Angeles, CA*

3/4 ounce (20 grams) dried seaweed (fureo wakame), soaked and finely shredded
1/2 cucumber, peeled
1/2 medium carrot, peeled
20 onion sprouts (may substitute with alfalfa or other fine sprouts)
one 5 inch daikon radish, peeled
1/2 cup hiashi fresh seaweed, optional
2 round or square wonton skins
1/4 cup slivered nori seaweed
2 tablespoons norigoma furikake flakes
2 tablespoons salad dressing, ZIP ginger dressing recommended

ZIP Ginger Dressing
2 cups Ponzu sauce
1 thumb-sized piece of ginger, peeled and grated
two 4 inch pieces orange pickled gobo, very finely minced
1/4 medium white onion, grated or very finely minced

Stir the ingredients for the dressing together. Put into a squeeze bottle or small pitcher. Use a Japanese rotary slicer to make fine threads of the cucumber and carrot in separate piles, or use a mandolin to slice very thin and then cut into very fine shreds. Slice daikon radish into thin strips by hand or with a mandolin and cut into very fine shreds. Cut 2 wonton skins into very thin strips. Deep fry in corn oil until crispy but not very dark. Drain on paper towels. Form the shredded vegetables, sprouts and seaweed into individual balls about 2 inches in diameter by pressing them in the palms of your hands. Arrange the balls close together in the middle of a dinner plate. In a layered ring around the vegetables, scatter the wonton strips, slivered nori and norigoma furikake flakes. Drizzle ZIP ginger dressing over the vegetable arrangement to taste. Present the dish with two forks or chopsticks and gently toss all the ingredients together before eating.

Serves 2

MyPyramid.gov

*Please see page 260 for a complete list of restaurant locations.

ALTHOUGH THERE ARE A NUMBER OF INGREDIENTS IN THIS RECIPE, THESE ITEMS ARE PERFECT ASIAN PANTRY BUILDERS BECAUSE THEY STORE WELL AND ARE USED OFTEN IN ASIAN COOKING. ALL OF THE SHREDDING, FRYING AND DRESSING FOR THE ZIP GINGER DRESSING CAN BE DONE SEVERAL HOURS AHEAD, COVERED AND REFRIGERATED AND ASSEMBLED JUST BEFORE SERVING. WE WERE TAUGHT FROM AN EARLY AGE IN KOREA THAT THE SEA IS NATURE'S STOREHOUSE OF BEAUTY PRODUCTS AND SEAWEED IS ONE OF THE BEST. OUR SIGNATURE ZIP SEAWEED SALAD FEEDS ALL OF THE SENSES AND HAS A CRUNCHY TEXTURE ADDED TO IT MAKING IT REALLY FUN TO EAT. —*JASON HA & SEAN AHN*

SHIITAKE PEPPERCORN CRUSTED SALMON SALAD

Jeff Liu • Bistro 88 • Austin, TX

Citrus Dressing
1/2 pound mixed salad greens
4 ounces fresh orange juice
2 teaspoons lime juice
2 teaspoons lemon juice
3 tablespoons extra virgin olive oil
1 tablespoon sugar
1 pinch white pepper
1 can of mandarin orange segments
12 red grape tomatoes, halved, quartered, or sliced into circles
1/4 cup nori strips— loose, not packed down

Mint Yogurt Sauce
4 ounces plain yogurt
1 ounce sugar
1 pinch white pepper
1-2 tablespoons mint leaves, torn

Peppercorn Salmon
24 ounces of salmon, cut into 3 ounce portions
2 ounces dried Shiitake mushrooms, processed to powder in spice grinder
2 tablespoons cracked peppercorn
2-3 tablespoons neutral vegetable oil (canola or corn oil) for searing

Citrus Dressing: Whisk olive oil into orange, lime and lemon juices until emulsified, then season to taste with sugar and white pepper. Refrigerate.
Mint Yogurt Sauce: Whisk yogurt with sugar, white pepper and mint leaves. Chill.
Peppercorn Salmon: On a plate, mix together powdered Shiitake mushrooms and peppercorn. Coat salmon fillets in mushroom and peppercorn mix. Heat oil in pan and sear salmon in hot skillet on all sides (a non stick pan is good for this and will require less oil), leaving center rare. Remove from pan and set aside. To plate the salad, toss the mixed salad greens and mandarin orange segments with citrus dressing. Garnish with grape tomatoes and nori strips. Portion out servings of salad onto large plates and arrange 2 salmon fillets on each plate next to the salad, not on top of the greens. Drizzle salmon with yogurt dressing.

PHOTO: James Fung

Serves 4

SHOJIN SALAD WITH PEANUT FLAVORED TOFU DRESSING

Mari Fujii • Fushiki-An • Kamakura, Japan

8 thin spears asparagus, woody ends removed
4 lettuce leaves, torn into bite-sized pieces
1 1/2 cups tomatoes, dice cut into 1/2 inch pieces

Dressing
1 block tofu (silken, if available)
2 tablespoons peanut butter, unsweetened
2 tablespoons rice vinegar or any white vinegar
2 tablespoons olive oil
2 teaspoons maple syrup
dash of black pepper
1 teaspoon salt
2 tablespoons lemon juice

Wrap the tofu in a paper towel, place a plate on top and refrigerate for about 30 minutes to remove excess moisture. To make the dressing, blend the tofu, peanut butter, rice vinegar, olive oil, maple syrup, black pepper, salt, and lemon juice in a food processor. Blanch the asparagus in boiling water, drain, plunge into cold water, then slice diagonally into 1 inch pieces. Spread the lettuce on a serving plate, arrange the asparagus, tomato, avocado and cucumber on top, and cover with the dressing.

Serves 4

THIS CREAMY PEANUT, LEMON AND TOFU DRESSING IS A GREAT WAY TO ENHANCE THE TASTE OF FRESH VEGETABLES. —*MARI FUJII*

SINGAPOREAN SLAW SALAD WITH SALTED APRICOT DRESSING

Susur Lee • Lee Restaurant • Toronto, Ontario*

1 pickled red onion
1 1/2 cups salted apricot dressing
2 green onions, both white and green parts, julienned
vegetable oil, for deep frying
1/2 fresh taro root, peeled and julienned
2 ounces rice vermicelli, broken into 3 inch pieces
1 large English cucumber, julienned
1 large carrot, peeled and julienned
1 small jicama, peeled and julienned
2 large Roma tomatoes, peeled, seeded, and thinly sliced
4 teaspoons toasted sesame seeds
6 teaspoons crushed roasted peanuts
4 teaspoons fresh edible flower petals
4 teaspoons fennel seedlings
4 teaspoons purple basil seedlings
4 teaspoons daikon sprouts
4 teaspoons fried shallots

Pickled Red Onion
1 red onion
1 cup rice wine vinegar
1 cup water
1/2 teaspoon salt
1/4 teaspoon black peppercorns
1/4 teaspoon fennel seeds
1 bay leaf
1 sprig thyme

Salted Apricot Dressing
1 cup salted apricot (ume) paste
1/2 cup rice wine vinegar
1 teaspoon mirin
1 teaspoon dashi
1 1/2 tablespoons onion oil (see recipe)
3 tablespoons sugar
1/2 tablespoon fresh ginger, peeled and chopped
1/4 teaspoon salt

Dashi
Makes approximately 3 cups

4 cups water
1 ounce kombu (dried seaweed)
2 ounces bonito flakes

Onion Oil
Makes approximately 2 cups

3 to 4 cups vegetable oil
4 cups loosely packed leeks, chopped and white parts only
4 green onions, chopped
2 medium onions, chopped

PHOTO: Koji Iwamoto

(recipe continued on following page)

(recipe continued from previous page)

Dashi: In a medium pot, combine water and kombu and let it soak for 2 hours. Once soaked, turn heat to medium-low until water starts to boil. Just before bubbles start to form, remove pot from heat, remove kombu and add bonito flakes. Return pot to low heat. When water begins to boil, turn off heat, cover, and let steep for 5 to 10 minutes. Strain dashi into bowl through fine mesh sieve, being careful not to agitate and cloud water. Dashi should be as clear as consommé. Store, covered in the refrigerator for up to 1 week or in the freezer up to 6 months.

Onion Oil: In a medium saucepan on high heat, combine oil, leeks, green onions and onions. Stirring occasionally, cook for 3 to 4 minutes. Decrease heat to medium high and continue cooking stirring occasionally until onions and leeks are crispy and brown. Remove from heat and strain oil into bowl. Let it cool before transferring oil to jar. Onion oil can be kept covered for up to 1 month.

Pickled Red Onion: Peel and julienne red onion and set aside in a medium bowl. In a small, non-reactive saucepan, bring vinegar and water to a boil. Season with salt, peppercorns, fennel seeds, bay leaf and thyme. Continue boiling for another 5 minutes. Pour over onions and set aside for 1 hour.

Salted Apricot Dressing: In a blender, combine apricot paste, vinegar, mirin, dashi, onion oil, sugar, ginger, and salt. Puree until smooth.

Salad: Soak green onions in very cold water to keep crisp. Meanwhile, heat a large pot of oil. When temperature reaches 400° F, deep fry taro root, half at a time, for 2 minutes, or until slightly golden and crispy. Remove from oil, drain on paper towels, and lightly salt. At the same temperature quickly deep fry vermicelli, half at a time, for 2 seconds, or until they curl up. Remove from oil, drain on paper towels, and lightly salt. Remove julienned green onions from bowl and drain. Place one quarter of fried vermicelli in the center of each of the 4 plates and on each plate, arrange one quarter of green onions, cucumber, carrot, jicama, tomatoes, and pickled red onions around vermicelli. Top with fried taro root. Sprinkle toasted sesame seeds and crushed peanuts over each salad. In a small bowl, combine edible flowers, seedlings, sprouts, and fried shallots. Sprinkle flower sprout-shallot mixture on salad and serve with salted apricot dressing alongside.

Serves 4

*Please see page 260 for a complete list of restaurant locations.

TOFU SALAD MALAY STYLE

(TAHU GORENG)

Chris Yeo • Straits Restaurant • San Jose, CA*

2 pieces firm tofu, deep fried in oil and strained
3 ounces cucumber, julienned
3 ounces bean sprout, scalded
1 egg, hard-boiled and cut into 4 wedges
1 bunch parsley or cilantro for garnish

Sauce
1 tablespoon peanuts, ground
3 tablespoons sugar
1 tablespoon tamarind concentrate
3 tablespoons dark soy sauce
1-2 teaspoons chili sauce to taste, optional

Mixed the peanuts, sugar, tamarind concentrate, soy sauce and chili sauce in a mixing bowl. Put the cooked tofu on a serving plate and garnish with hard-boiled egg wedges, bean sprouts and julienned cucumbers. Top with sauce. Garnish with a few sprigs of parsley or cilantro.

Serves 2-3

*Please see page 260 for a complete list of restaurant locations.

PHOTO: Ray Grefe

WOK SEARED BEEF FILET CUBES WITH SALAD DIJON MUSTARD VINAIGRETTE

(BO LUC LAC)

Michael Huynh • Bao Noodles • New York, NY*

Dressing

1 red onion, peeled and finely shredded
2 garlic cloves, finely minced
1/2 teaspoon sugar
1/2 teaspoon salt
1 teaspoon Dijon mustard
1/4 cup rice or distilled white vinegar
1/4 cup olive oil
freshly ground black pepper

Beef

1 pound beef sirloin or other tender cut
10 garlic cloves, minced
1 tablespoon of butter
1 tablespoon nuoc mam (Vietnamese fish sauce)
1 tablespoon soy sauce
1 teaspoon sugar
freshly ground black pepper
3 tablespoons of vegetable oil

Salad

1 head chicory (frisee)
1 small bunch of watercress
2 tomatoes or 1 pint cherry tomatoes
1 cup baby arugula
1 cup mache leaves

Combine the onion, garlic, sugar, salt, Dijon mustard, vinegar, olive oil and black pepper to taste in a large salad bowl. Mix well and set aside. Cut the beef against the grain into thin 1 inch cubes. In a bowl, combine the beef, half of the minced garlic (reserve remaining half for frying), fish sauce, soy sauce, sugar and ground black pepper to taste. Let stand for 1 hour. Clean the frisee, mache, watercress, arugula and tomatoes. Add the salad to the dressing. Preheat a large skillet over high heat and add the vegetable oil. Fry the remaining minced garlic until fragrant. Add the beef and sauté quickly, shaking the pan over high heat to sear, about 1 minute (the beef should be medium rare). Pour the seared beef meat over the greens and toss gently. Divide the warm salad among 4 individual plates. Sprinkle with fresh ground black pepper and serve with Jasmine rice or French bread.

Serves 6

*Please see page 260 for a complete list of restaurant locations.

YOU CAN CREATE YOUR OWN SALAD COMBINATIONS ACCORDING TO AVAILABILITY OF GREENS. —*MICHAEL HUYNH*

WOK SEARED SPICY CALAMARI SALAD WITH TATSOI, SRIRACHA, LIME AND TOASTED CASHEWS

Cliff Wharton • TenPenh • Washington, DC

1 pound calamari, cut into rings and tentacles
1 tablespoon chopped fresh cilantro
1 tablespoon chopped fresh mint
1 tablespoon chopped toasted cashew nuts
1 teaspoon sriracha sauce (Vietnamese hot paste)
1 cup tatsoi (may substitue with baby bok choy)
1 head Belgian endive (more could be used, according to taste)
1 ounce olive oil
2 ounces lime juice

In a bowl, mix calamari, cilantro, mint, cashews, and sriracha sauce. Season to taste and set aside. Place the tatsoi and endive on a serving plate and set aside. Over high heat, heat olive oil until smoking. Add calamari mixture to the hot pan and stir fry for 20 seconds. Add the lime juice and deglaze the pan. Remove from heat and pour the mixture over the greens.

Serves 4

PHOTO: This page, Courtesy of TenPenh

SOUPS

Soups are an important element in many Asian countries, none more so than China where it may be the costliest part of the meal. No imperial banquet is considered complete without a fine shark's fin or bird's nest soup. In Korea, chicken steamed for hours with ginseng and other herbs, is prized for its nutritional qualities and serves as a tonic. In China, doctors might prescribe soup as a medicine and in one famous herb restaurant in Singapore, there is a doctor on-site for pre-dining consultations.

CAMBODIAN SOUR SOUP WITH DUCK *(SOMLAH MACHOU TIEH)*

Longteine & Nadsa de Monteiro • Elephant Walk • Boston, MA*

1 whole duckling, chopped into 2 inch pieces, bone-in and skin-on
2 small stalks lemon grass, thinly sliced
10 wild lime leaves, deveined
2 large shallots, coarsely chopped
2 tablespoons galangal, peeled and coarsely chopped
12 garlic cloves, coarsely chopped
1 teaspoon turmeric
1 1/4 cups water
3 tablespoons vegetable oil
1 tablespoon Prahok (Cambodian preserved fish, optional)
5 cups water
4 tablespoons sugar
3 1/2 tablespoons fish sauce
2 tablespoons table salt
3/4 cup tamarind juice
1 pound Chinese watercress, or regular watercress cut into 1 1/2 inch pieces
4 branches curry leaves, toasted
bird's eye chilies, thinly sliced

To make the paste, blend all the ingredients in a blender until smooth, 2 to 3 minutes. Heat the oil in a stockpot over medium-high heat. Add the paste, duck pieces and Prahok (optional) and sauté for 8 to 10 minutes, stirring constantly until the flavors are released. Add the water, sugar, fish sauce and salt and bring to a boil. Reduce the heat to low and simmer for 30-40 minutes or until meat is tender. Add the tamarind juice, watercress, toasted curry leaves and cook, stirring occasionally, for 5 minutes longer. Transfer the soup to a serving bowl and serve with rice, with chilies on the side.

Serves 4-6

*Please see page 260 for a complete list of restaurant locations.

THIS IS ONE OF OUR FAVORITE DISHES. THE BROTH HAS AN INTRIGUING COMBINATION OF FLAVOR WITH THE SOURNESS OF THE TAMARIND, THE EARTHINESS AND DEPTH OF THE PRAHOK, WITH THE WONDERFUL FLAVOR OF BONE-IN DUCK AND TOASTED CURRY LEAVES ALL BLENDED TOGETHER. — *LONGTEINE & NADSA DE MONTEIRO*

CHILLED YELLOW TOMATO SOUP WITH ROMA TOMATO TARTARE AND BASIL PANEER

Vikram Garg • IndeBleu • Washington, DC

Soup
12 ripe yellow hothouse tomatoes
6 garlic cloves, minced
3 shallots, thinly sliced
1/2 tablespoon basil, chopped
1/2 tablespoon picked thyme
1/2 tablespoon rosemary, chopped
1/2 tablespoon oregano, chopped
1/2 tablespoon sage, chopped
2 tablespoons extra virgin olive oil
1/2 tablespoon coarse sea salt
1 tablespoon sugar
1/2 teaspoon fresh ground black pepper
1 teaspoon toasted coriander seed

Roma Tomato Tartare
4 firm Roma tomatoes
1 teaspoon extra virgin olive oil
fine sea salt to taste
crushed peppercorn to taste

Basil Paneer (*Paneer can be substituted with drained cottage cheese)
1 quart whole milk
1 tablespoon whole plain yogurt
1 tablespoon kosher salt
1/2 teaspoon lemon juice
1 bunch picked basil
1 tablespoon extra virgin olive oil

Soup: Cut yellow tomatoes in half width-wise and place together in a baking pan. Brush tomatoes with extra virgin olive oil. Season with garlic, shallots, herbs, salt, pepper, sugar and coriander. Roast uncovered at 200° F for 2 hours, then let cool. Liquefy tomatoes in blender, pass through fine mesh strainer and dilute with cold water to desired consistency. Season to taste and chill.

Roma Tomato Tartare: Blanch scored Roma tomatoes for 10 seconds and shock in ice water. Peel Roma tomatoes, remove seeds and dice into 1/4 inches. Marinate with olive oil, salt and freshly crushed pepper.

Basil Paneer: Bring salted milk to a simmer. Whisk in lemon juice and plain yogurt. Milk will curdle and whey will separate. Strain curdled milk through cheesecloth and hang until all the whey has passed through (about 3-4 hours). Bring 1 quart of salted boiling water to a rolling boil. Blanch picked basil for 10 seconds and shock in ice water. Puree basil with 1/4 cup cold water and place in coffee filter to remove water. Crumble paneer and fold in basil puree and extra virgin olive oil. Serve soup chilled with Roma tomato tartare and basil paneer.

Serves 4

CONSOMMÉ WITH BLANCHED FISH SLICES

H.K. & Pauline D. Loh • Food Writers & Cookbook Authors • Singapore

1 whole fish with firm flesh such as carp, threadfin or snakehead
1 head lettuce
1 1/2 quarts water
1 slice ginger, julienned
salt
sesame oil

Fillet the fish. Use a kitchen towel to absorb excess moisture. Pan fry the fish bones with ginger until fragrant, then add enough water to make a clear fish soup. Slice the filleted fish into the thinnest slices you can manage. Wash the lettuce and choose only the tender young leaves. Line a deep container with the lettuce leaves and layer the fish slices on top. Pour the boiling fish stock on top and cover immediately. Leave for 3 minutes, season with salt to taste, add a little sesame oil and scatter the julienned ginger on top.

Serves 4-6

Recipe adapted from Dad & Company, SNP Editions

This is a pretty dramatic dish that is literally cooked at the table. We first ate this at a restaurant serving Hunan cuisine and soon adapted it for the family table. —*H.K. & Pauline D. Loh*

CURRIED MUSSEL WONTON SOUP

Philippe Chin • CuiZine • Aiken, SC*

2 pounds Great Eastern or New Zealand green lip mussels
1 tablespoon butter
1 cup dry white wine, Muscadet
1/2 cup coconut milk
1 cup heavy cream
3 cups fresh or bottled clam juice
1 tablespoon onions, chopped
1 tablespoon shallots, chopped
1 tablespoon parsley, chopped
1 teaspoon Chinese curry powder
salt and pepper to taste
cornstarch as needed to thicken

Wontons
8 wonton skins
1/2 tablespoon cilantro, chopped
1/2 tablespoon fresh ginger, grated
1/2 reserved mussel meat
12 fresh whole cilantro leaves, for garnish

Heat a large pan with high heat. Sauté the butter, onions, shallots, and parsley for about 3 minutes. Add white wine and clam juice and bring to a boil. Add mussels. Cover and simmer for 8 minutes and strain. Put mussels aside. Whisk curry powder into cooking liquid and season to taste with salt and pepper. Add coconut milk, cream and cook another 5 minutes. Thicken with cornstarch if needed. Shell the mussels and coarsely chop mussel meat. Mix in ginger and cilantro. Season to taste with salt and pepper. Evenly distribute mussel mix on each of the wonton skins, moisten edges of skin with water or egg wash and fold into triangle shaped pockets. Bring the soup back to a boil and add wontons. Simmer for 3 minutes. Serve immediately in soup bowls and garnish with fresh cilantro leaves.

Serves 4

*Please see page 260 for a complete list of restaurant locations.

PHOTO: Tuck Loong

DRUNKEN FISH SOUP

Martin Yan • Yan Can • Santa Clara, CA*

1 pound skinless white fish fillets, such as catfish or cod
4 cups chicken stock
2 cups fish stock
1/4 cup good-quality Chinese rice wine (Shao Xing)
1 shallot, peeled and thinly sliced
3 small firm but ripe tomatoes, each cored and quartered
8 sprigs fresh dill
1/4 cup winter melon, julienned
2 tablespoons fish sauce
1/2 teaspoon sugar
1/4 teaspoon freshly ground white pepper

In a medium saucepan, bring the chicken, fish stock, wine and shallots to a boil over high heat. Add fish, reduce heat to medium-low and simmer for 1 minute. Skim any foam that rises to the surface of the broth. Add the tomatoes, 4 sprigs of the dill, winter melon, fish sauce, sugar and pepper. Cook until fish turns opaque and tomatoes soften, about 5 minutes. Remove and discard dill sprigs. Divide the fish, tomatoes, winter melon and broth between four soup bowls and garnish with remaining dill sprigs.

Serves 4

*Please see page 260 for a complete list of restaurant locations.

FRUIT SOUP *(SOP BUAH)*

Yono Purnomo • Yono's Restaurant • Albany, NY

2 jack fruit, peeled and large diced
3 mangos, peeled and large diced
two 1 pound papayas, peeled and large diced
12 ounces coconut milk
16 ounces champagne or sparkling wine (may substitute with fruit juice)
1 tablespoon chili oil
18 mint leaves for garnish
6 tablespoons fresh whipped cream (3 ounces liquid heavy cream whipped to form peaks)

Choose ripe fruit for this dish. Blend the peeled and large diced fruit and 1 cup of the champagne or sparkling wine (or fruit juice) in a food processor or blender till smooth. Put the remainder of the champagne and pureed fruit into a stockpot, bring to a quick boil, then add coconut milk and remove from heat. Chill for several hours. Garnish with whipped cream, fresh mint and a dash of chili oil.

Serves 6

PHOTO: Stephanie Liu Jan

GINGERED KABOCHA SQUASH SOUP

Robert Gadsby • Noe Restaurant at the Omni Hotel • Los Angeles, CA*

3 ounces unsalted butter
1 1/2 pounds kabocha squash, peeled, seeded and diced
4 ounces onions, peeled and sliced
4 ounces fresh ginger, peeled and chopped
3 1/2 cups water
coarse salt to taste
white pepper to taste

In a saucepan, melt the butter over medium heat. Sauté onions until translucent. Add the squash and ginger, season with salt and pepper. Cook for 15 to 20 minutes, stirring occasionally, until nicely caramelized but still firm. Add the water and raise the heat to high and bring to a boil. Reduce heat and simmer for 20 to 25 minutes or until squash is tender. Transfer the soup to a blender or food processor and puree until smooth. Adjust the seasonings. Ladle into bowls. Garnish with shaved, toasted almonds.

Serves 8

*Please see page 260 for a complete list of restaurant locations.

JUMBO PRAWN LEMON GRASS SOUP

David Bank • Land Thai Kitchen •
New York, NY

20 pieces jumbo prawns
10 cups water
1 pound fresh oyster mushrooms, sliced
3 stalks lemon grass, bruised with back of knife
2 cups lemon juice
10 pieces kaffir lime leaves, bruised in hand
1/2 cup fish sauce
1/2 cup regular milk
1 small piece galangal root, finely minced or grated
5 sprigs cilantro, leaves plucked and reserved, stems reserved
1 bottle or 8 ounces sweet and sour Tom Yum paste
10-15 pieces Thai bird chilies, minced with seeds, adjust spiciness to taste

Wash the prawns and shell them without removing the tails. Pour the water into a pan. Add lemon grass, kaffir lime leaves, cilantro stems and galangal root. Boil for 5 minutes. Add mushrooms, fish sauce, lime juice, milk, Tom Yum paste and simmer for 2 minutes or until mushrooms are tender. Add prawns and cook until they turn pink. Finish by adding Thai bird chilies to taste, and garnish with fresh cilantro leaves.

Serves 5

PHOTO: Martin Jansche

LITTLE SAIGON CHICKEN NOODLE SOUP

Norman Van Aken • Norman's • Coral Gables, FL*

Soup Base
2 tablespoons dark roasted sesame oil
2 tablespoons virgin olive oil
1 scotch bonnet chili, stem and seeds discarded, finely julienned
2 tablespoons garlic, finely chopped
1 1/2 tablespoons ginger
2 tablespoons butter
2 gobo root, peeled and cut thinly (optional)
1 carrot large diced
3 small celery stalks, large diced
1 tablespoon Thai red curry paste
1 cup sherry wine
7 cups light chicken stock
1 stalk lemon grass, peeled, ends cut off, cut in half lengthwise
salt and pepper to taste

Garnish
2 tablespoons peanut or canola oil
1 tablespoon dark roasted sesame oil
1 bunch scallions, trimmed and finely minced using about 1/2 of the green ends
1 cup raw mushrooms, sliced
1 poblano chili, stems and seeds, discarded and finely julienned
pre-prepared chicken stock

Noodles
10 ounces fresh oriental noodles
12 snow peas, blanched and julienned
12 chive sprouts or garlic chives, chopped into 1 inch lengths
salt and pepper to taste
1 tablespoon fish sauce or to taste

Soup Base: Heat a soup pot or large wok on medium heat. Add the sesame oil and olive oil. Allow it to warm. Add the scotch bonnet, garlic and ginger. Stir for about 1 minute. Add butter, gobo root, carrot and celery. Season to taste. Stir and cook for about 5 minutes. Stir in the curry paste and keep on medium heat. Cook and stir about 30 seconds and add the sherry. Allow to simmer, stirring all the time to help dissolve the curry paste for about a minute or two. Lower the heat to a low simmer and add the chicken stock. Add the lemon grass stalk and allow to cook about 1 1/2 hours, skimming as necessary. Strain off the soup. Set the vegetables aside. They can be saved for another use, such as stirred into some cooked rice or pasta.

Noodles: Heat a wok or soup pan on medium high heat. Add the oils and allow to get warm. Add the scallions, mushrooms and poblano chiles. Stir rapidly and allow to cook about 2 minutes. Add the prepared chicken stock and bring it to a high simmer. Drop in the chive sprouts, snow peas and cooked noodles. Season with the salt, pepper and fish sauce. Serve.

Makes 5 1/2 cups

MyPyramid.gov

*Please see page 260 for a complete list of restaurant locations.

The soup base can be prepared days ahead of time if desired. Just chill, strain and cover. I love to use the noodles known as "fen" for this soup. Fen noodles usually need to be pulled apart. I just pull them apart and drop them into the soup as it is heating up. They will separate in the simmering soup. If you like, you can use al dente cooked pappardelle noodles instead of fen. You can also increase the meatiness of this dish by adding cooked chicken pieces. Fen noodles tend to "gobble up the stock", so prepare to add a bit more stock if you are re-heating the soup in the following day or two. —*Norman Van Aken*

THAI STYLE COCONUT AND CHICKEN SOUP WITH PORTOBELLO MUSHROOMS

Cliff Wharton • TenPenh • Washington, DC

Soup Base
1/4 cup finely chopped lemon grass
1/4 cup galangal
2 tablespoons kaffir lime leaves
1 gallon canned coconut milk
6 ounces fish sauce
6 ounces lime juice
1/2 cup sugar
salt to taste

Chicken
1 pound chicken, thigh meat
4 ounces soy sauce
4 ounces white vinegar
2 bay leaves
1/2 tablespoon black peppercorns
3-4 garlic cloves

3 portabello mushrooms
2 garlic cloves
1 pint soy sauce
chives, to garnish

Combine all soup base ingredients in a stockpot. Bring to a boil over medium-high heat. After achieving a boil, reduce heat and let simmer for 15 minutes. Strain soup and reserve.

Chicken: Combine all ingredients in a stockpot. Bring to a boil over medium-high heat. Reduce heat and simmer until chicken is cooked through and tender. Remove from heat and reserve chicken.

Soup: Preheat the oven to 325° F. Place mushrooms in a baking dish with garlic and soy sauce. Marinate approximately 30 minutes. Roast the mushrooms in the oven until softened, approximately 20 minutes. Chop mushrooms and chicken. Divide equally among heated soup bowls and add soup. Garnish with chives.

Serves 10-12

PHOTO: Courtesy of TenPenh

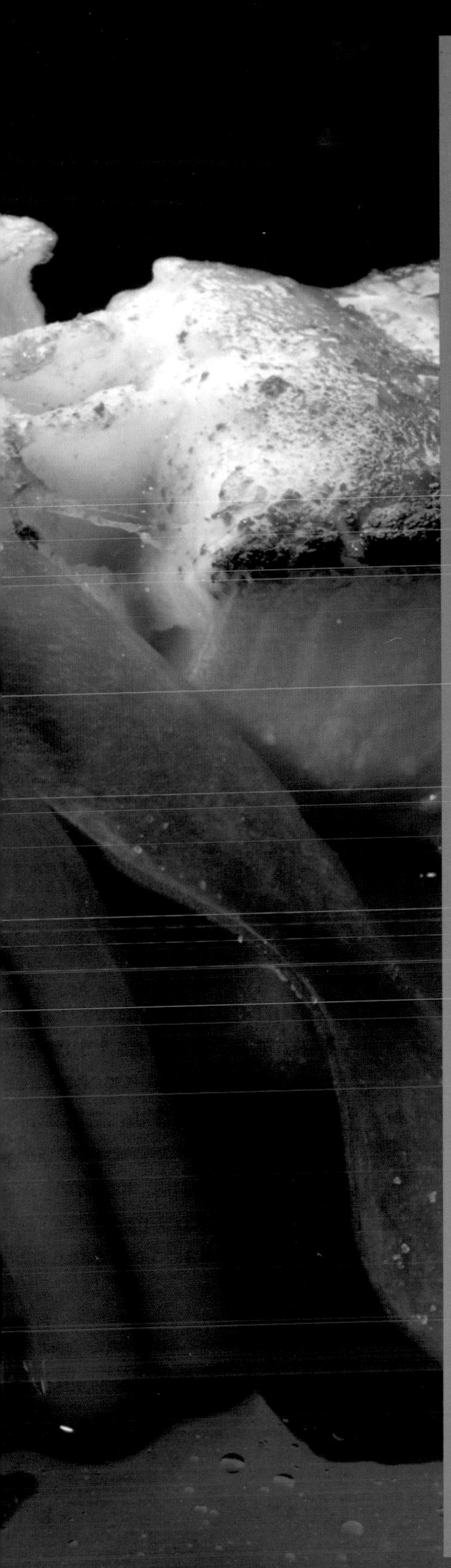

FISH & SEAFOOD

Asians fortunate enough to live near oceans, rivers or lakes are blessed with a daily staple of fish, shellfish and various aquatic vegetables. Freshness is traditionally of paramount importance, and fish that do not go from their watery homes to stoves in quick order are often kept alive in aquarium-like aerated tanks until the cooks are ready for them. Ordering fish this fresh in a Cantonese seafood restaurant is called Yau Sui Yu—a literal translation of "swimming fish." Steaming is a favored cooking method for thousands of years. Steaming brings out the natural flavor of fish, with little or no added fat, and a limited loss of nutrients. Fin fish and shellfish are also often stir fried, deep fried, poached, or are chopped and pounded into purees, seasoned, stuffed into vegetables, tofu pouches, or wonton skins, and then steamed, braised or deep fried.

The popularity of sushi has opened up new ways to consume fish for many. The health benefits of FDA-approved fish as a lean source of protein are well documented, and the American Heart Association recommends 3 servings of fish every week to help reduce the risk of heart disease. Seafood is a prime source of healthy fats like omega-3 and omega-6 fatty acids. These fatty acids, which are a form of polyunsaturated fat contribute to general good health. Salmon, trout, mackerel, and sardines are among the highest in omega-3 fatty acids.

With so many healthful benefits, it is no wonder we collected the most number of fish and seafood recipes from our chefs.

AHI TUNA SAUCE

Jimmy Wu • Ahi Sushi • Studio City, CA

2 1/2 carrots, peeled
1 1/2 red onions, chopped
1 piece ginger, peeled and coarsely chopped
1 1/2 garlic cloves
1/4 bunch cilantro, coarsely chopped
2 cups vinegar
2 cups soy sauce
2 cups sugar
1/8 cup sesame oil
1/2 tablespoon black pepper
16 ounces either olive or light sesame oil
2 1/2 ounces chili seco dried chili powder

Blend ingredients in a food processor, adding oil slowly to emulsify. Blend until smooth. The sauce can be stored for up to one month in refrigerator. Stir before each use.

Makes 1 gallon

I'VE SPENT YEARS MODIFYING THIS SAUCE TO GET THE RIGHT TASTE AND TEXTURE. IT'S HEALTHY AND GOES GREAT WITH ANY KIND OF SEAFOOD. EVERYONE LOVES IT AND IT'S VERSATILE ENOUGH FOR DIPPING, SALADS AND A GARNISH. —*JIMMY WU*

BAKED BLUE POINT OYSTERS WITH PORT WINE

Wai-Keung Kwong • T'ang Court at Langham Hotel Hong Kong • Kowloon, Hong Kong

4 pieces fresh Blue Point oysters with shells
1 tablespoon garlic, minced
1 tablespoon Port wine
1 teaspoon light soy sauce
1/8 teaspoon sugar
1/4 teaspoon sesame oil
6 ounces corn flour
oil for deep frying
parsley or cilantro and radish (optional) for garnish

Cook oysters in boiling water for 1 minute. Strain well. Coat oysters with flour and deep fry in a wok of hot oil until golden brown. Pour a little oil into wok and add garlic, light soy sauce, sugar and sesame oil. Stir fry with oysters. Add Port wine to wok and stir gently. Put lid on wok and cook for approximately 1 minute. Place each oyster back into a clean shell. Place oysters on plate and garnish before serving.

Serves 4

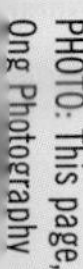

BHUTANESE RED RICE AND ROCK SHRIMP STIR FRY

Arnold Eric Wong • EOS • San Francisco, CA*

12 ounces whole rock shrimp, deveined and rinsed
2 cups Bhutanese red rice
1/2 small yellow or white onion, diced small
1 cup Chinese long beans, cut into 2 inch pieces
1 small red bell pepper, stem, seeds and ribs removed, julienne cut
4 large Shiitake mushrooms, stems removed and sliced
2 ounces peanut, grapeseed or light tasting olive oil
4 ounces light chicken stock
1/4 bunch green or spring onions, sliced very thin
1 tablespoon black sesame seeds

Sauce
1/2 cup dry Sherry wine
1/2 cup Port wine
1/3 cup oyster sauce
1 1/2 ounces light soy sauce
1 ounce fresh lemon juice
1 ounce red wine vinegar
1 tablespoon sambal chili sauce
1 1/2 tablespoons fish sauce
2 teaspoons fresh garlic, minced
2 teaspoons fresh ginger root, minced
1/2 bunch Thai basil leaves
6 tablespoons or 1/4 bunch cilantro, minced (including stems)
1/4 cup scallions, sliced thin
2 tablespoons cornstarch

Steam the rice till tender. Remove from the steamer or pot and set aside in a separate bowl. Whisk the sauce ingredients together and set aside. Clean the shrimp under cold water and drain well and set aside. Prepare the vegetables as specified and set aside. In a large sauté pan or wok, heat the oil till it just begins to smoke. Add the onions, long beans, peppers and mushrooms. Sauté on high heat for about 5 minutes or until the onions are translucent. Add the shrimp and sauté an additional 2 to 3 minutes (the shrimp should be about half cooked at this stage). Add the rice and stir well. Add half of the chicken stock and cook to steam

IF YOU CANNOT FIND BHUTANESE RED RICE, OTHER TYPES OF RICE MAY BE SUBSTITUTED, SUCH AS BROWN RICE. TOFU, CHICKEN OR BEEF MAY BE SUBSTITUTED FOR THE ROCK SHRIMP. —*ARNOLD ERIC WONG*

the rice through. Shake or stir the sauce to distribute the cornstarch that may have settled at the bottom. Pour in half of the sauce into the rice mixture and toss or stir well. Add additional chicken stock and or additional sauce as desired. Season with salt and pepper. Garnish with thin sliced green onions and black sesame seeds.

Serves 6

*Please see page 260 for a complete list of restaurant locations.

PHOTO: Ray Grefe

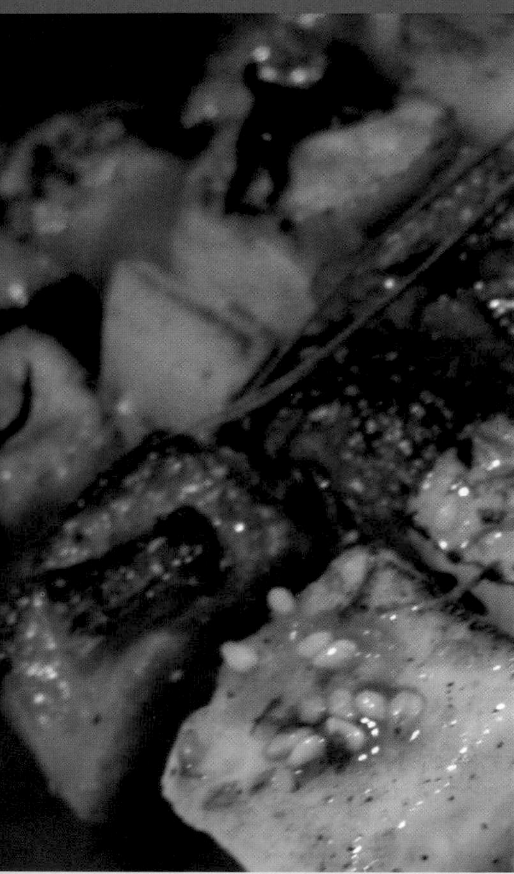

BLACK COD AND EGGPLANT KUSHIYAKI

Noriyuki Sugie • Asiate at The Mandarin Oriental • New York, NY

2 pounds black cod
1 Japanese eggplant
8 bamboo skewers
oil for deep frying

Marinade
3 teaspoons foie gras
2 teaspoons white miso
1 teaspoon mirin
2 teaspoons sake
1 teaspoon sugar
2 teaspoons chives

Combine sake, sugar, and mirin. In a saucepan over medium heat, cook off alcohol, then add white miso and foie gras. Mix well. Cut black cod into 1 inch cubes and eggplant into 1 inch pieces. Alternate onto skewers. Deep fry until fish is cooked through and eggplant is golden brown, remove from fryer, drain on paper towels to remove excess oil and then dip into the marinade. To finish, sprinkle with chives.

Serves 4

BLACK COD IN MISO

Nobu Matsuhisa • Nobu New York • New York, NY*

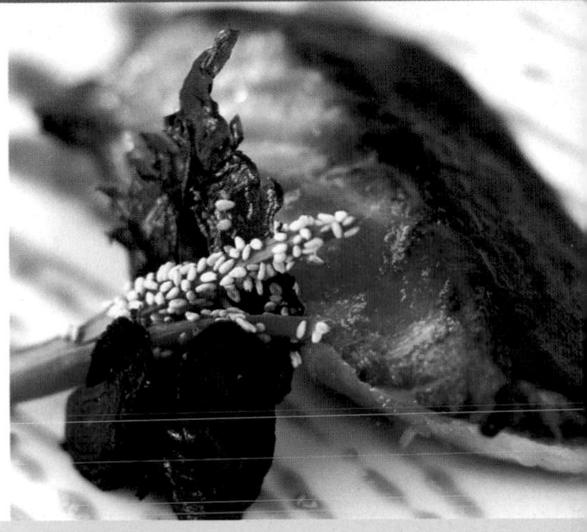

4 black cod fillets, about 1/2 pound each
3 cups Nobu style Saikyo Miso
1 stalk hajikami per serving (ginger pickled in sweet vinegar, see recipe below)

Nobu-style Saikyo Miso (for 3 cups)
sake
3/4 cup mirin
2 cups white miso paste
1 1/4 cups granulated sugar

Bring the sake and mirin to a boil in a medium saucepan over high heat. Boil for 20 seconds to evaporate the alcohol. Turn the heat down to low and add the miso paste, mixing with a wooden spoon. When the miso has dissolved completely, turn the heat up to high again and add the sugar, stirring constantly with the wooden spoon to ensure that the bottom of the pan doesn't burn. Remove from heat once the sugar is fully dissolved. Cool to room temperature. Pat the fillets thoroughly dry with paper towels. Slather the fish with Nobu-style Saikyo Miso and place in a non-reactive dish or bowl and cover tightly with plastic wrap. Leave to steep in the refrigerator for 2 to 3 days. Preheat the oven to 400° F. Preheat the grill or broiler. Lightly wipe off any excess miso clinging to the fillets but don't rinse it off. Place the fish on the grill or in a broiler pan and grill or broil until the surface of the fish turns brown. Then, bake for 10 to 15 minutes. Arrange the black cod fillets on individual plates and garnish with hajikami. Add a few extra drops of Nobu style Saikyo Miso to each plate.

Hajikami Ginger Pickled in Sweet Vinegar: Peel and cut ginger thinly into 6 inch lengths. Briefly plunge the sliced ginger into a pot of boiling water to which rice vinegar has been added (1 tablespoon per 1 quart of water). Drain and sprinkle thoroughly with sea salt. Let cool to room temperature. In a glass jar or container, put amazu marinade (1 cup rice vinegar, 1/4 cup water, 3 tablespoons sugar) and add ginger into marinade. Ginger will turn pink. Amazu ginger can keep in the refrigerator for up to 4 months.

Serves 4

*Please see page 260 for a complete list of restaurant locations.

PHOTOS: Left, Courtesy of The Mandarin Oriental, NY

BLACK COD IN RED CURRY MISO

Rodelio Aglibot • Yi Cuisine •
Los Angeles, CA

four 6 ounce black cod fillets

Marinade
2 cups mirin
2 cups sake
2 cups sugar
4 cups miso paste
1 teaspoon red curry paste

Garnish
1/4 cup red cabbage, finely chopped
1 green onion, thinly sliced

In a medium pan, bring mirin and sake to a boil to burn out the alcohol. Add miso and simmer until smooth. Stir in sugar and curry and then let cool. Marinate black cod overnight in a tightly wrapped container. Remove cod from marinade and wash. Broil fish to the temperature of your liking and then garnish before serving.

Serves 4

BRAISED THAI SNAPPER WITH JAPANESE PLUM, SAKE AND POTATOES

Troy N. Thompson • Jer-ne Restaurant and Bar at The Ritz-Carlton • Marina del Rey, CA

6 ounces Thai snapper fillets, scaled and bones removed
6 pieces umeboshi plum (Japanese pickled plum)
6 finger potatoes, very thinly sliced
6 white mushrooms, very thinly sliced (optional)
2 cups sake
2 tablespoons butter
4 tablespoons olive oil
salt and pepper

In a pan, add all of the ingredients and bring up to a small simmer. Cover and cook for 6 to 10 minutes till the fish is tender. Take out of the pan and let rest. Reduce liquid by 3/4 and add butter and olive oil at the end.

Serves 6

PHOTO: Josh Dearing

CHILEAN SEA BASS YAKIBITASHI WITH TOMATO AND GRAPEFRUIT SAUCE

Yorinobu Yamasaki • Kai • New York, NY

two 4 ounce fillets of Chilean sea bass
1 bunch bok choy
3 ounces green beans (boiled, shocked and cut into 2 inch lengths)
1 cup grapefruit juice
1/2 teaspoon tomato powder

Marinade
4 tablespoons soy sauce
2 ounces mirin
2 ounces sake

Marinate Chilean sea bass in marinade for one hour. Heat grapefruit juice over medium heat. When juice is reduced to half, mix in the tomato powder. Grill Chilean sea bass. Boil bok choy and strain. Top Chilean sea bass with tomato and grapefruit sauce. Serve with green beans and bok choy.

Serves 2

CHINESE-STYLE STEAMED WHOLE MOI WITH SIZZLING HOT PEANUT OIL

Roy Yamaguchi • Roy's • Honolulu, HI*

4 (12 ounce) whole moi, cleaned
8 dried Shiitake mushrooms, soaked overnight in water, drained, and thinly sliced
2 tablespoons ginger, finely julienned
3 scallions (green parts only), finely julienned
2 leeks (white parts only), cut into 2 inch lengths and julienned
3/4 cup soy sauce
2 tablespoons sake
1/2 cup fish stock or chicken stock
2 tablespoons sugar
1 teaspoon salt
1/2 cup peanut oil
20 cilantro sprigs
steamed rice for serving

In a steamer, bring 1 or 2 inches of water to a boil and add the whole moi. You may have to steam two fish at a time. Cover and steam for 2 minutes. Transfer to a rimmed dish that can fit inside the steamer. Place the Shiitake mushrooms, ginger, scallions and leeks on top of the fish. Combine the soy sauce, sake, stock, sugar and salt in a bowl and stir to blend. Pour over the fish. Place in the steamer, cover and steam for about 14 minutes, or until opaque throughout. Heat the peanut oil in a small heavy saucepan over high heat until smoking. Transfer the moi with the mushrooms and the sauce to warmed plates and garnish with the cilantro. Pour the oil over the fish and serve with the steamed rice.

Serves 4

Recipe courtesy of *Roy's Fish & Seafood: Recipes From The Pacific Rim* by Roy Yamaguchi with John Harrisson (Ten Speed Press 2005)
*Please see page 260 for a complete list of restaurant locations.

PHOTO: Martin Jansche

THIS MANDARIN-STYLE DISH IS A POPULAR ITEM ON OUR MENU. IT HAS AN EYE-CATCHING PRESENTATION WHETHER SERVED IN OUR DINING ROOM OR YOURS. THE DRIED MUSHROOMS GIVE THE DISH AN EARTHY PRONOUNCED FLAVOR, BUT THE SIZZLE, THE AROMAS AND THE VISUAL APPEAL ENGAGE ALL THE SENSES. —*ROY YAMAGUCHI*

COD EN PAPILLOTTE WITH COCONUT LIME SAUCE

Simpson Wong • Jefferson Grill • New York, NY*

4 cod fillets, 5 ounces each
4 pieces okra, thinly sliced lengthwise
1 cup sugar snap peas
10 cherry tomatoes, cut into halves
1 tablespoon oil
salt and pepper

Sauce
2 cans coconut milk
1/2 cup lemon grass, chopped
1/4 cup galangal, chopped
2 tablespoons galangal flower, chopped
10 kaffir lime leaves, shredded by hand
3 pieces bird's eye chili, seeds removed
3 tablespoons fish sauce
3 tablespoons sugar
3 tablespoons of lime juice
salt and pepper

Gently simmer coconut milk in a pot. Add lemon grass, galangal, galangal flower, lime leaves and chilies. Cook for 20 minutes over low heat, strain and add fish sauce, sugar and lime juice. Season with salt and pepper to taste. Set aside. Place a small portion of sugar snap peas at the center of a 15 inch x 15 inch parchment paper. Layer the cod over the peas. Top off with okra and add the halved tomatoes. Pour some of the coconut sauce over the fish. Secure the content by tying the four corners of the paper together at the center with a twine. Place parcels on a sheet pan. Bake in a 375° F preheated oven for 12 to 15 minutes. When it is ready, open parcels, garnish with cilantro and basil leaves. Serve immediately with steamed black sticky rice or baguette.

Serves 4

*Please see page 260 for a complete list of restaurant locations.

CRAB CAKE-CRUSTED AHI

Rodelio Aglibot • Yi Cuisine •
Los Angeles, CA

1/2 pound lump crab meat, preferably Dungeness
2 (4 ounce) tuna steaks, about 1 inch thick
2 teaspoons fresh ginger, grated
2 tablespoons fresh cilantro, finely chopped
1 tablespoon fresh chives, finely chopped
1/4 cup Panko bread crumbs
3 large egg whites
2 teaspoons corn starch and 2 tablespoons water to make a slurry
Kosher or sea salt
freshly ground black pepper
2 teaspoons vegetable oil
2 cups daikon sprouts or mixed greens
2 teaspoons sweet-hot mustard

To make the crab cake mixture, combine the crab meat, ginger, cilantro, chives, bread crumbs and 2 egg whites in a large bowl. In a little bowl, whisk the cornstarch and water together with a fork to make a slurry. When the cornstarch is dissolved, pour half of it into the crab mixture, reserving the rest for the tuna. Fold the ingredients together gently but thoroughly, taking care not to mash the flaky crabmeat. Season with salt and pepper. Beat the remaining egg whites until frothy and brush it on the top side of each tuna steak. Now, brush the remaining cornstarch slurry over the egg whites to create extra glue for the crab cake to grab onto. Divide the crab mixture in half and pat a layer on the two pieces of tuna so it sticks and covers the top. Wrap it in plastic and store in the fridge for at least 8 hours or up to overnight so the crab and tuna can bond together. Place a large nonstick skillet over medium-high flame, drizzle with oil, and just when it begins to smoke, lay the tuna steaks in the hot pan, crab-side down. Let them cook for a full 5 minutes without moving the tuna around, until the crab cake has firmed up into a golden crust. Using a spatula, carefully flip the tuna over and sear the bottom side for 10 seconds just until the flesh of the tuna turns white. Remove from the heat and place the tuna on a cutting board. Cut the crab cake-crusted tuna into even slices, about 4 slices per steak. To serve, pile the daikon sprouts on a plate and arrange the tuna slices on top in a row. Dollop each piece of tuna with a little bit of sweet-hot mustard.

Serves 4

MyPyramid.gov

This dish has become a signature favorite at my restaurant Yi Cuisine in Los Angeles. It perfectly marries sweet crab with buttery tuna, two great tastes that work wonderfully together. I find it's best to assemble this dish the night before you plan to cook it. The crab cake mixture has time to set and adhere well to the tuna, so it doesn't clump off in the pan when cooked. —*Rodelio Aglibot*

PHOTOS: Left, Martin Jansche; This page, BarePixels.com

CRAB MEAT, AVOCADO AND LEMON GRASS SALAD WITH GRAPEFRUIT VINAIGRETTE

Simpson Wong • Jefferson Grill• New York, NY*

2 cups lump crab meat
1 haas avocado, peeled and thinly sliced
1 cup of tomatoes, peeled, seeded and diced
1/4 cup of chopped grapefruit, seeded
2 tablespoons grapeseed oil
2 tablespoons lemon grass, finely chopped
salt and pepper to taste

Vinaigrette
1/2 cup of grapefruit juice
1/2 cup of tomato water (see recipe below)
1/4 cup of extra virgin olive oil
1 tablespoon of Dijon mustard
salt and pepper to taste

Tomato Water: Puree three tomatoes in a blender, strain through extra fine cheesecloth. Let it drip overnight. You should have about 1/4 cup.
Combine grapefruit juice, tomato water, and Dijon mustard in a bowl. Gradually mix in olive oil by using a handheld blender. Season with salt and pepper and set aside.
Salad: In a bowl, mix crab meat, tomatoes, grapefruit, lemon grass and grapeseed oil together, toss well and season with salt and pepper. Place a ring mold at the center of a serving plate, layer avocado at the bottom and top with the crab mixture. Make sure that the mixture is packed tightly. Finish the top layer with mixed herbs. Gently pour the vinaigrette and serve.

Serves 4

*Please see page 260 for a complete list of restaurant locations.

CRAB MEAT MANGO GINGER CUCUMBER SLAW

Hiroshi Noguchi • Renaissance Orlando Resort at Marriott• Orlando, FL

1 1/2 ounces crab meat
4 ounces mango, julienned
3 1/2 ounces tomatoes, julienned
2 1/2 ounces onions, julienned
2 ounces cucumber, julienned
2 ounces pickled ginger, julienned
2 teaspoons cilantro, chopped
2 teaspoons parsley, chopped

Dressing
3 teaspoons white balsamic vinegar
2 teaspoons rice vinegar
juice of 1 lemon
1 teaspoon honey
salt and pepper to taste

Peel all fresh vegetables, except cucumber, and julienne. Julienne pickled ginger. Chop cilantro and parsley. Mix all the ingredients. Pour dressing ingredients in a small mixing bowl and blend well. Add dressing to the mixture and season with salt and pepper.

Serves 4-6

NOTE: This recipe can be an entrée or used as an accompaniment to other fish dishes. See Chef Noguchi's reccommendation on page 108.

PHOTO: Martin Jansche

CRISPY LOBSTER ROLL

Julian Medina • Zocalo • New York, NY*

2 small 1 to 1 1/4 pound lobsters
1 cup Panko bread crumbs
1 cup flour
3 eggs, beaten
salt and pepper
4 flour tortillas
1 small jicama, julienned
8 slices of avocado
1 sliced pickled red onion

Chile de Arbol Salsa
2 plum tomatoes, diced
1/2 cup toasted black sesame seeds
3 toasted Chinese chilies
1/4 cup rice vinegar
1 tablespoon honey
salt and pepper

Mix salsa ingredients in a bowl. Season and set aside. Open the lobsters with scissors and cut the tail in half lengthwise. Remove the meat. Open the claws as well. Flour, egg and bread the lobster meat. Place a skewer in the middle of the tail so it does not curl up. Season meat with salt and pepper. In a hot oiled pan, fry the lobster until golden brown, remove. Add more salt. Slice the red onion and cover with white vinegar for 1 hour and drain. Pulse all salsa ingredients together in a blender until smooth. Add salt and pepper to taste. Heat flour tortillas using a grill, remove sides. Place jicama, avocado slices, crispy lobster and pickled onion in the tortilla. Roll the tortillas and then cut the roll in 1/2 inch pieces. Serve with salsa on top.

Serves 4

*Please see page 260 for a complete list of restaurant locations.

CRISPY WHOLE FISH WITH LESSER GINGER AND THAI HOT BASIL SAUCE

Ian Chalermkittichai • Kittichai • New York, NY

1 whole fish (about 2 pounds) stripe bass, scaled and gutted
1 quart cooking oil for frying fish
7 ounces rice flour
10 leaves Thai hot basil, deep fried

Lesser Ginger Sauce
2 tablespoons grapeseed oil
3 ounces red curry paste
7 ounces lesser ginger (may substitute with young ginger)
2 pieces fresh red chili pepper
17 ounces coconut milk
1 1/2 ounce fish sauce
1 tablespoon white sugar
20 leaves Thai basil

Crispy Whole Fish: Pat fish dry. Using a sharp knife, cut the fish on the bias side and dust with rice flour then fry in the hot oil at 300° F for 7 minutes.

Lesser Ginger Sauce: In a wok, heat 2 tablespoons of grapeseed oil with medium heat and roast the red chili paste, fresh red chili, and lesser ginger for 2-3 minutes until fragrant. Pour in the coconut milk and bring to a boil. Simmer for 10 minutes, season with fish sauce and white sugar to taste. Pour the sauce on to a 12 inch plate and place the fish on top of the sauce and sprinkle with fried hot basil and serve.

Serves 6

PHOTO: David Paler

FISH DUMPLINGS

Frank Yang • Din Tai Fung Dumpling House • Arcadia, CA*

2 cups of hot water dough (see recipe below)
1/3 pound of celery
1/3 pound of onions
2/3 pound of ground sole fish

Seasonings
1 teaspoon of salt
1 teaspoon of sugar
1/8 teaspoon of pepper
1 tablespoon of vegetable oil
3 tablespoons of sesame oil
1 tablespoon of cooking wine (Shao Xing or dry sherry)

Hot Water Dough: In a food processor, add 1/4 cup of boiling water to 2 cups of flour. Then, add 1/4 cup of cold water. Remove from processor and knead dough by hand to form a ball. Do not over knead.

Stuffing: Chop celery and onions finely, add to ground fish. Add all seasonings and mix well. Make dough into small balls. Roll each ball into a circle. Place a little stuffing in the center of each dough circle, fold over, press edges tightly to seal. Steam in a steamer on medium for 10 minutes. Remove and serve.

Serves 4

NOTE: Consider putting dumplings on a blanched piece of large Napa cabbage leaf before steaming, to avoid sticking and breaking the skin when removing from the steamer.

*Please see page 260 for a complete list of restaurant locations.

GOAN SPICED CRAB CAKES

Salim Mohmed & Santok Singh • Gaylord India Restaurant • Sausalito, CA*

16 ounces crab meat, cleaned and picked over for shells
1/4 cup corn oil
1 white onion, diced
1 tablespoon fresh ginger, minced
1/2 tablespoon fresh garlic, minced
1 teaspoon ground cumin seeds
1/4 teaspoon ground coriander seeds
1/4 teaspoon paprika
2 lemons, zested and juiced
8 springs fresh cilantro, chopped
1/2 teaspoon cayenne pepper
1 egg, beaten
1/2 green bell pepper, seeded and diced
1/2 yellow bell pepper, seeded and diced
salt and pepper to taste
1 cup Panko bread crumbs
1 serrano green chili, chopped

In a large sauté pan, heat 1 tablespoon of corn oil. Add ginger, garlic, diced onions and sauté for 5 minutes over medium heat. Add bell peppers, ground spices and green chili and continue sautéing until mixture dries. Remove from heat and cool. In a large mixing bowl, combine crab meat, the cooled onion mixture, lemon zest, lemon juice, cilantro, beaten egg and 3 tablespoons of Panko bread crumbs. Then, season with salt, pepper and cayenne. Mix well so that all ingredients are well incorporated. Divide mixture into 4 equal portions. Form into balls and flatten to form patties. Put the rest of the bread crumbs on a cutting board. Place the patties in the bread crumbs and coat evenly. Heat oil in a heavy-bottomed skillet over medium heat. Fry the crab cakes. When cakes turn a light golden color, flip them over and cook the other side. Remove when done and drain on a paper towel. Serve hot.

Serves 4

PHOTO: Ray Grefe

*Please see page 260 for a complete list of restaurant locations.

GRILLED FISH IN A BANANA LEAF *(IKAN PEPES)*

Yono Purnomo • Yono's Restaurant • Albany, NY

six 6-ounce fillets of grouper, corvina or red snapper
2 tablespoons butter
1 tablespoon olive oil
2 tablespoons shallots, minced
1 teaspoon garlic, minced
1 teaspoon sambal oelek (ground chilies or Vietnamese chili garlic sauce)
1 1/2 inches fresh ginger, finely minced or grated
4 lime leaves
1 ounce coconut milk, to make a paste
1 teaspoon cumin
1 teaspoon coriander
6 banana leaves
salt to taste

Sauté fish lightly in butter and olive oil, then remove from pan and set aside In the same pan, add shallots, garlic, sambal, ginger, lime leaves, cumin, coriander and 1 ounce of coconut milk to make a paste. Sauté to combine. Lay out the banana leaves. Rub the fish with the paste. Place the rubbed fish on the banana leaves and wrap a few times and secure with bamboo skewers that have been soaked briefly in water. Grill for about 6 minutes on each side. Serve with Jasmine rice.

Serves 6

GRILLED FISH WITH SUMATRAN BBQ SAUCE *(IKAN PANGANG PADANG)*

Stoney Chen • Xótik Kitchen • Culver City, CA

1 pound sea bass or any white fish, cut into 4 pieces

Marinade
Sumatran BBQ Sauce
2 candlenuts, crushed
1 teaspoon tamarind juice
2 Thai chilies
2 inches ginger
4 whole lemon grass, white part only
2 inches fresh turmeric
4 garlic cloves
1/2 teaspoon sea salt
6 shallots
1 tablespoon fresh lemon juice
2 tablespoons brown sugar
1 cup coconut cream

Garnish
kaffir lime leaves, finely shredded
1 lime, cut into wedges
drizzle of coconut cream

Take all marinade ingredients and place into a food processor. Process to a fine paste. Marinate fish with half the sauce for 1 hour in the refrigerator. Bring to room temperature and spread the remaining sauce over the fish. Bake in oven at 475° F to 500° F for 8 to 10 minutes, depending on the thickness of the fish. Drizzle with coconut cream and garnish with finely shredded kaffir lime leaves. Serve with lime wedges.

Serves 4

This dish is also great with chicken, pork, lamb or beef and will taste even better if broiled or grilled. The marinade can be prepared up to a week in advance and kept refrigerated. —*Stoney Chen*

GRILLED SHRIMP WITH A STRAWBERRY BEET REDUCTION

James McDevitt • Restaurant Budo • Napa, CA

2 prawns, deveined and dried with a paper towel
3 pea shoots
1 piece of candied ginger, thinly sliced
3 large strawberries, 1 sliced for use in plating
1 large beet
1 tablespoon sugar
oil for grilling
salt and pepper

Strawberry Beet Reduction: Juice the beets and the strawberries separately. Combine juices and place in small saucepot over high heat. Boil until volume has reduced by 1/2 or the liquid has a light syrup consistency and coats the back of a spoon. Chill and set aside.

Prawns: Brush prawns with a little oil and grill. Season with salt and pepper. Brush the plate with a little strawberry beet reduction. Lay pea shoots down. Then layer with a few slices of candied ginger, slices of strawberry and top with the grilled prawns.

Serves 1

HIBACHI TUNA WITH "ASIAN AU JUS" AND AN ORIENTAL MUSHROOM SALSA

Norman Van Aken • Norman's • West Hollywood, CA*

Tuna
4 tuna steaks (about 6 ounces each)
2 to 3 tablespoons pure olive oil to coat the fish with
1 to 2 teaspoons Sichuan peppercorns, freshly toasted and ground
salt and pepper to taste

Asian Au Jus
1/2 quart water
1/8 inch piece kombu (kelp)
10 to 12 Sichuan peppercorns, bruised and lightly toasted
1/4 cup bonito flakes
3 tablespoons light soy sauce
2 tablespoons sake
1 tablespoon rice wine vinegar
1 tablespoon mirin

Oriental Mushroom Salsa
1 tablespoon butter
2 tablespoons dark roasted sesame oil
5 shallots, peeled and sliced
1 scotch bonnet chili pepper, stem, seeds removed and minced
2 cups Shiitake mushrooms, stems discarded, sliced into 1/8 inch slices
1 small tomato, seeded and diced
2 scallions, ends discarded, sliced medium fine on bias cut
2 tablespoons cilantro leaves washed, spun dry and minced
2 cloves garlic, minced
1 teaspoon ginger, minced
2 tablespoons rice wine vinegar
1/4 teaspoon sugar
1 teaspoon salsa sriracha (Vietnamese prepared chili sauce)
1 1/2 teaspoon mushroom soy
salt and pepper, to taste

Tuna: Rub the tuna all over with olive oil. Sprinkle the Sichuan peppercorns, salt and pepper and set aside. ***Asian Au Jus:*** Simmer the kombu on medium heat in water for approximately 30 minutes or until just 2 cups remain. Add the remaining ingredients for Asian Au Jus and allow standing 30 minutes. Strain and reserve until needed. ***Oriental Mushroom Salsa***: Heat a large skillet on medium high heat. Add butter and sesame oil. When it is just beginning to foam, add the scotch bonnet pepper and shallots and stir. Cook for about 30 seconds. Add the sliced Shiitake mushrooms and stir well. Allow the mixture to cook for about one minute. Remove the mix to a bowl. Combine the cooked mushrooms with the remaining ingredients for the dish. Season to taste. To serve, heat a grill until very hot. This can be done quite well in a grill pan too. Heat the Asian Au Jus and the Oriental Mushroom Salsa and keep warm. Grill the tuna steaks about 2 minutes on each side. Place the four tuna steaks onto four warm plates. Scatter the salsa over the top of each steak and divide the Asian Au Jus between four little teacups. Serve the cups right on the plates or in saucers on the side. Your guest can either sip the jus between bites or pour it over the tuna if they like. Serve.

Serves 4

PHOTO: Ray Grefe

*Please see page 260 for a complete list of restaurant locations.

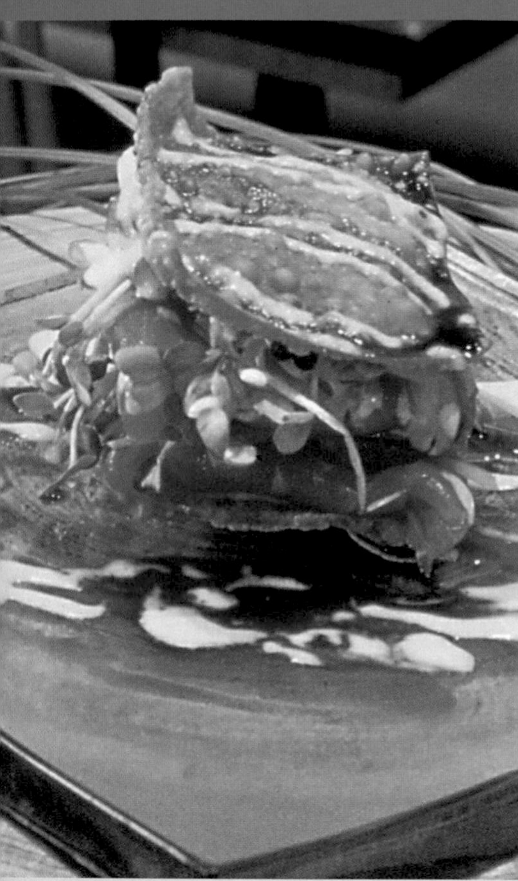

HOUSE SMOKED SALMON AND CRISP WONTON NAPOLEON WITH KAIWARE SPROUTS AND CHINESE MUSTARD HONEY AIOLI

Cliff Wharton • TenPenh • Washington, DC

Salmon and Wonton Napoleon
2 pounds smoked salmon, cut into 1 ounce pieces (3-4 ounces per dish)
1 large red onion, julienned
1 bunch Kaiware sprouts
1 bottle eel sauce (also called kubiyaki sauce)

Chinese Mustard Honey Aioli
1 large egg
3 tablespoons rice wine vinegar
5 tablespoons honey
2/3 cup Dijon mustard
2 cups blended olive oil (25% canola oil, 75% olive oil)

Wonton Crisps
24 wonton wrappers
vegetable oil for frying

Chinese Mustard Honey Aioli: Combine egg, vinegar, honey and mustard in a blender over medium-high speed. Slowly add oil until incorporated. Reserve.

Wonton Crisps: Heat oil to 375° F and fry wontons until crisp and golden. Remove wontons from oil with slotted spoon. Place on paper towels to absorb excess oil. Reserve.

Salmon and Wonton Napoleon: Fill one squeeze bottle with aioli and one with eel sauce. Squeeze small amounts of aioli in the center of the plate to secure the first wonton crisp. Place one wonton crisp in the center of the plate. Cover with 1 ounce smoked salmon, a small amount of red onions, a few Kaiware sprouts and a few drops of aioli. Repeat this twice, ending with a wonton crisp. Drizzle aioli and eel sauce over top of dish and serve.

Serves 8

JAPANESE CEVICHE *(SUNOMONO)*

Kazuo Yoshida • Geisha • New York, NY

2 legs king crab, boiled (about 1/4 pound)
1/4 pound octopus, boiled
1 seedless cucumber (about 1/2 pound)
1/4 pound yamaimo (Japanese Mountain Yam)
10 pieces seedless grapes
2 ounces Tosazu vinegar
rice crackers

Tosazu Vinegar
1 teaspoon sake
2 teaspoons mirin
2 tablespoons water
4 teapoons rice vinegar
1/2 teaspoon soy sauce
1 1/2 teaspoons yuzu juice
3/4 ounce bonito flakes
1 piece kombu seaweed, 2 inch square
1/4 ounce gelatin leaf

Boil all ingredients, except the gelatin. After boiling, remove the bonito flakes and seaweed. Add the gelatin leaf and mix well. Dice the cucumber and yamaimo into 1/3 inch pieces. Cut the seedless grapes into thin slices. Dice the king crab and octopus into 1 inch pieces. Mix the crab meat, octopus, cucumber, yamaimo and grape slices in a bowl with Tosazu vinegar. Serve on a plate with cracked black pepper and rice crackers.

Serves 4

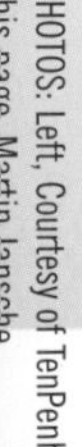

JUMBO PRAWNS WITH SWEET AND SOUR GLAZE

Alan Yu • Zengo • Washington, DC

5 large prawns
2 tablespoons chopped ginger
2 tablespoons chopped lemon grass
1 teaspoon chopped garlic
2 tablespoons chopped scallions
1 tablespoon cornstarch mix with 2 tablespoons of cold water

Seasonings
5 tablespoons ketchup
1/2 cup sugar
juice of 1 lemon
zest of 1/2 lemon
1 tablespoon garlic chili sauce
freshly ground black pepper to taste
2 teaspoons salt

Garnish
cilantro sprigs

Cut the prawns from the back, keep the shells on and remove the vein. Pat the prawns dry with a paper towel. Heat some oil to sauté the chopped ginger, then add lemon grass and cook until fragrant. Add shrimp and cook for about 2 minutes on each side. Add in seasonings and cook until the sauce is reduced slightly. Thicken the sauce with cornstarch water and sprinkle with chopped spring onions. Ready to serve. Garnish with cilantro sprigs.

Serves 2

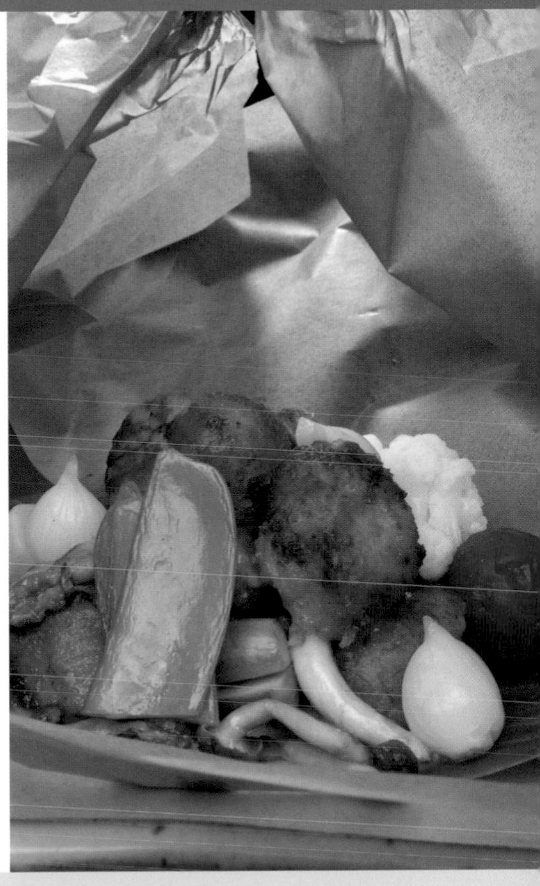

KAI-STYLE SCALLOPS PAPILLOTE WITH THREE MUSHROOMS

Yorinobu Yamasaki • Kai • New York, NY

6 pieces fresh scallops
10 Shiitake mushroom caps, stems removed, sliced
1/2 package of fresh enoki mushrooms, sliced
10 small oyster mushrooms, sliced, stems removed
salt and freshly ground black pepper
15 inch square parchment paper

Kinome Miso (can be kept for one month)
35 ounces white miso
5 egg yolks
1 cup sake
1 cup mirin

10 leaves fresh basil

Mix kinome miso ingredients very well in a saucepan over low heat for about 40 minutes. Take 3 tablespoons of heated miso base. Blanch 10 basil leaves. Blend the miso and basil in a blender until smooth. Preheat oven to 350° F. Season scallops with salt and ground pepper. Sear the scallops with vegetable oil and add kinome miso. Sauté mushrooms with salt and ground pepper. Place scallops and mushrooms on the parchment paper. Wrap and squeeze the top of the paper. Bake in the oven for 10 minutes.

Serves 2

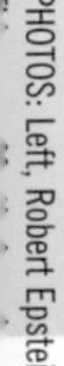

LILLIPUTIAN TOWER OF LOBSTER AND LUMP CRAB WITH MARINATED MANGO AND CURRY OIL

Vikram Gag • IndeBleu • Washington, DC

Tower
1 1/2 pounds Maine lobster tail, cooked
4 ounces Phillips lump crab meat
1 teaspoon shallots, minced
1 teaspoon sour cream
4 drops lemon juice
1 twist crushed black pepper
salt to taste

Marinated Mango
1 mango, peeled and diced
1 slice pickled ginger, minced
1/2 ounce red bell pepper, diced
1/4 teaspoon fresh cilantro, shredded
1/4 teaspoon fresh spearmint, shredded
4 drops lime juice
pinch of sugar
salt and crushed black pepper to taste

Curry Oil
1 teaspoon Madras curry powder, mild
1/4 cup, olive oil
1/4 cup, orange juice
salt to taste

Garnish
4 plantain chips
20 pine nuts, toasted
4 ounces mixed lettuce

Tower: Poach 1 1/2 pounds lobster in boiling water for 7 minutes and let it cool. Remove tail and slice thinly. Remove any shells from crab meat (Phillips Brand is best for this because it is usually the most shell free). Marinate crab meat with sour cream, lemon juice, shallots, salt and crushed black pepper.

Mango Salsa: Peel and dice ripe mango and red bell pepper in tiny cubes. Mince pickled ginger and shred mint and cilantro leaves. Mix all these ingredients together and add lime juice, salt, sugar and crushed pepper.

Curry Oil: Heat half of the olive oil in a pan, add curry powder, deglaze with orange juice and cook for 3 to 4 minutes. Remove from heat, whisk in rest of the olive oil and adjust seasonings.

SERVE WITH A CHILLED GLASS OF GEWURZTRAMINER. — *VIKRAM GAG*

Plantain Chips: Peel semi ripe plantain and slice thin. Deep fry at 325° F until crisp.
Garnish: Toast pine nuts in oven and season with sea salt. Pick lettuce and refresh in cold water. Separate prepared lobster, crab meat and mango salsa into equal parts. In the middle of each plate, place a small 1 1/2 inch diameter round ring. Place one serving of lobster into the bottom of each ring. Then, place crab meat on top of the lobster and mango salsa on top of the crab meat. Remove the ring so you have a tower in middle of plate. Decorate each tower with one plantain chip and each plate with 5 toasted pine nuts, a leaf of lettuce and drizzle curry oil around the tower.

Serves 4

PHOTO: Lisa Masson Studio

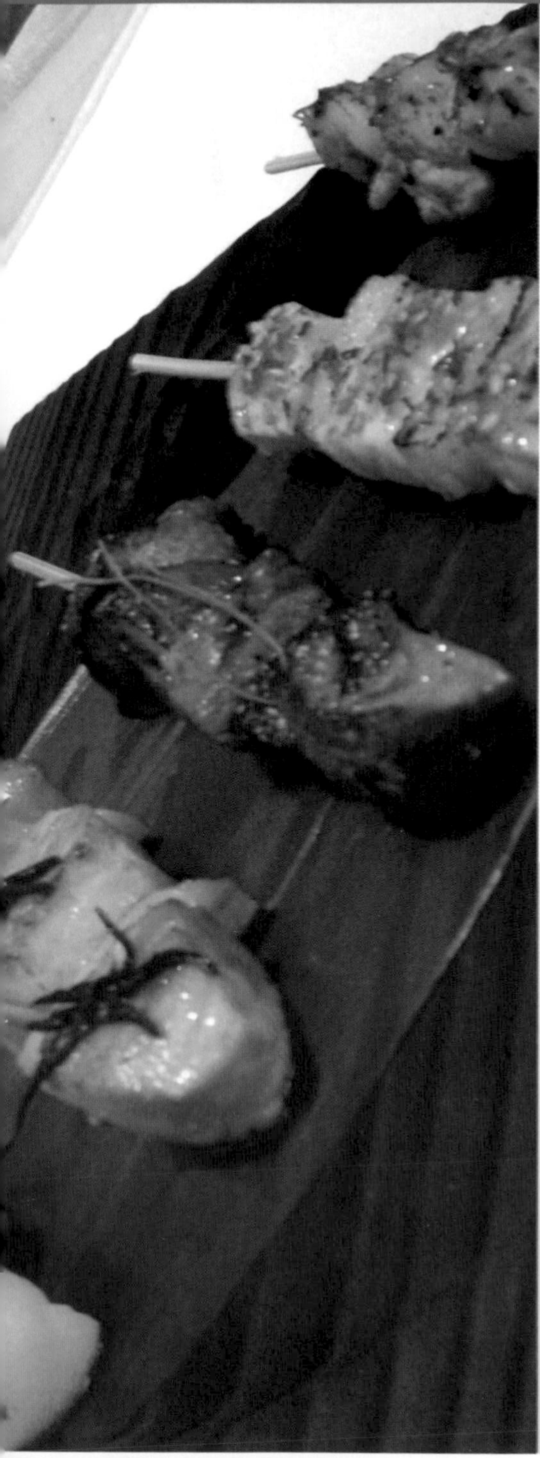

LOBSTER AND CHICKEN KUSHIYAKI

Noriyuki Sugie • Asiate at The Mandarin Hotel • New York, NY

2 lobster tails
3 pounds of chicken
1 mango, pureed
1 teaspoon curry powder
1 teaspoon Earl Gray tea
1 teaspoon sea salt

Marinade
fresh mango puree
curry powder
Earl Gray tea
sea salt

Combine tea, salt and curry. Set aside. Cut lobster tail and chicken into 1 inch cubes. Alternate onto skewer. Cook quickly. Brush marinade onto skewer and quickly grill again.

Serves 4

MAINE LOBSTER SHABU-SHABU

Troy N. Thompson • Jer-ne Restaurant and Bar at The Ritz-Carlton • Marina del Rey, CA

1 1/2 pounds live Maine lobster, blanched in boiling water for five seconds

4 cups water
1 cup light soy sauce
1/2 of a medium onion
1/2 a bunch chrysanthemum leaves
3 pieces romaine lettuce heart leaves
5 pieces fresh Shiitake mushrooms
1/2 a bunch of green onions
5 pieces thin asparagus
12 ounces Shiratake noodles

Choose one of the following:
3/4 ounce dried Shiitake mushrooms
1/4 ounce dried kombu
1/4 ounce dried bonito flakes

Lobster: Leave the claws in for three minutes. Ice down and then, take the lobster meat out of the shell. Save the head for the shabu-shabu water. On a portable burner, make the stock out of water and one of the dried ingredients (dried Shiitake mushrooms, or dried kombu or dried bonito flakes). Bring to a boil and simmer for 10 minutes. If you choose to use the bonito flakes, you will have to strain and discard it before adding the other ingredients. Add the soy, the lobster head and onions and simmer. In a bento box or on a small serving plate, nicely arrange the sliced raw lobster meat, lobster claws, mushrooms, chrysanthemum leaves, romaine leaves, green onions and asparagus. Place the noodles in a small bowl. Take a pair of chopsticks and cook the vegetables and the lobster meat in the simmering stock. After you are finished simmering the vegetables and lobster meat, spoon the broth over the noodles.

Serves 1

PHOTO: Courtesy of The Mandarin Oriental, NY

SHABU-SHABU IS A POT OF BOILING WATER USED TO COOK FOOD AT THE TABLE. PAPER-THIN SLICES OF MARBLED BEEF OR CHICKEN ARE COOKED BY DIPPING THEM INTO A POT OF SIMMERING KOMBU (KELP) BROTH FOR FEW SECONDS. TO JAPANESE EARS, SHABU-SHABU IS THE SOUND MADE WHEN ONE SWISHES THE MEAT IN THE BROTH. THE MORSELS OF MEAT ARE EATEN WITH EITHER A SESAME FLAVORED SAUCE (TARE) OR CITRON FLAVORED SAUCE (PONZU). OTHER INGREDIENTS SUCH AS TOFU, CABBAGE, CHRYSANTHEMUM LEAVES (SHUNGIKU), SCALLIONS, AND MUSHROOMS ARE SIMMERED IN THE STOCK AS WELL. — *TROY THOMPSON*

MINCED PRAWNS IN PURPLE ENDIVE

Larry Chu • Chef Chu's • Los Altos, CA

8 to 12 purple endive leaves, separated

Filling

2 ounces raw prawns, shelled, deveined and coarsely minced
1 tablespoon jicama or water chestnuts, coarsely minced
1 teaspoon white part of green onions, minced
1 teaspoon ginger, minced
pinch of salt
1/2 egg white
1 tablespoon canola oil
1 teaspoon toasted pine nuts

Place separated endive leaves in ice water until needed. Drain and pat dry before use. To make filling, combine all ingredients in a small bowl. Using your hand and fingers as a whisk, whip to incorporate air into the mixture. Continue whipping until the mixture becomes fluffy. To stir fry, heat canola oil in a sauté pan until hot, lower heat to medium high and add filling mixture. Stir fry for about 1 to 1 1/2 minutes until prawns turn opaque and are done. Remove to a strainer and drain for 1 minute. To assemble, place 1 teaspoon filling in the middle of each endive leaf. Top with a few pine nuts. Arrange attractively on a plate.

Serves 4

The filling can be served in red radicchio leaves, small hearts of romaine, ivory endive, butter lettuce or iceberg lettuce cups, proportioning a larger amount to fit the leaves. You can use pickled ginger slivers or sprigs of fennel for an alternative garnish. —*Larry Chu*

MISO-MARINATED RED SNAPPER WITH SHIITAKE MUSHROOMS

Hiroshi Noguchi • Renaissance Orlando Resort at Marriott • Orlando, FL

4 red snapper fillets, 6 ounces each
12 pieces Shiitake mushrooms

Marinade
12 tablespoons miso
12 tablespoons sweet sake
2 1/2 tablespoons soy sauce
6 tablespoons sugar

Accompaniments
1 cup green beans, cooked and shocked
lemon wedges

Marinate red snapper fillets for 3 hours. Clean the marinade off the fillets and grill or sauté. Grill Shiitake mushrooms. Garnish with green beans and a lemon wedge.

Serves 4

IF DRY, SERVE WITH SOY SAUCE OR LEMON SOY SAUCE. —*HIROSHI NOGUCHI*

PHOTOS: Left, Ray Grefe;

MISO-MARINATED YELLOWTAIL TATAKI WITH WASABI MAYONNAISE AND CRAB MEAT MANGO GINGER CUCUMBER SLAW

Hiroshi Noguchi • Renaissance Orlando Resort at Marriott • Orlando, FL

16 ounces yellowtail fillets
1 cup marinated miso sauce (see recipe below)
2 soy sheets
4 ounces crab meat
mango ginger cucumber slaw (see recipe on page 89)
4 teaspoons wasabi mayonnaise
4 sheets wonton skin
8 pieces young romaine lettuce
1 ounce soy sauce
1/2 ounce gelatin powder
1/2 ounce water

Marinated Miso Sauce
1/2 cup miso paste
1/2 cup mirin
1 teaspoon garlic, finely chopped
1 teaspoon seven spices (shichimi)
dash of salt

Gelatin: Place gelatin powder and water into a small bowl and allow gel to soften for ten minutes. Place bowl over a pot of hot, steaming (not boiling) water until gelatin dissolves completely. Do not stir too much as air bubbles will form in gel.
Wasabi Mayonnaise: For every 3 teaspoons of prepared mayonnaise, add 1 teaspoon of prepared wasabi paste. Stir briskly to combine, check seasoning for salt and/or sugar. Hold for later use.
Fish: After cleaning the fish, marinate for 24 hours in one cup of the miso marinating sauce. Clean sauce and sear on hot flame all around. Take from flame and wrap fillet in the soy sheet. Brush on gelatin. When finished, wrap in plastic to cool down in iced water bath. Cool down, take out water and keep in refrigerator until ready to serve.

Wonton Cup: Cut wonton skins round. Put in sake cup to mold to form of cup. Fill cup with raw, uncooked rice to hold wonton skins in place. Place in the oven at 350° F. Cook for 20 minutes, discard rice. Brush on soy sauce. Cook for 5 minutes more until dry.

Presentation: Cut the yellowtail into 8 pieces. Place 2 small pieces of young romaine lettuce onto each plate. On top of lettuce, place 2 pieces of yellowtail. Add wasabi mayonnaise into a pastry bag, then squeeze it onto the fish. Fill up the wonton cup with crab meat mango ginger cucumber slaw. Put the remaining mayonnaise on the romaine lettuce and serve.

Serves 4

PHOTO: Eri Noguchi

ORIGAMI SALMON

Chris Yeo • Straits Restaurant • San Jose, CA*

one 6 ounces salmon fillet
2 tablespoons fish sauce
9 tablespoons beer
1/2 teaspoon sesame oil
1/2 teaspoon sugar
pinch of pepper
2 slices of ginger, cut into strips
1 ounce green bell peppers, cut into strips
1 ounce red bell peppers, cut into strips
1 ounce yellow bell peppers, cut into strips
1 ounce Shiitake mushrooms, cut into strips
1/2 ounce wolfberry or dry berry
1/2 ounce dry longan (optional)

Place the salmon fillet into a pasta bowl, then place bell peppers, wolfberry, longan (optional), and Shiitake mushrooms on top of the salmon fillet. Then, pour the fish sauce, beer, sesame oil, sugar and pepper on top. Place the pasta bowl in a steamer for 5 minutes in medium to high heat. Serve with rice.

Presentation: Use parchment paper to make the origami box. Go online to get instructions if necessary.

Serves 1

*Please see page 260 for a complete list of restaurant locations.

PAN-FRIED SALMON WITH TARO PUFFS

Wai-Keung Kwong • T'ang Court at Langham Hotel Hong Kong • Kowloon, Hong Kong

7 ounces fresh salmon, cut into 1 inch squares
2 3/4 ounces fresh salmon, diced small
3 1/2 ounces taro, cooked and mashed
1 1/2 ounces dried Chinese ham, diced
1/3 ounce Chinese celery, diced
2 pieces fermented red bean curd, form paste
1 teaspoon sugar
1 teaspoon sesame oil
2 teaspoons Chinese rose wine

Wrap the diced salmon, Chinese celery and dried Chinese ham with the mashed taro. Deep fry the taro puff until golden brown. Serve as a side dish. Dredge the sliced salmon with corn flour. Deep fry until golden brown. Set aside. Cook fermented bean curd, sesame oil and sugar until melted. Return deep fried salmon. Stir fry for 1 minute on low heat. Dish the deep fried salmon. Add Chinese wine along plate and set flame. Please be careful when performing the flaming procedure.

Serves 4

PHOTOS: Left, Ray Grefe;
This page, Ong Photography

PAN ROASTED OCEAN SCALLOPS WITH BACON, KALAMANSI AND SAKE

King Phojanakong • Kuma Inn • New York, NY

4 large sea scallops
1 teaspoon canola oil
salt and pepper to taste
1 teaspoon bacon lardons
1 tablespoon kalamansi
(may substitute with lemon or lime)
1 tablespoon sake
(may substitute with white wine or omit)
1 teaspoon unsalted butter

Accompaniment
seasonal greens, sautéed

Heat and lightly oil pan. Sauté bacon lardons until brown. Season scallops to taste. Sear scallops evenly on both sides (approximately 3-4 minutes). Remove scallops from pan and deglaze pan with kalamansi and sake. Finish sauce with butter. Serve over sautéed greens.

Serves 1

The acidity of the kalamansi works well in cutting the richness of the scallops. Kangkong (water spinach) or mulunggay (horseradish) leaves are great for sautéing. —*King Phojanakong*

PASSION FRUIT MARINATED TUNA WITH DRAGON FRUIT, ALMOND AND DIJON

Michael Bloise • Wish at The Hotel • Miami Beach, FL

Marinade
4 tuna loin portions, 6-8 ounces
1 fresh passion fruit, pureed
3 tablespoons soy sauce
1 tablespoon parsley, chopped

Salad
1 dragon fruit, peeled and diced into 1/4 inch chunks
4 portions spinach or watercress or red oak
1/2 cup almonds, slivered
1 red onion, small juilenne
6 ounces Dijon dressing

Dressing
1 shallot, peeled and sliced
2 thyme sprigs
1 1/2 tablespoons Dijon mustard
2 tablespoons honey
3 tablespoons rice wine vinegar
2 cups vegetable oil

PHOTOS: Left, Martin Jansche; This page, Michael Bloise

(recipe continued on following page)

(recipe continued from previous page)

Marinade: Combine all ingredients in a bowl and marinate tuna for 2 hours in the refrigerator.

Dressing: Combine all the ingredients, except oil, in a food processor. After mixture is semi smooth, slowly drizzle in the oil until dressing has reached proper consistency. You may need to add more or less oil, depending on your preference. Season with salt and pepper to taste. Reserve in the refrigerator. Grill the tuna, slice and serve over dressed salad.

Tuna: Set grill to have three "zones"—High for searing, medium for cooking without burning the exterior, and low for holding without additional cooking. Wipe excess marinade from tuna portions, but reserve. Wipe grill surface clean with a rough cloth. Place tuna pieces directly over the hottest part of the grill and sear for 30 seconds to 1 minute on each side. Move tuna to medium hot part of grill and continue to cook tuna for 2-3 minutes on each side, depending on the degree of doneness you prefer. During this stage you may brush on small amounts of the reserved marinade, be careful not to let too much drip onto the coals below this will cause flare-ups and burning. Move tuna aside. Dress and assemble salad on plates. Remove tuna from grill, slice into 5 or 6 slices per portion and arrange on top of the salad. Drizzle a bit more dressing over the tuna and serve immediately.

Serves 4

This is a wonderful dish that combines the heartiness of the summer grill with the lightness of fresh local tropical fruit! Enjoy! —*Michael Bloise*

RED-ROASTED SNAPPER WITH SHAVED CUTTLEFISH AND LEEK FONDUE

Cheong Liew • Grange Restaurant at the Hilton Adelaide • Adelaide, Australia

Fish
approximately two 1/2 pound snapper fillets
2 ounces peanut oil

Marinade
1 spring onion, finely sliced
1 inch knob ginger, finely sliced
1 tablespoon light soy sauce
2 tablespoons rice wine
1 tablespoon peanut oil
1 teaspoon sugar
1 tablespoon dark soy sauce
salt and pepper

Sauce
2 green chilies
1 tablespoon coriander leaves and roots, chopped
2 tablespoons celery leaves, chopped
1 tablespoon brown bean paste
2 tablespoons spring green onion, chopped
1 teaspoon sesame oil
1 tablespoon oyster sauce
1/2 tablespoon ginger, chopped
1/2 tablespoon sugar
1/2 tablespoon rice wine
2 1/2 tablespoons fish stock
1/2 tablespoon ginger juice
1 tablespoon peanut oil
1 garlic clove, chopped

Leek Fondue
3 ounces butter
3 1/2 ounces crème fraiche
1 bunch leeks, white only, finely sliced
3 tablespoons white wine (Noilly Prat recommended)
salt and freshly ground white pepper

Cuttlefish Shavings
1 cuttlefish, cleaned and gutted
1 tablespoon peanut oil
1 slice ginger
salt and freshly ground black pepper

Fish: For the whole fish, remove the head, gills, guts and scales, then fillet and remove all bones.

Marinade: Combine all marinade ingredients. Marinate fish for 30 minutes. Remove from marinade, pat dry and shallow fry with a little oil, skin-side down, until brown and crisp. Turn over, cook for 1 minute, and then remove.

Sauce: Blend or pound the chillies, coriander, celery leaves and spring green onions into a green paste. Heat peanut oil and sesame oil. Add garlic, ginger and brown bean paste. Add in sugar and rice wine. Then, add green paste and sauté gently for 2 minutes. Strain mixture through a fine sieve and push as much of the paste through as possible with the back of a spoon. Return the green jus to the heat. Add fish stock, oyster sauce, ginger juice and reduce to one-third.

Leek Fondue: In a pan, heat up 2/3 ounces of butter and toss in the leeks. Stir for a few minutes, then add white wine. Add in the crème fraiche. Reduce to thicken then add remaining butter. Slowly cook for about 20 minutes until the leeks are very tender. Season with salt and pepper. *(recipe continued on following page)*

(recipe continued from previous page)

Cuttlefish Shavings: Cut the cuttlefish into halves, lengthwise. Thinly slice from the inside at an angle. Marinate in half the oil and some salt. Heat the remaining oil in a pan with a slice of ginger. With a shake of the pan, instantly sauté and separate the cuttlefish slices if they stick together. Season with salt and pepper.

Plating: Spread one generous tablespoon of leek fondue onto the center of the plate. Place the red-roast snapper on top of the fondue. Warm the sauce through and add unsalted butter whisking to incorporate. Pour around the leek fondue, placing a tablespoon on top of the snapper. Garnish with the cuttlefish shavings.

Serves 6

This is an intense dish both for the chef to prepare and for the diner to enjoy. The outer skin of the fish is very distinctly caramel in flavors but inside, there is soft and delicate meat. It can be garnished with very quickly sautéed snowpea shoots. This roast is very slightly braised with the sauce, exuding a delicate flavor. The leek fondue goes well with the flavors and texture of the snapper, and the green sauce brings together the separate elements of the dish. The cuttlefish shavings add another dimension. This recipe is also applicable for barramundi. —*Cheong Liew*

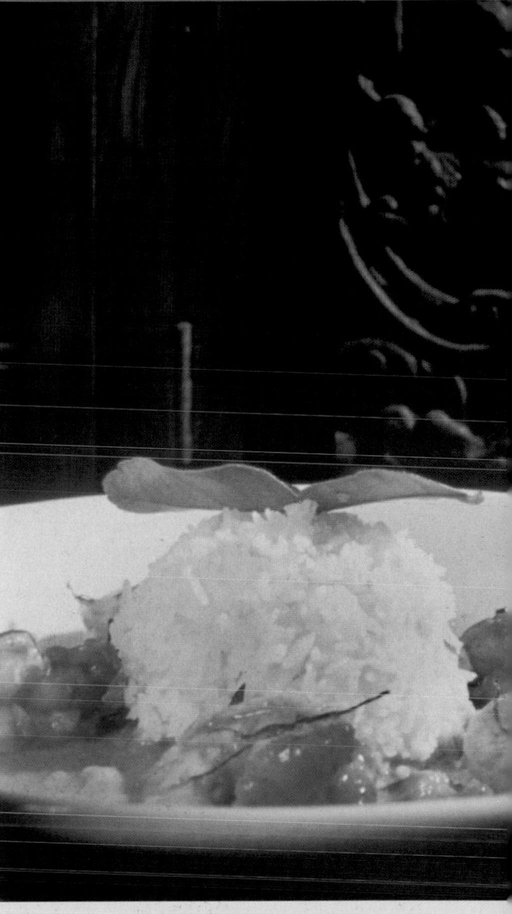

RED THAI CURRY SHRIMP WITH GOLDEN PINEAPPLE AND STEAMED JASMINE RICE

Cliff Wharton • TenPenh • Washington, DC

Curry Paste
1/3 cup red chilies
1 cup lemon grass, chopped
1/4 cup galangal
1 1/2 cup garlic, chopped
1 1/2 cup onions, chopped
1/2 tablespoon shrimp paste
1/2 cup olive oil
1/4 tablespoons coriander seeds, toasted

Sauce
2 cups curry paste
four 10 ounce cans coconut milk
1/2 cup palm sugar
1/3 cup fish sauce

Shrimp
100 shrimp (26-30 shrimp per pound)
1 tablespoon olive oil
10 tablespoons fresh pineapple

40 ounces cooked Jasmine rice
10 julienned kaffir lime leaves to garnish

Curry Paste: Purée all ingredients in a blender and pour into a shallow saucepan. Simmer until thick and aromatic. Be careful not to burn.

Sauce: Combine all ingredients over low heat in a medium saucepan. Simmer for 45 minutes. Reserve.

Shrimp: Peel and devein shrimp. Chop pineapple into 1/2 inch cubes. Heat 1 tablespoon olive oil in a saucepan. Sauté the shrimp over medium heat until they are almost pink. Quickly add the sauce and the pineapple cubes. Cook for about 5 minutes. Place 4 ounces of Jasmine rice in the center of each plate. Pour shrimp curry (approximately 10 shrimp per person) over rice. Garnish with julienned kaffir lime leaves.

Serves 10

PHOTO: This page, Courtesy of TenPenh

ROASTED BUTTER CLAMS, BOUCHOT MUSSELS AND BABY SQUID WITH FERMENTED SOYBEAN PASTE

David Chang • Momofuku Noodle Bar • New York, NY

1 pound of Bouchot or PEI mussels, clean and de-beard (PEI designates Prince Edward Island, a producer of superior quality mussels)
1 pound of butter clams or cockles, clean and wash well
1/2 pound of baby calamari, clean and remove body, tentacles, entrails and beak
1/2 cup sake

Soybean Sauce
1 cup of daen jang (fermented soy bean paste)
1 tablespoon of ginger, minced
1/4 cup of grapeseed oil
1/4 cup of mirin
1 tablespoon of red chili peppers, minced
1 bunch of scallions, finely chopped
coarse black pepper

For fermented soybean sauce, mix all ingredients well and check for seasoning. Heat medium sized pot on high heat, add sake and cook off alcohol. Add clams and cover with lid. After 3-4 minutes or till clams begin to open, add mussels and calamari. In addition, add soybean sauce and mix well. Cover till mussels have opened. Place shellfish in a large bowl and garnish with more chopped scallions. Serve with a side of rice.

Serves 2

SALMON AND GREEN ASPARAGUS KUSHIYAKI

Noriyuki Sugie • Asiate at The Mandarin Oriental • New York, NY

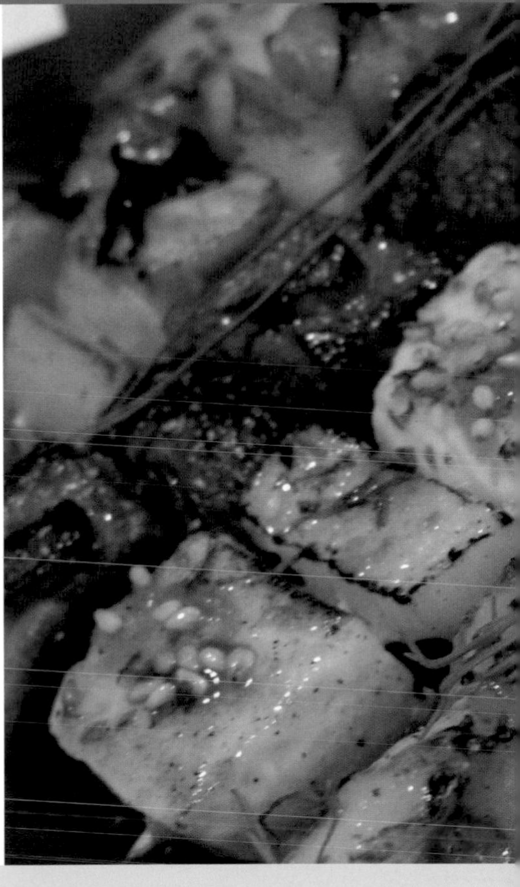

1 1/2 pound salmon
8 green asparagus stalks (medium size)
vegetable oil
10 inch bamboo skewers

Marinade
2 tablespoons sake
1 tablespoon soy sauce
1/2 tablespoon mirin
1/2 tablespoon white truffle oil

Soak bamboo skewers in water for at least one hour. Combine sake, mirin, soy sauce, white truffle oil. Mix well. Cut salmon into 1 inch cubes. Cut asparagus to same size. Alternate 1 piece of salmon with two parallel pieces of asparagus onto a skewer. Brush with vegetable oil. Cook on the grill until salmon is slightly under cooked. Remove from grill, brush on marinade and return to the grill to complete cooking. Serve hot from grill.

Serves 4

I CHOSE KUSHIYAKI-STYLE CUISINE, AS I WORKED AT A KUSHIYAKI RESTAURANT CALLED TORINOSU TO PAY FOR MY COOKING SCHOOL. BASICALLY, IT IS A "SHISH-KEBAB" THAT IS TYPICALLY MADE ON THE STREETS OF OSAKA. IT'S PERCEIVED TO BE FUN, COMFORT FOOD, FROM WHICH I HAVE WORKED TO BUILD MY STYLE OF CUISINE. THE METHOD FOR ALL MENU ITEMS I TO MAKE THE MARINADE, ASSEMBLE THE PROTEIN AND VEGETABLES ON THE SKEWERS. COOK THE SKEWER, DIP IN MARINADE AND THEN COOK AGAIN QUICKLY. KEBABS ARE NOT MARINATED PRIOR TO COOKING. —*NORIYUKI SUGIE*

PHOTOS: This page, Courtesy of The Mandarin Oriental; Left,

SEARED SALMON WITH SESAME AND GARLIC PONZU DRESSING

(TIRADITO DE SALMON)

Ricardo Zarate • Zuma • London, England

16 ounces fresh salmon, wild if available
4 teaspoons Ponzu sauce
4 tablespoons olive oil
1 tablespoon garlic puree
2 tablespoons sesame oil
1 tablespoon white sesame seeds
mixed leaf salad for 4 people

Dressing
1/4 cup soy sauce
2 tablespoons lemon juice
2 tablespoons rice vinegar
2 tablespoons dried bonito flakes
1/2 cup grapeseed oil or canola oil
seasoning

Dressing and Garnish: Add soy and bonito flakes to a pot and bring to a boil. Remove and cool. Then, strain out flakes and keep sauce. Add chilled soy sauce, lemon and vinegar to taste. Slowly whisk or blend with oil for dressing. Season for consistency and taste. Slice salmon into thin strips and marinate with Ponzu sauce and minced garlic for 5 minutes. Then, rinse off lightly and pat dry. Place strips on a heatproof plate. This is only to sear the salmon with hot oil. Heat oil in a pan until it smokes. Do not burn. Carefully pour over the salmon strips to sear them. Place mixed leaves on 4 dishes and place seared salmon strips on top. Garnish with dressing and sesame seeds. Serve.

Serves 4

SEARED SEA BASS WITH WOK-SAUTÉED RICE NOODLES, PORK, AND SHRIMP

Roy Yamaguchi • Roy's • Honolulu, HI*

Rice Noodles, Pork and Shrimp

8 ounces extra-large shrimp (about 8) peeled, deveined and halved lengthwise
1 pound white rice noodles
3 tablespoons soy sauce
3 tablespoons fish sauce
2 tablespoons palm sugar
1/2 cup thinly sliced pork belly or pork butt (pork shoulder)
1/4 cup sesame oil
2 teaspoons garlic, minced
2 red Thai chilies, seeded and minced
1 shallot, minced
1 cup bean sprouts
4 baby bok choy, quartered
2 tomatoes, quartered
1/4 cup packed fresh mint leaves

Sea Bass

4 sea bass fillets, about 7 ounces each
2 tablespoons sesame oil
salt and freshly ground black pepper

Combine the soy sauce, fish sauce, and palm sugar in a bowl and stir until the palm sugar dissolves. Set aside. Heat a wok over high heat and add the pork. Cook for 2-3 minutes until some of the pork fat is rendered. Add the oil, and when hot, add the garlic, chilies, and shallots. Stir fry for about 1 minute until the garlic begins to brown, and then add the shrimp. Cook until the shrimp begin to curl slightly, about 1 minute. Do not overcook or the shrimp will become tough. Add the rice noodles, bean sprouts, bok choy, tomatoes and mint leaves. Stir fry 1 minute longer. Pour in the soy sauce mixture and stir to deglaze the wok. Set aside and keep warm. While cooking the noodles, prepare the fish. Heat the sesame oil in a sauté pan or skillet over medium-high heat. Season the fillets with salt and pepper to taste and add to the pan. Sauté for 3 minutes on each side, or until opaque throughout. Transfer to warmed plates and serve the rice noodle mixture on the side.

Serves 4

*Please see page 260 for a complete list of restaurant locations.

STIR FRIED NOODLES MAKE A TASTY BED FOR FISH DISHES, AND THE PARTICULAR INSPIRATION FOR THIS RECIPE COMES FROM THAI-STYLE RICE NOODLES, WHICH ARE A FAVORITE OF MINE WHENEVER I EAT OUT AT THAI RESTAURANTS. PORK ADDS ANOTHER FLAVOR AND TEXTURE DIMENSION TO FISH AND SEAFOOD DISHES AND THE SHRIMP SERVES THE SAME PURPOSE. USE PALM SUGAR FOR THIS RECIPE IF YOU CAN, AS THE FLAVOR IS SUPERIOR TO THAT OF REFINED SUGAR. —*ROY YAMAGUCHI*

SHRIMP IN LIGHT GREEN CURRY

J.K. Paul • Maurya • Beverly Hills, CA

2 pounds tiger shrimp
3 ounces onions
3 ounces tomatoes
4 ounces cilantro
6 green chilies
2 cups coconut milk
1/2 cup canola oil
1 teaspoon turmeric powder
1 teaspoon cumin seeds
2 cinnamon sticks
12 cloves
2 tablespoons tamarind pulp
2 bay leaves
salt to taste

Shrimp: Remove shell, devein and wash the shrimps. Pat dry and marinate with salt and turmeric powder.

Vegetables: Peel, wash and chop onions. Wash and chop 2 teaspoons of cilantro for garnish and keep the rest for paste. Remove stems, wash, slit and deseed green chilies. Blanch, remove skin and chop tomatoes. Put cilantro, green chilies, cinnamon sticks, cumin seeds and cloves in a blender and make a fine paste. Heat oil in a cooking pan. Add bay leaves and stir. Add chopped onions and sauté till golden brown. Add chopped tomatoes and cook for another 8 to 10 minutes. Add cilantro paste and cook for 3 to 4 minutes. Now, add marinated shrimp and sauté till the oil leaves the spices (this means that the spices are properly cooked). Add the tamarind pulp and fresh coconut milk. Simmer on a low flame for 3 more minutes. Add salt to taste. Serve hot with rice or any Indian bread garnished with chopped cilantro.

Serves 4-6

This traditional shrimp curry is from the region of Konkan. Like most of the Goan, this is spicy but delicious.
—J.K. Paul

STEAMED CHILEAN SEA BASS

Peng S. Looi • Asiatique • Louisville, KY*

12 ounce piece Chilean sea bass
6 romaine lettuce leaves
3 tablespoons vegetable oil
2 limes for lime juice

Sauce
10 red chilies
2 garlic cloves
3 lemon grass stalks
1 whole red onion
1 teaspoon turmeric
1/2 cup water

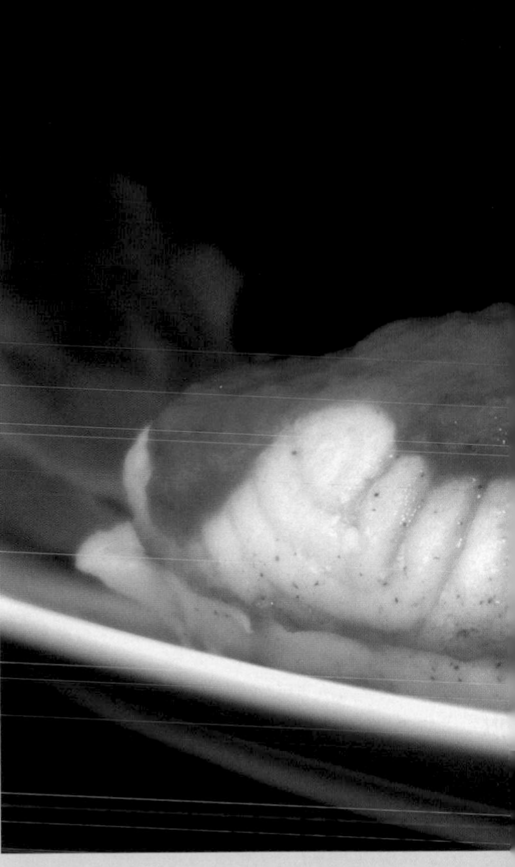

Cut all sauce ingredients into small pieces. Place in blender to mince. Stop when consistency is thick. In medium heat, place all sauce ingredients in a sauté pan. Stir constantly until fragrant. Add salt to taste. Add lime juice and remove from heat. Let cool. Pour half the sauce on top of fish to marinate for 20 minutes. Steam fish on a rack over boiling water until done. Arrange romaine lettuce on a platter and pour half the remaining sauce on lettuce. Place steamed fish on platter and pour the rest of the sauce over fish. Serve immediately.

Serves 2-3

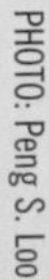

*Please see page 260 for a complete list of restaurant locations.

STEAMED HALIBUT WRAPPED WITH NAPA CABBAGE AND FRESH CHILI LIME SAUCE

David Bank • Land Thai Kitchen • New York, NY

2 pounds halibut (make four portions, 8 ounces)
8 large pieces of Napa cabbage leaves
20 pieces cherry tomatoes
3 pieces shallots
1/4 pound Chinese celery
10 pieces Thai bird chilies
1 bunch scallions
10 pieces cilantro

Sauce
1 cup fish sauce
2 cups lime juice
10 ounces palm sugar

Blanch Napa cabbage leaves and let cool. Then, wrap the halibut. For sauce, put the fish sauce, lime juice and palm sugar in a pot and boil for 5 minutes. Cool down the sauce to room temperature. Cut cherry tomatoes in half, slice shallots and chop the fresh bird chilies, scallions, Chinese celery and cilantro. Put halibut pieces in a steamer for 7 to 10 minutes until cooked. Combine sauce and all vegetables together and pour over the fish. Serve with Jasmine rice.

Serves 4

STEAMED MANILLA CLAMS WITH SQUID INK PASTA AND LOTUS ROOT

Brooke Williamson & Nick Roberts • Beechwood • Venice, CA*

1 pound Manila clams, cleaned
large handful of fresh squid ink pasta, or partially cooked dried squid ink pasta
1/2 lotus root, peeled and sliced horizontally into paper thin pieces (hold in water to avoid browning)
4 garlic cloves, sliced
1 tablespoon Italian parsley, chopped
2 tablespoons canola oil

Broth

2 stalks lemon grass, chopped
1 yellow onion, diced
3 dried Thai chilies
juice of 1 lemon
2 tablespoons light brown sugar
1/8 cup soy sauce
1 tablespoon sesame oil
4 cups water

Place all broth ingredients in a sauce pot and bring to a boil. Take the pot off the heat and let it sit for 20 minutes, then strain, discarding the solids and reserving the broth. Place a large pot on high heat and add the canola oil. When the oil is hot, add the clams and sliced garlic. Just as the garlic begins to brown and the clams begin to open, add the lotus root and then the broth. Cover the pot until most of the clams are open, and then uncover and add the pasta. Taste the broth and add salt to season as needed. When the pasta is hot, and all the clams are open, add the parsley and serve.

Serves 4

*Please see page 260 for a complete list of restaurant locations.

PHOTOS: Left, Martin Jansche;

WE LIKE THE SURPRISING MIX OF FLAVORS IN THIS RECIPE. SQUID INK PASTA IS A STAPLE OF ITALIAN COOKING BUT ADDING LOTUS ROOT AND GIVING THE BROTH A TOUCH OF ASIAN FLAVOR GIVES THIS DISH FAR EASTERN FLAIR. —*BROOKE WILLIAMSON & NICK ROBERTS*

STEAMED SEA BASS WITH TIGER LILIES

Khai Duong • Ana Mandara • San Francisco, CA

4 ounces sea bass fillets
1 ounce cellophane noodles
1 tablespoon fish sauce
1 tablespoon red miso
2 tomatoes, small slices
6 strands of dried tiger lily buds
4 Thai basil leaves
2 oyster mushrooms
1 white scallion, thinly sliced
1 1/2 inch piece ginger, peeled, thinly sliced and cut into sticks
1 pinch black pepper
1 small fresh chili, thinly sliced
cilantro sprigs for garnish

In a small bowl, cover the lily buds with hot water and soak until soft, about 10 minutes. Rinse well and squeeze dry. Cut the hard knobs off the ends of the buds and tie the buds in single knots. In a small bowl, soak the cellophane noodles in cold water until pliable, about 3 minutes. Drain and set aside. Put the fish on a round plate that fits onto the rack of a steamer. Rub the fish with miso, fish sauce, sprinkle with black pepper. Cover and surround the fish with the lily buds, mushrooms, ginger, scallions, basil, tomatoes, chilies. Then, place the cellophane noodles on top. Bring the water in the steamer to a boil then put the plate into the steamer and cover over high heat and steam the fish for about 10 to 12 minutes, until just cooked through. Remove the fish from steamer and garnish with cilantro sprigs on top.

Serves 1

STIR FRIED FRESH LOBSTER WITH SPRING ONION, RED ONION AND SHALLOTS

Wai-Keung Kwong • T'ang Court at Langham Hotel Hong Kong • Kowloon, Hong Kong

1 1/2 pound lobster, chopped into bite size pieces
2 1/2 ounces onion, shredded
4 ounces red onion, sliced
1 1/2 ounce shallots, sliced
2 tablespoons soy sauce
"Fa Dew" Chinese wine to taste
peanut oil for frying

Heat the wok with 2 tablespoons of peanut oil and stir fry the shallots until they turn golden yellow. Set aside. In the same wok over high heat, stir fry the spring onions, red onions and then add lobster pieces. Add soy sauce and a splash of "Fa Dew' wine and continue to stir fry briefly. Sprinkle the shallots on top and serve.

Serves 4

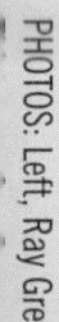

STRIPED BASS MANILENA WITH GRILLED PLANTAINS

King Phojanakong • Kuma Inn •
New York, NY

4 ounce fillet of striped bass
1 teaspoon canola oil
salt and pepper to taste
3 1/2 inch thick plantains slices, cut on a bias and grilled

Salsa
1 teaspoon canola oil
1 tablespoon onions, minced
1 tablespoon green peppers, minced
pinch of garlic, minced
2 tablespoons tomatoes, peel removed
salt and pepper to taste
1 tablespoon Kalamansi juice (may substitute with lemon or lime)

Heat and lightly oil pan. Season fish to taste in a very hot pan, sear fish skin side down until crisp. Turn fish and cook through. Remove fish from pan and plate with grilled plantains. Add oil to pan and sauté onions, peppers, garlic and tomatoes and season. Finish with kalamansi and spoon over fish.

Serves 1

TYPICALLY BANGUS (MILK FISH) IS USED IN THIS DISH. BASS, SNAPPER OR ALMOST ANY WHITE FLESH FISH WORKS WELL AS A SUBSTITUTE. THE SALSA MIXTURE IS USUALLY STUFFED INSIDE THE FISH OR SERVED ON TOP. —*KING PHOJANAKONG*

SWORDFISH AND MOUNTAIN POTATO KUSHIYAKI

Noriyuki Sugie •Asiate at The Mandarin Oriental • New York, NY

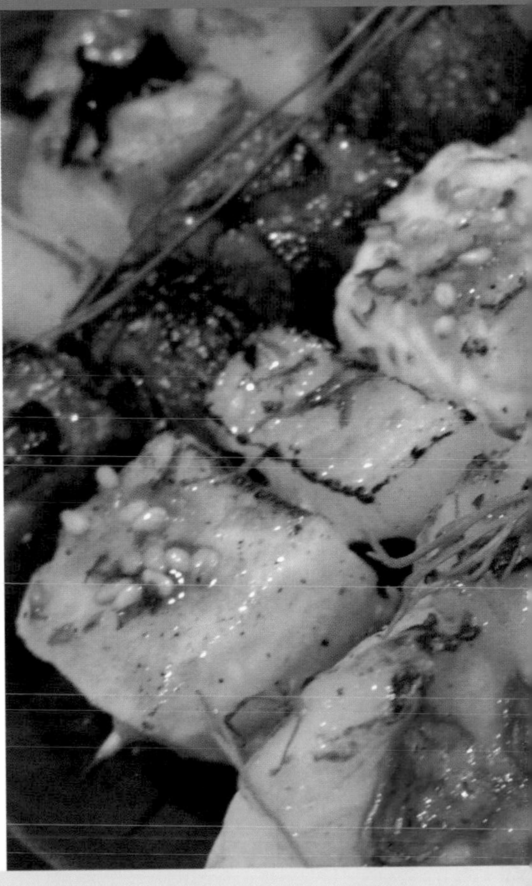

3 pounds swordfish
1 Japanese mountain potato
3 teaspoons butter
1 teaspoon mirin
2 teaspoons soy sauce
1 teaspoon yuzu kosho
(spicy Japanese condiment)
1 teaspoon white sesame seeds

Marinade
butter
mirin
soy sauce

To make brown butter, heat butter in sauté pan, then add soy sauce and mirin. Cut swordfish and potatoes into 1 inch cubes and alternate onto skewer. Cook on the grill. Dip in marinade. Cook quickly again. Finish with yuzu kosho and white sesame seeds.

Serves 4-6

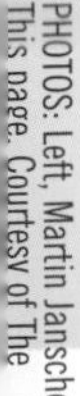

TERIYAKI TUNA LOIN WITH SUSHI RICE AND WASABI

Philippe Chin • CuiZine • Aiken, SC*

8 ounces tuna loin, cut in 2 to 3 inch bars
1 tablespoon olive oil
4 pieces nori
2 cups steamed sushi rice
2 teaspoons rice vinegar
1 tablespoon toasted black and white sesame seeds
1/4 cup water or chicken broth
1 tablespoon ginger, chopped
1 teaspoon garlic, chopped
2 tablespoons scallions, chopped
1 cup soy sauce
1/2 cup brown sugar
1 teaspoon sesame oil
1 tablespoon wasabi powder
2 tablespoons water

In a saucepan over medium heat, simmer the chicken broth with the ginger, garlic, scallions and brown sugar for 5 minutes. Add soy sauce, 1 teaspoon rice vinegar and sesame oil. Let chill and strain. Marinate the tuna in the chilled sauce for 1 hour turning it around every 15 minutes. Mix sushi rice with sesame seeds and 1 teaspoon vinegar. Mix wasabi powder with the water gradually to get a paste like consistency. In a large sauté pan, sear the tuna over high heat for 1 minute on each side. Cut the tuna into 1/2 inch thick medallions. Place the nori onto the serving plates, top with the sushi rice molded into a circle with a 3 inch ring (try using a can of tuna open at each end). Place 3 medallions of tuna and drizzle with the wasabi.

Serves 4

*Please see page 260 for a complete list of restaurant locations.

THREE'S COMPANY *(SAM BAI TAO)*

Pathama Parikanont • Thep Phanom • San Francisco, CA

4 large size scallops
4 large size prawns, deveined
4 medium size calamari, cut into rings
1 cup unsweetened coconut milk
2 finely sliced kaffir lime leaves
1 tablespoon fresh lemon grass, sliced
1 teaspoon fresh ginger, sliced
1 teaspoon Thai fish sauce
1 teaspoon oyster sauce
I teaspoon fresh lime juice
pinch of white pepper and sugar

Accompaniments
2 sliced cabbages, cut into about 1 inch pieces, boiled until soft
2 Roma tomatoes, cut into large pieces

Garnish
2 sprigs of cilantro
2 thin slices of lime

In a saucepan, add coconut milk, kaffir leaves, lemon grass, ginger, fish sauce, oyster sauce, lime juice, white pepper and sugar. Stir until blended and bring to a boil. Add scallops, prawns and calamari. Stir occasionally until all seafood is cooked. Do not overcook. Add in cabbage and tomatoes. Stir gently. Garnish with cilantro and sliced lime. Best served with steamed rice.

Serves 2

PHOTO: This page, Aniruin Pom Limkul

TUNA, CRAB AND AVOCADO WITH FRIED YUCA, CUCUMBER AND YUZU SOY

Michael Cressotti • Sushi Samba • New York, NY*

2 ounces sushi grade tuna
1 1/2 ounces Alaskan king crab
1/2 of a whole haas avocado (large dices)
1 teaspoon red onion, finely diced
1/2 teaspoon cilantro, chopped
1 tablespoon fresh lime juice
1 teaspoon mayonnaise
salt and pepper to taste
3 thinly sliced English cucumbers, about 6 inches long
9 yuca fried strips
extra virgin olive oil, drizzle as garnish
pink sea salt for garnish
a few mache leaves for garnish

Yuzu Soy
3 tablespoons Ponzu sauce
1 tablespoon yuzu juice

Place tuna in the center of a lightly oiled plastic wrap. Cover with another sheet of plastic wrap and gently pound with a flat surfaced meat tenderizer into a 6 inch circle. Store in refrigerator. Gently mix crab, avocado, red onions, cilantro, lime juice, mayonnaise in a mixing bowl. Season with salt and pepper. Keep refrigerated in an airtight container. Fry julienned yuca strips in fryer until golden in color.
Yuzu Soy: Mix 3 parts Ponzu sauce with 1 part yuzu and keep chilled. The quantity of these ingredients may be increased or decreased at will as long as they remain in ratio of 3:1. 3 tablespoons of Ponzu to 1 tablespoon of yuzu should be sufficient for 1-3 portions.
Tuna: Simply fill the pounded tuna with crab and avocado mixture and slowly fold up all the sides to form a small package. Form into a ball and refrigerate. Arrange three overlapping pieces of cucumber, horizontal on a white rectangle plate. Place the tuna atop the cucumber in the center of the plate. Spoon a generous amount of the yuzu soy sauce over the tuna and cucumber. Pierce tuna with the fried yuca to create a sea urchin effect. Garnish the plate with sea salt, a drizzle of olive oil and mache.

Serves 1

*Please see page 260 for a complete list of restaurant locations.

TUNA TARTAR

Todd English • Olives • New York, NY*

1 pound grade "A" sushi tuna
4 ounces sushi rice
2 sheets nori paper
2 stalks scallions, finely julienned
1 ounce ginger, freshly grated
1 ounce siracha aioli
1 bunch fresh cilantro, chopped
1 ounce sesame oil
1 ounce rice wine vinegar
1 cucumber, peeled and seeded, then julienned
1/2 teaspoon salt
1/2 ounce fresh lime juice
3 ounces mayonnaise

Sriracha Aioli: Combine sriracha sauce, lime juice and mayonnaise.
Tartar: Cook sushi rice in salted water for 30 minutes. As a rule of thumb, you generally use 2 parts water to 1 part rice. When the rice is cooling, add the sugar, salt and rice wine vinegar. Place tuna on a clean cutting board and remove any silver skin or sinew. Cut tuna into small cubes. Always work with raw tuna in a clean iced bowl. Add the ginger, aioli, cilantro, sesame oil, salt and pepper. Mix gently and set aside. Place rice on parchment paper and flatten with your fingers or a rolling pin. Cut the rice into 2 inch squares. Cut the nori paper into squares just smaller than the rice and place the nori on top of the rice. Place the tartar on top of the nori paper. Place the julienned cucumber on top of the tuna tartar. Garnish with finely julienned scallions. Drizzle with any left over sriracha aioli.

Serves 4

*Please see page 260 for a complete list of restaurant locations.

I LOVE SUSHI AND TUNA IS ONE OF MY FAVORITES. I LOVE DISCOVERING THE DIFFERENT CULTURES THAT EAT RAW AND MARINATED FISH, AND WHEN I WENT TO ITALY I WAS VERY SURPRISED TO SEE THAT IT WAS ONE OF THEM. THE JAPANESE ARE THE MOST OBVIOUS, BUT I THINK ABOUT EATING OYSTERS AND LITTLENECKS ON THE HALF-SHELL IN NEW ENGLAND, CONCH CEVICHE IN THE BAHAMAS, AND ALL THE CEVICHES OF SOUTH AND CENTRAL AMERICA. —*TODD ENGLISH*

TURMERIC FLAVORED SHRIMP

Peng S. Looi • Asiatique • Louisville, KY*

24 large shrimp
one 14 ounce can coconut milk
1 stalk lemon grass, cut into 1 inch lengths
5 fresh hot peppers such as Serrano or Thai bird chilies
20 baby squash, yellow squash or zucchini, split in half lengthwise

Paste
1 teaspoon ground turmeric
8 shallots
3 chilies, dried
salt and pepper to taste

Place the ingredients for the paste in a spice grinder to form paste. In a medium sauce pot, add 1 tablespoon of cooking oil. Add blended paste and stir until fragrant. Add coconut milk, lemon grass and fresh hot peppers and simmer for 30 minutes. Add baby squash and shrimp and keep stirring. Remove from heat when shrimp and baby squash are cooked, about 3 minutes. Serve immediately.

Serves 6

*Please see page 260 for a complete list of restaurant locations.

FISH & SEAFOOD

PHOTO: Peng S. Looi

MEAT & POULTRY

Meats and poultry are consumed in smaller amounts and with less frequency in Asian cuisine. A Chinese home cook will take a single chicken and portion it out, stretching it over several meals for the family. Typically, the back, neck and feet go directly into the stock-pot. The breast is cut and stir fried or steamed with vegetables while the legs and thighs are chopped through the skin, meat and bone into small chunks, marinated and steamed or braised with preserved vegetables and dried mushrooms. This is a perfect example of the sensibilities of Asian chefs practicing a sustainable lifestyle and their aversion to waste. In other words, all foods are used and nothing is wasted. Though historically, poultry was consumed once a week, today, it is more practical to recommend small amounts taken a few times a week, but always with an eye toward keeping the intake of animal fats at a healthful level. Red meats have traditionally been more limited on the table in rural Asia and then, always mixed with vegetables and served with a big mound of rice or another grain-based accompaniment. Today, Asians consume meat and poultry in greater amounts. Scientists behind the pyramid acknowledge that meat and poultry can be eaten with greater frequency, but its intake must be in moderation for a healthy diet. Again, the strategic word is moderation.

BEEF RENDANG

Carol Selva Rajah • Chef, South East Asian Cuisine • Sydney, Australia

1 1/4 pounds stew beef, cubed
2 stalks lemon grass
1 1/4 inch length galangal
1 1/4 inch length ginger
3 garlic cloves
2 teaspoons chili powder or 5 dried chilies (soaked in hot water for 6 minutes)
2 tablespoons vegetable oil
2 Spanish onions, sliced
2 cups beef stock or water
2 tablespoons mixed curry powder mix (see below for proportions)
1 pandan leaf, optional
1 tablespoon thick soy sauce
salt and sugar to taste
3/4 cup desiccated coconut, dry roasted

Curry Mix Powder
1 tablespoon dry roasted cumin powder
1/2 tablespoon dry roasted fennel powder
1 tablespoon coriander powder
1 star anise, ground
6 cloves, ground
1/2 teaspoon black pepper, ground

Blend the lemon grass, ginger, galangal, garlic and chilli with 1 tablespoon of oil to a paste in a food processor or mortar and pestle. Coat the meat well with the paste. Heat the remaining oil in a wok and sauté the onions until golden. Add the meat and stir well. Lower the heat, cover the wok and cook for 10 minutes. Add water or stock, curry mix and stir well with spices and pandan. Cover and cook for 20 minutes or more. Stir until beef is tender. The liquid will reduce. If beef is still tough, add more water as needed. Add the thick soy sauce, balance salt and sugar to taste. Bring to a boil and cook uncovered for 5 minutes, stirring continuously. Reduce sauce on high heat, add the desiccated coconut and stir for another 5 minutes. The curry should be quite dry by the time you've finished. Remove the pandan leaf. Serve with rice.

Serves 6

This is an aromatic Rendang without coconut milk. Its rich flavors depend on the ground spices, blended herbs, the pandan and the dessicated coconut. Remember to slowly sauté the meat until aromatic to bring out the best flavors; this may take 5 minutes on low heat. Patience is necessary when cooking Rendang. Rendang stores well because of all the spices and the slow cooking. —*Carol Selva Rajah*

BEEF SPARE RIB TERIYAKI YOGURT STEW WITH ORIENTAL VEGETABLE

Hiroshi Noguchi • Renaissance Orlando Resort at Marriott • Orlando, FL

3 1/2 pounds beef spare ribs
5 ounces peanut oil
2 cups soy sauce
4 cups brown sugar
8 cups sake
4 cups water
2 teaspoons salad oil
5 teaspoons corn starch in 5 teaspoons water
20 ounces plain yogurt
salt and pepper to taste

Oriental Vegetables
1 carrot, cut
1 can (4 ounces) bamboo shoots, sliced
8 ounces lotus root, 1/2 inch slices cut into 4
4 small taro roots, 1/2 inch slices
24 pieces fresh green beans, precooked
4 fresh Shiitake mushrooms, cut into quarters
1 cup rice
1 cup water
12 pieces lotus root, thinly sliced (1/4 inch)
1 cup salad oil
1 teaspoon dashi powder in 2 cups of water
dash of shichimi powder (Japanese pepper)

Fried Lotus Root: Heat salad oil in a frying pan. Put in the lotus roots. When brown, remove from pan. Sprinkle the shichimi powder. Put on paper towel
Rice: Wash rice, add water and cover. Bring rice to a boil and then lower the heat. When water is all gone, put in the oven until ready to serve.
Stew: Take bones off spare ribs and clean. Cut the meat into big cubes. Heat oil in fry pan and sear diced spare ribs and brown them. Place soy sauce, brown sugar, sake and water in a saucepan and heat. Add the diced spare ribs and bring them to a boil, cover and simmer for 1 1/2 hours. Cook all the vegetables for 5 minutes in dashi water (1 teaspoon dashi and water). Cut precooked green beans into 2 inch pieces, then cook for 5 minutes. After 1 1/2 hours take out the meat. Mix corn starch and water, then add to thicken the sauce. Take off from the heat. Add yogurt to taste, then add beef and vegetables, mix them together well. Place steamed rice on a plate with stew on top. Decorate with fried lotus roots before serving.

Serves 4

PHOTO: Ronald Leong

BLACK PEPPER STEAK OVER COCONUT RICE

Kimmy Tang • Michelia • Los Angeles, CA

1 pound cubed filet mignon
1 cup Jasmine rice
1 cup water
2 ounces coconut powder
1 teaspoon shallots
1 teaspoon butter
salt to taste
1/2 teaspoon crushed black pepper
1 teaspoon soy sauce
1/4 teaspoon sugar
1/2 teaspoon mirin
2 tablespoons vegetable oil
1 tablespoon butter
2 teaspoons sake

Mix rice and water in cooker. After the rice is cooked, let set for another 15 minutes in covered cooker. Preheat the sautéed pan in minimum heat and add butter and shallots. Stir fry until it is golden brown. Add rice, coconut powder and salt. Place it on a serving plate and set aside in a warm place. While rice is cooking, marinate beef with soy sauce, sugar, mirin, 1/2 of the sake, and black pepper for 15 minutes. Heat wok with high heat. When the wok is hot, add oil and then the mignon. Quickly stir fry for about 2 minutes, searing beef cubes on all sides. When beef is seared, add butter to wok and stir rapidly to incorporate it without burning. When butter has been melted into beef, remove beef from wok and sprinkle with remaining sake. Serve over coconut rice.

Serves 4

BRAISED BEEF SHIN

H.K. & Pauline D. Loh • Food Writers & Cookbook Authors • Singapore

1 whole beef shin
3/4 cup light soy sauce
1/2 cup chicken stock
2 cups water
2 tablespoons rock sugar

Wash and dry beef shin. Trim off surface tendons and blanch the shin in boiling water for five minutes. Remove shin from boiling water and rinse with cool water. Bring light soy sauce, chicken stock and water to a rolling boil. Add rock sugar to taste and reduce heat to a simmer. Place beef shin in the stock and simmer for about 1 hour 30 minutes. Remove beef from stock, drain and cool. Refrigerate until needed. Cut into very thin slices and serve chilled.

Serves 4-6

Recipe adapted from *Dad & Company*, SNP Editions

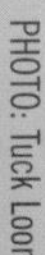

PHOTO: Tuck Loong

BRAISED DUCK DRUMSTICKS WITH BLACK DATES

Kwok Chan • Hua Ting Restaurant at Orchard Hotel Singapore • Singapore

4 duck drumsticks
vegetable oil for wok frying

Seasoning Sauce
4 1/2 cups chicken stock
2 teaspoons chicken powder
1/3 teaspoon salt
pinch of sugar
4 ounces black dates, washed
2 garlic cloves, minced
1 ginger slice, minced
1 spring onion, finely sliced
1/2 teaspoon bean paste
1/2 teaspoon cornstarch, dissolved in cold water

Garnish
1 1/4 pound seasonal vegetables,
boiled until tender

Lightly stir fry the duck drumsticks in a wok with a little vegetable oil, then transfer to a pot and add the black dates. Set aside. Mix the ingredients for the seasoning together in a saucepan and bring to a boil. Reheat the wok with some vegetable oil and stir fry the garlic, ginger, spring onions and bean paste until fragrant. Add the seasoning sauce and bring the mixture to a boil. Pour mixture over drumstick. Continue cooking over high heat for about 10 minutes. Then, reduce the heat and simmer for another 30 minutes until the duck drumstick meat is tender. Arrange the cooked drumsticks on a serving plate. Add dissolved cornstarch into the wok to thicken the sauce and then pour sauce over the stewed duck. Add a serving of cooked seasonal vegetables on the side and serve hot.

Serves 4

BRAISED SHORT RIBS

Richard Chen• Wing Lei at Wynn Las Vegas • Las Vegas, NV

4 Black Angus short ribs
1 gallon veal demi glaze*
20 star anise
6 cloves of garlic, peeled
1 green jalapeno pepper
1 bunch green onions, cleaned with roots removed
1 bunch cilantro, cleaned with leaves removed
1 small piece of ginger, peeled
2 small carrots
1 large onion
7-8 sprigs of thyme
12 pieces of asparagus
12 baby turnips
8 stalks Chinese broccoli
4 tablespoons white truffle oil
salt and pepper
"micro" greens, for garnish
3 cups Jasmine rice

Season short rib meat with salt and pepper. Pan sear short ribs until golden brown on both sides, then set aside. Roast onion, carrots, garlic, ginger, jalapeno at 350° F until golden brown. In a deep saucepan, roast star anise gently to bring out flavor. Put veal demi glace into saucepan and bring to a boil. Put cilantro stalks, thyme and green onion into liquid, then add meat and browned ingredients. Cover with lid and simmer at low heat (or in oven at 250° F). Braise until fork tender (when meat is falling off the bone). Remove meat gently, discard other contents, strain and keep half the liquid reducing it to a thicker consistency. Cut asparagus, baby turnips and Chinese broccoli to about 1 1/2 inches. Blanch asparagus and Chinese broccoli in salted water. Put baby turnips in cold water with a bit of salt. Shock all vegetables to stop from over-cooking. Place meat in the center of the plate, add cooked vegetables around the meat, and pour sauce (reheat if cold) over both meat and vegetables. Garnish with micro greens. Served with steamed Jasmine rice on the side.

Serves 4

*Demi glaze is an expensive gourmet sauce available from better retailers. The generous use of demi glaze in this recipe suggests serving this dish for a celebratory meal.

PHOTOS: Left, Kwok Chan;

CASHEW NUTS WITH CHICKEN

H.K. & Pauline D. Loh • Food Writers & Cookbook Authors • Singapore

4 boneless chicken thighs, 1 1/2 pounds
1 red bell pepper
1 yellow bell pepper
7 ounces sugar peas
4 cloves garlic
7 ounces cashew nuts
1/2 cup stock
1/4 cup soy sauce
1 tablespoon sugar
1/2 teaspoon salt
1/2 teaspoon freshly ground black pepper
1/4 cup Shoa Xing Chinese wine
1 teaspoon dark sesame oil
2 tablespoons cornstarch

Cut chicken meat into cubes and marinate with soy sauce, sugar, salt, pepper, Chinese wine, sesame oil and cornstarch for about 10 minutes. Seed bell peppers and cut into wedges. Top and tail sugar peas. Mince garlic. Roast cashew nuts in hot oil until crisp and lightly golden. Drain on kitchen paper. Heat 1 cup oil in pan to medium heat and run chicken pieces through the oil until just cooked. Drain on kitchen paper. Brown garlic in pan, add bell peppers, sugar peas and chicken. Add stock, adjust seasoning and simmer until liquid is reduced. Add cashew nuts just before serving and toss to combine. Serve at once.

Serves 4-6

Recipe adapted from *Dad & Company*, SNP Editions

In every Chinese restaurant from San Francisco to Shanghai, this is a menu staple. Try this classic and you will understand why. —*H.K. & Pauline D. Loh*

CHAR-GRILLED CHICKEN *(AYAM PANGGANG)*

Yono Purnomo • Yono's Restaurant • Albany, NY

3 whole chicken breasts, split in two to yield 6 pieces
1 stalk lemon grass
8 lime leaves
1 tablespoon Sambal Oelek (ground chilies or Vietnamese Chili garlic sauce)
12 candlenuts or macadamia nuts, ground
2 garlic cloves, minced
4 shallots, finely sliced
12 ounces coconut milk
1/3 cup Kecap Manis (Indonesian Sweet Soy)
1/2 tablespoon cumin
1/2 tablespoon coriander
sea salt and pepper to taste

Sauté shallots, garlic, lemon grass, sambal, lime leaves and candlenuts for 3-4 minutes. Add cumin, coriander, salt, coconut milk and Kecap Manis. Cook and stir together one minute. Add chicken breasts and simmer for 6 minutes, turning halfway through to cook evenly. Remove chicken from sauté pan, then continue cooking on a hot grill (charcoal preferably). Baste with liquid from the sauté pan as the chicken continues to cook on the grill. Continue simmering any additional liquid in the sauté pan and pour over chicken when plating.

Serves 6

PHOTO: Tuck Loong

Delicious with fruit salad and Indonesian Gado-Gado salad with peanut dressing. — *Yono Purnomo*

CHICKEN ADOBO *(ADOBONG MANOK)*

King Phojanakong • Kuma Inn • New York, NY

approximately 3 pounds, whole chicken, cut up
8 garlic cloves, crushed
1 tablespoon black peppercorns
5 bay leaves
1 cup distilled white vinegar
1/2 cup soy sauce
1/2 cup water
1/4 cup coconut milk (optional)

Combine all ingredients and let stand for at least 1/2 hour. Bring to a simmer, cover and braise for 40 minutes or until tender. If desired, finish sauce with coconut milk and serve over rice.

Serves 4

ADOBO IS THE NATIONAL DISH OF THE PHILIPPINES. IT EMBODIES THE INFLUENCE OF THE MEXICANS, SPANISH AND CHINESE IN FILIPINO COOKING. ADOBO WAS A POPULAR DISH AMONG TRAVELING SEAMEN BECAUSE OF ITS LONG SHELF LIFE DUE TO ITS HIGH SALT CONTENT AND ACIDITY. —*KING PHOJANAKONG*

CHICKEN AND VEGETABLE SKEWERS *(TAK SANJOK)*

Hi Soo Shin Hepinstall • Cookbook Author & Food Consultant • Silver Spring, MD

2 chicken breast halves, about 8 ounces each, boned, skinned and sliced into 16 thin pieces, about 3 inches long
8 bamboo skewers, 7 inches long, soaked in water for 30 minutes
8 oyster mushrooms, cut into 16 pieces or 16 pine mushrooms (matutake), sliced
8 Korean hot green peppers, halved, seeded, deribbed, each 2 1/2 inches long
8 Korean hot red peppers, halved, seeded, deribbed, each 2 1/2 inches long
8 ounces Napa cabbage, firm stem part only, cut into 16 pieces, each 1 inch by 2 1/2 inches
16 pieces Napa cabbage kimchi stems, stuffing shaken off, 1 by 2 1/2 inches
1 pound extra firm tofu sliced into 16 pieces, 1 1/2 by 1 1/2 by 2 1/2 inches
1 bunch large sweet green onions, halved lengthwise, cut into 2 1/2 inch pieces, tender white and pale green part only
5 tablespoons olive oil for cooking

Marinade
Kajin Yaknyomjang (Allspice Sauce)
3 regular green onions, white and some green part only
8 garlic cloves, peeled
1 tablespoon Korean hot red pepper flakes
1 tablespoon sugar
1 tablespoon toasted sesame seeds
4 walnut halves
1 1/2 teaspoon Korean fine sea salt
2 teaspoons freshly ground black pepper
5 tablespoons dark soy sauce
1 1/2 cup Korean rice wine or dry vermouth
1 tablespoon grain syrup
1 tablespoon dark sesame oil
4 tablespoons freshly squeezed lemon juice

Garnish
1 tablespoon well packed Korean hot red pepper threads, snipped into short pieces
2 tablespoons toasted pine nuts, coarsely chopped
1 tablespoon stone ear mushrooms, reconstituted in warm water and slivered
20 gingko nuts, pan toasted and skewered on 8 toothpicks

PHOTO: Martin Jansche

(recipe continued on following page)

(recipe continued from previous page)

On a large tray, arrange ingredients in the following order: bamboo skewers, chicken, mushrooms, green peppers, red peppers, Napa cabbage kimchi, tofu and large sweet green onions. In the same order, skewer the ingredients and repeat once, skipping the chicken. Replace the last green onion with a piece of chicken. In a food processor or a blender, add the green onions, garlic, hot red pepper flakes, sugar, toasted sesame seeds, walnut halves, sea salt and ground black pepper. Give a few pulses and add the remaining marinade ingredients. Blend all well with a few more pulses. On a large cookie sheet, brush 1 tablespoon olive oil. Add all the skewers and spoon over the marinade. Wrap the pan tightly with plastic wrap and marinate in the refrigerator for 15 minutes. Preheat the oven broiler for 15 minutes. Take pan out from the refrigerator, remove plastic wrap and drizzle the remaining olive oil over the skewers. Place the pan about 4 inches from the heat source. Broil for about 5 to 6 minutes per side, or to desired doneness. Turn only once. Grilling is another excellent way to cook. Place 2 skewers on individual plates, garnish with Korean hot pepper, pine nuts, stone ear mushroom slivers and toasted ginko nut skewers. Serve with pan toasted ginko nut skewers, leaf lettuce salad and rice.

Serves 4

Recipe adapted from *Growing Up In A Korean Kitchen: A Cookbook, Berkeley*: Ten Speed Press, 2001

SANJOK IS AN IMPORTANT DISH AT A TRADITIONAL KOREAN ANCESTRAL CEREMONY. THE ORIGINAL VERSION USUALLY INCLUDES BEEF AND MOUNTAIN VEGETABLES, SUCH AS BELLFLOWER ROOTS AND FERNBRACKEN. IT IS DUSTED IN FLOUR, EGG COATED AND THEN PAN FRIED. MY MORE CASUAL RECIPE DOES NOT OBSERVE THE STRICT RULES OF SHAPE, SIZE AND APPEARANCE. THESE SKEWERS ARE A HARMONIOUS GATHERING OF COLORS, FLAVORS AND NUTRITIOUS INGREDIENTS. CHICKEN, VEGETABLES, MUSHROOMS, KIMCHI, TOFU AND HOT PEPPER MINGLE IN A SPICY MARINADE. EASY TO PREPARE, TAK SANJOK MAKES A HANDSOME ENTRÉE OR APPETIZER.
—HI SOO SHIN HEPINSTALL

CHICKEN LOB *(LOB GICE)*

Penn Hongthong • Cookbook Author • Middle Island, NY

1 pound extra-lean chicken or turkey, ground
2 tablespoons lime or lemon juice
1/2 teaspoon salt
1 1/2 tablespoons fish sauce
1/2 teaspoon crushed hot pepper, optional
1 teaspoon galangal powder
2 kaffir lime leaves, minced
1 tablespoon rice powder
1 stalk scallion, chopped
1/2 cup cilantro, chopped
1/2 cup mint, chopped

Rice Powder (Koa Kore)
1/2 cup plain uncooked rice

Put the uncooked rice in an old unwanted pan. Place on top of the stove on high heat. Stir and shake the pan occasionally until the rice is dark brown, 8 minutes. Let it cool for 10 minutes. Transfer to a coffee grinder and grind until it turns to powder, about 15 seconds. Store in an airtight container for few months or refrigerate for a year. Makes 1/3 cup. Cook the chicken in nonstick wok (do not use oil) on medium heat. Stir constantly until the chicken is just about cooked, about 10 minutes. Do not brown or overcook. Transfer to a large mixing bowl and let cool for 10 minutes. Add lime juice, salt, fish sauce, pepper, kalanga powder, kaffir lime leaves, and rice powder. Crumble the meat with both hands (use gloves if desired) and mix well. Add scallions, cilantro, and mint. Mix lightly so as not to bruise the herbs. Accompany with fresh vegetables and serve with sticky rice.

Serves 2

PHOTO: Larry G. Hepinstall

LOB IS A TRADITIONAL LAOTIAN DISH. WE SERVE LOB ON HOLIDAYS AND SPECIAL OCCASIONS. IT IS ONE OF THE FEW DISHES THAT IS SERVED WITH WINE. LOB CAN BE MADE WITH CHICKEN, FISH, DUCK, AND WILD GAME. THE MOST COMMON LOB IS BEEF. IT IS ALWAYS SERVED WITH STICKY RICE AND ACCOMPANIED WITH FRESH AND BITTER VEGETABLES SUCH AS LETTUCE OF ANY KIND, GREEN CABBAGE, CHINESE CABBAGE, BOK CHOY, CUCUMBER, CAULIFLOWER, RADISH, LONG GREEN BEANS, WATERCRESS, MUSTARD GREENS, BROCCOLI RABE, ESCAROLE AND GRILLED BITTER MELON. —*PENN HONGTHONG*

CHICKEN TIKKA KABAB

Salim Mohmed & Santok Singh • Gaylord India Restaurant • Sausalito, CA*

3 whole chicken breasts, skinned, boned and cut into 1 1/2 inch cubes
2 tablespoons chopped ginger
2 tablespoons chopped garlic
1/2 teaspoon white pepper powder
1/4 cup non fat yogurt
1/2 teaspoon ground cumin
1/2 teaspoon ground nutmeg
1/4 teaspoon ground cardamom seeds
1/2 teaspoon red chili powder
1/2 teaspoon ground turmeric
1/4 cup lemon juice
2 teaspoons vegetable oil
salt to taste

Combine the ginger, garlic, white pepper powder, yogurt, cumin, nutmeg, cardamom, chili powder, turmeric, lemon juice in a food processor and blend. Drizzle the oil into the mixture blending it into a smooth paste. Empty the mixture into a non-reactive bowl. Add the chicken pieces to the marinade and mix well to coat all the chicken pieces. Cover and let marinate for 3-4 hours in the refrigerator. Preheat oven to 375° F (in the absence of a tandoor). Skewer the chicken pieces about an inch apart. Place the skewers on a rack over a pan and broil for about 10-12 minutes per side or until done. Serve hot.

Serves 6

*Please see page 260 for a complete list of restaurant locations.

MARINADES CAN ADD GREAT FLAVOR TO A MEAL WITHOUT EXTRA FAT AND/OR SODIUM. MAKE THIS DISH EARLY IN THE DAY AND GRILL RIGHT BEFORE SERVING. COMBINE THIS RECIPE WITH 1 CUP OF RICE AND A SERVING OF SPINACH (SAAG) TO ROUND OUT THE MEAL. —SALIM MOHMED & SANTOK SINGH

GREEN CHICKEN CURRY WITH EGGPLANTS *(GAENG KHIEW WAAN GAI)*

Vichit Mukura • Baan Rim Vaam at The Oriental • Bangkok, Thailand

1 pound sliced chicken thighs
7 ounces round eggplant (quartered)
1 ounce Thai pea eggplant (mabua puong)
1 tablespoon green peppercorns
1 tablespoons long green bell pepper, shredded
2 teaspoons big red chilies, shredded
2 tablespoons sweet basil leaves (bai horabha)
1/2 teaspoon lesser galangal roots, shredded
1/2 teaspoon kaffir lime leaves, shredded

Green Curry Paste
1 tablespoon small green chilies
1 tablespoon shallots
4 teaspoons garlic cloves
3 teaspoons lemon grass
1/2 teaspoon fresh yellow turmeric
1 teaspoon coriander roots
1 tablespoon galangal roots
1 teaspoon kaffir lime rinds
2 teaspoons shrimp paste, wrapped with banana leaf and grilled
1/4 teaspoon coriander seeds, roasted and ground
1/4 teaspoon cumin seeds, roasted and ground

Green Curry Sauce
17 ounces thick coconut milk
6 ounces hot water
2 1/2 ounces green curry paste
3 ounces fish sauce
1 ounce palm sugar
3 cups thin coconut milk

Green Curry Paste: In a mortar or electric spice grinder, pound small green chilies, shallots, garlic cloves, lemon grass, fresh yellow turmeric, coriander roots, galangal roots, kaffir and lime rinds together until a smooth paste is obtained. Add shrimp paste, coriander seeds, cumin seeds and mix thoroughly with the pestle. ***Green Curry Sauce:*** Heat thick coconut milk over medium high heat, leave it to reduce until coconut oil comes to the surface. Add hot water. Add green curry paste to stir fry until fragrant and season with fish sauce and palm sugar. Add the chicken thighs to stir fry, then add round eggplants (quartered) and pea eggplants. Keep stirring until cooked. Add thin coconut milk and keep boiling. Mix in the green peppercorns, long green bell pepper, big red chilies, sweet basil leaves, lesser galangal, kaffir lime leaves. Leave it to boil again. Serve with steamed Jasmine rice.

Serves 4

PHOTO: Ray Grefe

GRILLED SKIRT STEAK WITH THAI CHILI DIPPING SAUCE *(NEUR YANG NAM TOK)*

Taweewat Hurapan • Hurapan Kitchen • New York, NY

8 ounces skirt steak, cleaned and trimmed

Marinade
2 ounces oyster sauce
1 ounce Maggi brand seasoning sauce
1 ounce garlic, chopped
4 ounces sugar, granulated

Thai Chili Dipping Sauce
1 ounce fish sauce
1 ounce lime juice
1 teaspoon garlic, sliced
1 kaffir lime leaf, julienned
1 teaspoon sugar, granulated
1 teaspoon red chili, crushed and dried

Combine all ingredients of the marinade and pour over the steak. Marinate the steak for 15 minutes only or it will be too salty. Mix the ingredients of dipping sauce. Grill the steak until medium or medium-rare. When steak is done, cut into slices and serve with dipping sauce.

Serves 4

HERBED MINCED CHICKEN AND SWEET CORN IN PASTRY SHELLS

Vichit Mukura • Baan Rim Vaam at The Oriental • Thailand

Pastry Shells
1 1/4 cups rice flour
1/4 cup tapioca flour
1/2 cup wheat flour
1/2 cup plain water
1/2 cup lime water
1/2 cup thick coconut milk
1/4 tablespoon salt
1 chicken egg
1/2 tablespoon black sesame seeds

Stuffing
2 1/2 ounces chicken, minced
8 ounces sweet corn, shaved
3 ounces onion, diced
1 teaspoon coriander roots and garlic, make paste
1/8 teaspoon turmeric powder
1 teaspoon salt
3 tablespoons white sugar
1 ounce cooking oil
3 tablespoons boiled lotus seed, chopped
4 ounces chicken broth

Shells: In a bowl, mix together rice flour, tapioca flour, wheat flour and salt. Combine plain water, lime water, thick coconut milk and chicken egg together until well mixed, then gradually pour into the mixture bowl. Stir until smooth batter forms. Strain. Add black sesame seeds to the batter and mix well. Heat oil until 375° F. Dip the mold bottom into the batter and deep fry. Remove pastry shell from the mold and keep deep frying until golden brown.
Stuffing: Heat cooking oil over medium heat. Add coriander roots and garlic to stir fry until fragrant. Add minced chicken and chicken broth to stir fry until cooked. Then, add the onions until softened. Add the sweet corn to stir fry over high heat until cooked, and then add the lotus seeds, curry powder, and turmeric powder. Season with salt and white sugar. Keep stirring until well mixed. To serve, fill the stuffing into pastry shells, garnish with coriander leaves and shredded big red chilies.

Serves 4

PHOTO: Left, Martin Jansche

KOREAN GRILLED MARINATED FLANK STEAK WITH MARINATED SHIITAKE MUSHROOMS, PINE NUTS, RED CHILI PEPPERS AND SCALLIONS

David Chang • Momofuku Noodle Bar • New York, NY

Flank Steak

2 pieces of flank steak (12-14 ounces each)
8 pieces of garlic, peeled
one 2 inch piece of ginger, peeled and freshly grated
3 whole white Spanish onions
2 cups soy sauce
1/2 cup white sugar
1 cup of fresh apple juice or pear juice
1/8 cup of sesame oil
1 lemon
salt and fresh coarse cracked black pepper

Marinated Mushrooms (Do this ahead of time)

12-16 Shiitake or oyster mushrooms, stems removed
2 bunches of greens scallions, finely chopped
3 red chili peppers, seeded and thinly sliced
4 tablespoons of rice wine vinegar
1 tablespoon of sesame oil
2 tablespoons of soy sauce
canola oil for cooking
roasted pine nuts

Flank Steak: Combine sugar, soy sauce, sesame oil, garlic, sliced onions, juice of lemon and apple or pear. Taste for seasoning. Add flank steak and marinate for 4 to 6 hours.

Mushrooms: Over medium high heat, add 3 tablespoons of canola oil to pan. Add mushrooms. Season with salt and black pepper. Cook for 2-3 minutes, transfer to a bowl to rest. Add scallions, red chili peppers and pine nuts. In a separate bowl, add sesame oil, soy sauce and rice wine vinegar. Mix well and pour it over vegetables to marinate. Heat grill or sauté pan and cook flank steak for 4-5 minutes per side. Let meat rest for 2-3 minutes. At the same time, sauté marinated onions till tender. Slice meat and serve over a bed of cooked onions. Spoon vegetables and mushroom mixture over steak. Serve with a side of rice.

Serves 4-6

PHOTO: Martin Jansche

KUMQUAT CHICKEN

Kimmy Tang • Michelia • Los Angeles, CA

2 pieces of boneless and skinless chicken breasts (about 20 ounces total)
1 egg, beaten
8 ounces Panko bread crumbs
1 tablespoon fried shallots
2 cups vegetable oil, or enough to cover the bottom of a medium frying pan

Marinade
1/4 teaspoon salt
1/4 teaspoon sugar
1/2 teaspoon mirin

Sauce
1 tablespoon plum sauce
1 tablespoon kumquat sauce
1 piece red chili, diced
1 small onion, diced small
1/2 cup water
1 tablespoon garlic and shallots
1 teaspoon oil

Marinate chicken breasts with salt, sugar and mirin for 20 minutes. To make sauce, heat oil in saucepan with high heat, add garlic and shallots and stir until fragrant. Add plum sauce, kumquat sauce, chili, onions and water and bring to boil. Simmer for 3 minutes and set aside. Grind fried shallots to a powder and combine with Panko. Dip chicken breasts into beaten egg and then into Panko and shallots mixture. Preheat oil in the frying pan with medium heat, deep fried until golden brown. Transfer to plate and pour the kumquat sauce over the chicken and serve.

Serves 4

NAVARIN OF LAMB ORIENTAL WITH NOODLES AND FRESH CHILLI

Paul Rankin • Cayenne • Belfast, United Kingdom*

3 pounds lamb shoulder, trimmed of fat, and cut into 1/2 inch dices
3 1/2 ounces dark soy sauce
3 tablespoons fresh ginger, chopped
3 tablespoons sesame oil
2 tablespoons garlic, chopped
1 tablespoon white peppercorns
10 whole star anise
4 tablespoons vegetable oil
3 tablespoons flour
4 1/2 cups water
2 large carrots, peeled and quartered
1 large onion, peeled and quartered
1 leek, split at the top and washed thoroughly
2 packets of fresh thick Shanghai noodles
2 teaspoons sesame oil
4 small green chilies, deseeded
6 spring onions
3 tablespoons fresh coriander
salt and pepper

To marinate the lamb, combine the soy sauce, ginger, sesame oil, garlic, white pepper and star anise in a large non-reactive bowl. Add the lamb pieces and toss them thoroughly to coat each piece well with the marinade. Cover and leave to marinade in the refrigerator for at least six hours or ideally overnight. To cook the lamb, heat the oil over high heat and then add the lamb in batches. As the lamb browns, sprinkle it with the flour, and continue to cook for two minutes more. Drain the pieces in a colander as they finish browning and then place in a heavy casserole dish. Add the water, carrots, onions and leeks. Bring to a simmer and skim off any access fat or scum. Cover and cook over low heat for approximately 1 1/2 hours or until lamb is tender. Now, strain the juices through a fine sieve and again, skim off any excess fat. Pick the cooked onions, carrots and leeks out of the meat and pour the strained juices back onto the meat. Check the seasoning and add a little salt and pepper if needed. Cook the noodles in 1 1/2 gallons of boiling water for approximately 5 minutes or until soft. Drain and toss with sesame oil. To serve, divide the noodles into warmed bowls, and place a ladle or two of the navarin on top. Finish it off by sprinkling over the chillies, spring onions, and coriander, all freshly chopped.

Serves 6

*Please see page 260 for a complete list of restaurant locations.

This is a remake of the very satisfying French classic 'navarin d'agneau'. We've twisted it about a bit in the seasonings and added some noodles, but feel free to serve it with whatever you fancy. When I was a lot younger, my wife Jeanne and I travelled the world and worked in kitchens to earn a bit of cash along the way. We visited many countries including Singapore, Malaysia, Thailand, Hong Kong and even spent three months in mainland China which is where we fell in love with spices and Pan-Asian food in general. It was from our travels that we got the idea for our restaurant Cayenne, where we serve casual, hip food made with lovingly bought Irish produce but cooked with a twist. As the name suggests, the food we serve here has a touch of spice, which adds zest and zing, verve and vigor with it. Food becomes alive and jumps off the plate. —*Paul Rankin*

NEW ZEALAND RACK OF LAMB *(IGA KAMBING)*

Yono Purnomo • Yono's • Albany, NY

2 New Zealand lamb racks

Marinade
1 teaspoon shallots, minced
1 teaspoon garlic, minced
1 tablespoon parsley, chopped
1 ounce pernod
1 ounce balsamic vinegar
1/2 cup olive oil
1/4 teaspoon cumin
1/4 teaspoon coriander
1/4 teaspoon salt
1/4 teaspoon black pepper

Sauce
1/2 teaspoon shallots, minced
1/2 teaspoon garlic, minced
2 lime leaves
1 teaspoon Indian Madras curry powder
1 tablespoon Thai yellow curry paste, prepared or canned
1/2 teaspoon turmeric
3 tablespoons mango chutney
1 cup coconut milk
1/2 cup lamb stock
1/4 teaspoon sambal (Vietnamese chili garlic sauce)
2 tablespoons olive oil
1/4 teaspoon cumin
1 teaspoon coriander
salt and pepper to taste

Marinade: Combine marinade ingredients with a wire whisk. Marinate the lamb for 12 hours. Mark the lamb racks on a hot grill, then finish in the oven to desired serving temperature.

Sauce: Heat olive oil in a sauté pan, add shallots, garlic, lime leaves and sambal then cook until shallots are translucent. Add curry paste and chutney. Deglaze the pan with lamb stock, add curry powder, cumin, coriander and turmeric then reduce by half. Add coconut milk, reduce again to serving consistency. Adjust seasoning with dry spices if desired.

Serves 4 (3-4 chops each)

PAN FRIED CURRIED LAMB ROLLS WITH FRESH TOMATO SAUCE

Susanna Foo • Susanna Foo Chinese Cuisine • Philadelphia, PA

8 ounce coarsely ground lamb shoulder
1 tablespoon soy sauce
1 tablespoon brandy
1 teaspoon sesame oil
1/4 cup light vegetable oil or soybean oil
1/2 cup finely chopped shallots (about 2 large shallots)
1 tablespoon plus 1 teaspoon curry powder
2 jalapeno peppers, stemmed and finely chopped
1 cup finely chopped fresh Shiitake mushrooms
16 very thin "Shanghai style" square wonton wrappers
1/2 cup chicken stock
1 teaspoon tapioca powder with 1 tablespoon water
1 cup peeled grape tomatoes
Kosher salt and freshly ground pepper
small fresh basil or coriander leaves

In a medium bowl, mix the ground lamb with soy sauce, brandy and sesame oil. Cover and set aside. Heat 2 tablespoons oil in a small saucepan, add shallots. Cook until soft, add curry powder and jalapeno peppers and cook for another 30 seconds. Mix in the chopped Shiitake mushrooms, stir and cook for 30 seconds. Turn off the heat. Transfer to a large bowl. Let cool. Mix the marinated lamb with the curried mushrooms and mix well. Set aside one small bowl of water. Place one wrapper on a clean cutting board. Moist the wrapper with your fingers, spoon 1 tablespoon of lamb filling in the center of the wrapper. Fold and roll the wrapper over, pinch and seal both open ends. Repeat. Make 16 curried lamb rolls. Heat a large non-stick skillet over medium heat, add 1 tablespoon of oil, then line half (8 pieces) the lamb rolls on the skillet. Pour 3 tablespoons water. Cover tight and turn the heat to medium and cook for about 5 minutes. The bottom of the rolls will turn crispy gold. The meat should cook through. In the meantime, heat 1 tablespoon of oil in a medium saucepan. Add garlic and 1 teaspoon curry powder, cook until soft. Add the stock and tapioca. Bring to a boil and cook for 2 minutes. Turn the heat to medium, add tomato and cook for 30 seconds. The tomatoes should be slightly soft but still holding its shape. Turn off the heat. Taste with salt and freshly ground pepper. Place 4 pieces of curried lamb rolls on four plates (crispy side up) and spoon over the tomato sauce. Decorate with basil or coriander and serve.

Serves 4

PISTACHIO CRUSTED FOIE GRAS WITH JALAPENO LYCHEE MARMALADE

Cedric Tovar • Peacock Alley,
Waldorf=Astoria • New York, NY

1 small lobe of duck foie gras
(about 14 ounces)
1 cup water
1/2 cup granulated sugar
1 pound, fresh lychees, peeled and pitted
3 tablespoons pistachios, roasted and roughly chopped
1 jalapeno pepper, thinly sliced
1 fresh Thai bird chili, thinly sliced
1 tablespoon mirin vinegar
chive flowers
1 teaspoon extra virgin olive oil
sea salt and black pepper

Lychee Marmalade: Combine the water and sugar in a pot and bring to a boil. Add two thin slices of jalapeno peppers and a quarter of the Thai bird chilies. Reduce to a simmer and poach the lychees for 10 minutes. Let cool at room temperature. Strain the lychees and cut into quarters. Combine them with the rest of the jalapeno slices, the chili slices, and the olive oil. Reduce a quarter of the syrup to caramel. Deglaze with the mirin vinegar. Save at room temperature.
Foie Gras: Remove the foie gras from the refrigerator 45 minutes before cooking (to allow to come to room temperature). Season the foie gras with salt and pepper on both sides. Sear in a dry medium heat pan on its presentation side. Once you have obtained a nice brown color, flip the foie gras and start to baste it with the rendered foie fat. After one minute, rub the foie with one spoon of the lychee caramel and sprinkle with 2 tablespoons of the chopped pistachios. Baste one more time and remove from the fire. Let rest one minute in the pan. Slice the foie gras in four equal parts. Place in the middle of a rectangle serving plate with a spoon of lychee marmalade on one side and a teardrop of lychee caramel across the plate. Finish with sea salt and crushed black pepper.

Serves 4

I LOVE FOIE GRAS, ESPECIALLY SEARED AND ALSO ENJOY LYCHEES, WHICH I ATE BY THE POUND WHEN I WAS A CHILD. THEREFORE, THIS RECIPE CAME TOGETHER NATURALLY. MY VERSION OF THE MARMALADE IS JUST SWEET, SOUR AND SPICY ENOUGH TO COMPLEMENT THE RICHNESS OF THE FOIE GRAS AND THE ACIDITY OF THE VINEGAR, WHICH PERFECTLY BALANCE ITS FLAVOR. —*CEDRIC TOVAR*

PORK TENDERLOIN *(BABI KECAP)*

Yono Purnomo • Yono's Restaurant • Albany, NY

2 1/2 pounds pork tenderloin (trimmed), sliced into 1 1/2 ounce pieces
2 shallots, pureed
2 garlic cloves, pureed
1 1/2 teaspoon cumin
1 1/2 teaspoon coriander
1 inch fresh ginger, minced
1 tablespoon orange rinds, finely grated
1/2 cup Kecap Manis (Indonesian Sweet Soy)
3/4 cup coconut milk
1/2 tablespoon Sambal (Indonesian chili paste)
1 cup flour, to dredge
3 tablespoons oil
salt and pepper to taste

Accompaniments
steamed Jasmine rice
stir fried vegetables

Dredge the pork slices in flour, shaking off excess. Heat oil in a sauté pan, then sauté pork slices for two minutes on each side until golden brown. Remove pork from pan and set aside. In the same sauté pan, add shallots, garlic and ginger. Cook until translucent. Add orange rinds, sambal, spices and coconut milk. Bring to a boil, stirring, for two minutes. Return the sautéed pork to the pan, add the Kecap Manis and continue cooking 3-5 minutes until sauce is reduced, and napes the back of a spoon. Serve with Jasmine rice and stir fried vegetables.

Serves 6

PHOTOS: Left, Brett Mensh;

ROASTED DUCK BREAST, BAKED EGGPLANT, WASABI AND WATERCRESS SALAD

David Myers • Sona • Los Angeles, CA

4 duck breasts (approximately 6 ounces each)
3 tablespoons wasabi paste
4 Japanese eggplants
1/2 cup soy sauce
2 bunches watercress
4 tablespoons olive oil
1/2 lemon
salt and freshly ground pepper
2 tablespoons honey
2 tablespoons butter

Duck: With a knife, score the duck skin lengthwise. Heat a large sauté pan, place duck breasts skin side down and render the fat from the breasts until crisp. Season the flesh side of the breasts with salt and pepper. Place them on a rack atop a baking sheet with the skin side down in a 400° F oven for 8 minutes. Take the sheet out of the oven and brush the breasts with soy sauce and let rest in a warm place.
Eggplant: Cut eggplants in half lengthwise and score the skin side. Season with salt and pepper and 2 tablespoons of olive oil and 1 tablespoon of soy sauce. Place eggplants, flesh side down on a parchment lined baking sheet. Place in a 350° F oven for 11 minutes or until soft.
Wasabi: Mix 3 tablespoons wasabi, 2 tablespoons soy sauce, 2 tablespoons of melted butter, and 2 tablespoons honey. Mix well and reserve.
Watercress Salad: Season watercress with salt and pepper and toss in 2 tablespoons of olive oil and lemon juice.
Plating: On a warm plate, place a duck breast in the middle, place 2 eggplant pieces, crosshatched next to the duck. Place one tablespoon of wasabi sauce and watercress salad on top of the duck.

Serves 4

SHICHIMI CRUSTED LAMB LOIN, GINGER, LEMON GRASS JUS, CORN AND KABOCHA SAUCE

Hide Yamamoto • The Mandarin Oriental, Tokyo • Tokyo, Japan

Lamb
24 ounces lamb loin (domestic or Australian)
1 ounce kochujang paste (Korean miso, available in Korean food stores)
1/3 ounces shichimi (a mix of seven Japanese chili peppers)
2 teaspoons butter
1 teaspoon vegetable oil

Ginger and Lemon Grass Jus Sauce
4 ounces lamb jus or chicken soup
1 cinnamon stick
1/2 ounce gingerroot, peeled and sliced
1 star anise
1/4 ounce soy sauce
1/4 ounce sake
1/4 ounce lemon grass, sliced

Corn and Kabocha Sauce
5 ounces corn juice
5 ounces kabocha squash juice
2 ounces chicken soup
1 tablespoon butter
salt and pepper

Vegetables
1 ounce cooked higiki (cooked with dashi and soy sauce)
1 ounce Japanese mountain potato, peeled and cut
1 ounce micro-shiso leaf sprouts
1/4 ounce salty plum paste
1/4 ounce extra virgin olive oil
1/4 ounce lemon juice
salt and pepper

(recipe continued on following page)

(recipe continued from previous page)

Lamb: Remove fat and bones, salt slightly and heat vegetables in a sauté pan with oil and butter. Place lamb and grill the surface, brush Kochigian miso and sprinkle shichimi peppers. Preheat oven to 250° F. Cook to medium rare, set aside, and keep warm.

Ginger Lemon Grass Jus: Combine ingredients together in a medium-sized saucepan and simmer until approximately 2 ounces. Strain the jus and set aside.

Corn Kabocha Sauce: Make corn kabocha squash juice with a juicer machine. Strain the juice and transfer to a separate saucepan. Heat slowly until it becomes thick, and once heated, add chicken soup. Add butter for finishing.

Vegetables: Combine salty plum paste, lemon juice and olive oil together to make a vinaigrette sauce. Add higiki, Japanese mountain potato and micro shiso leaf sprouts. Mix gently, sprinkle salt and pepper on top for additional taste. Serve corn kabocha sauce, then ginger lemon grass jus on top. Cut the cooked lamb into 4 portions. Place in the middle of the two sauces and decorate vegetables on top of the lamb.

Serves 4

SLOW-ROASTED ORGANIC PORK, WILD PEPPER AND TRUFFLED TARO ROOT PUREE

Cedric Tovar • Peacock Alley, Waldorf=Astoria Hotel • New York, NY

6 pound rack of organic pork (ask your butcher to remove the loin from the bone and chop the bone into small pieces for you to use for the pork jus)
4 shallots, roughly sliced
1/2 carrot, roughly sliced
1 sprig thyme
1 bay leaf
1 head garlic
1 ounce ginger, peeled and sliced
1 stick lemon grass, pounded and chopped
4 tablespoons olive oil
4 baby bok choy, split in two
1/2 pound fava beans (after blanched and peeled will be 2 tablespoons)
1 pound taro root
1 tablespoon black truffle
4 tablespoons butter
2 cups milk
2 cups water
sea salt
wild black peppercorns (from North Vietnam also known as a variety of Szechwan pepper in South China)

PHOTOS: Left, Steve Legato;

(recipe continued on following page)

(recipe continued from previous page)

Marinade: Combine a teaspoon of cracked wild peppercorn, shallots, carrots, thyme, bay leaf, lemon grass, ginger, olive oil and 5 crushed cloves of garlic. Rub the loin of pork with this mixture. Marinate in the refrigerator for one day.
Slow Roasted Organic Pork: On the day you wish to prepare, preheat the oven to 230° F. Clean and save the marinade from the pork loin. Season the pork with sea salt and crushed wild pepper. Sear on all sides in a medium heat pan with a spoon of butter just until all sides have a nice caramelized color. Place in a roasting pan. Add the marinade, the rest of the garlic cloves and then put everything in the roasting pan with the pork. Put in the oven and cook for approximately 1 hour to get a perfect medium temperature. Turn the oven off and let rest in the oven until ready to serve.
Truffled Taro Root Puree: Peel the taro root and dice into large pieces. Place in a pot with 1 1/4 cups of milk and the water. Season with salt. Bring to a boil and cook slowly for 30 minutes. Place the taro root into a food processor with 2 tablespoons butter and 1/4 cup milk. Process just until smooth. Add the tablespoon of chopped truffle. Save in a warm spot. Blanch the bok choy in salted water. Shock in ice water and remove. Gently sponge dry with a clean towel. Sauté the bok choy and the fava beans with a tablespoon of butter. Slice the pork loin in twelve pieces. Rub them with the cooking fat and reseason them with the crushed wild pepper and sea salt. Strain the natural jus left in the pan. Divide the bok choy and fava beans on four serving plates. Place three slices of pork on each plate. Finish with a spoon of truffled taro root puree and a spoon of natural jus. You can also garnish this dish with lotus root or taro root chips.

Serves 4

This recipe uses a slow temperature cooking technique. With this technique, a protein cooked slowly to reach an internal temperature of 134°F to 152°F (temperature of transformation of protein). This is done in an oven generally between 190°F to 220°F. This will allow you to have a perfect temperature on a large piece of meat like a whole rack of pork, rib eye, turkey fillet...etc. and to keep all the flavors and the moisture. This technique was developed for cryovac cooking purposes and is widely adapted in restaurants now. The wild pepper we are using here is a variety of Szechwan pepper. It grows in the mountains of North Vietnam and has a very powerful and unique flavor. The taro root is used as a potato and carries perfectly the flavor of the truffle. The fusion of these two very local and geographically opposite elements, truffle and wild pepper, make this dish a surprising and delicious combination. —*Cedric Tovar*

SQUAB AND MUSHROOM KUSHIYAKI

Noriyuki Sugie • Asiate at The Mandarin Hotel, New York • New York, NY

2 whole squab breasts (four lobes)
8 Shiitake mushroom caps, stems removed
3 teaspoons Port
1 teaspoon soy sauce
1 teaspoon hazelnut oil
1 teaspoon Sanshou pepper

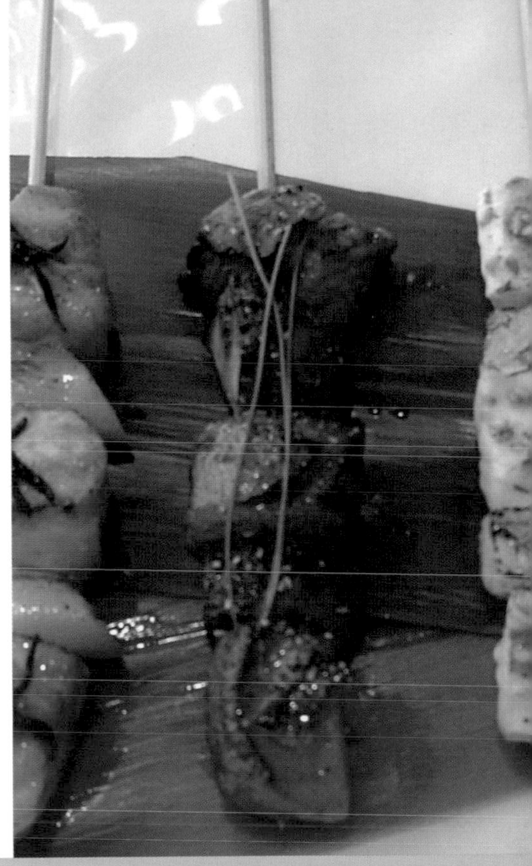

Combine Port, soy sauce and hazelnut oil. Mix well. Cut squab and Shiitake mushrooms into 1 inch cubes. Alternate onto skewer. Cook on grill. Dip in marinade. Cook quickly again. Finish with Sanshou pepper.

Serves 4

PHOTO: Courtesy of The Mandarin Oriental NY

MyPyramid.gov

STEAMED SESAME CHICKEN WITH MUSHROOM AND GINGER

Chris Yeo • Straits Restaurant •
San Jose, CA*

10 ounces boneless chicken meat,
cut into cube pieces
1 tablespoon fresh ginger, julienned
1 tablespoon Shiitake mushrooms, soaked with water until soft and sliced across

Marinade
2 tablespoons Xiao Shing wine
(may substitute with good quality dry sherry)
1 teaspoon sesame oil
1 teaspoon light soy sauce
1/2 teaspoon cornstarch
1/2 teaspoon sugar
dash of salt and pepper

Place chicken, ginger and mushrooms into a mixing bowl and marinate with the ingredients above. Marinate for 20 minutes and place onto a serving plate. Put into a steamer and steam on high for 20 minutes. Remove the plate from steamer and serve.

Serves 4

*Please see page 260 for a complete list of restaurant locations.

STICK OF BEEF MEDALLION AND RED ONION ROLL WITH ROASTED EGGPLANT

Didier Corlou • Le Beaulieu & The Spices Garden, Hotel Sofitel Metropole Hanoi • Hanoi, Vietnam

1 pound beef fillet, cut into 8 small medallions
2 ounces minced beef
1 large red onion, sliced
1 tablespoon red vinegar
4 pieces dry rice paper (4-6 inches diameter, rehydrate individually in a bowl of hot tap water for 10 seconds)
4 kumquats (may substitute with lime)
1 teaspoon granulated sugar
1 teaspoon honey
1 1/2 ounce caramel sauce
2 tablespoons fish sauce
4 pieces long eggplant
4 pieces lemon grass
salt and pepper to taste
olive oil for frying

Sauce
1/2 cup green tea
2 teaspoons tamarind juice

Sauté red onion slices in pan with olive oil. Season with 1 tablespoon fish sauce, pepper and red vinegar. Blend 1/3 of sautéed onion with some water and set aside. Mix minced beef with remaining onion in a bowl. Make 4 rolls by spooning beef and onion into the middle of rice paper. Tie with a lemon grass leaf. Marinate beef medallions with 1 tablespoon fish sauce, honey, caramel sauce and pepper. Skewer 2 beef medallions on each lemon grass stick. Marinate for 2 hours. Blanch eggplant in salted boiling water. Marinate cooked eggplant with same marinade as the beef medallions. In a small saucepan, cook kumquats in a little water with sugar, salt until well done. Deep fry the rolls in oil. Pan fry the beef stick quickly, and finish cooking at 375° F for 10 minutes. Place cooked eggplants in marinade in the oven at 370° F, basting from time to time until eggplant is soft. Deglaze the cooking pan with tea, tamarind juice and kumquat cooking juice until reduced to half. To serve, place eggplants in the middle and place a stick of beef medallion on the eggplant. On the side, place a fried roll and put one small glass of pureed onion sauce by its side. Spoon the reduction sauce on the beef.

Serves 4

PHOTO: Left, Ray Grefe

SWIFT IN PHOENIX (CHICKEN WITH BIRD'S NEST)

H.K. & Pauline D. Loh • Food Writers & Cookbook Authors • Singapore

3 pieces bird's nest, 1/2 ounce
1 small silky black chicken, 1 1/2 pound
2 chicken breasts, 1 1/2 pound
salt
1 ounce goji seeds, washed (optional)

Soak the bird's nest in warm water for 3 hours until soft. Drain and split the silky chicken along the breastbone, wash and dry. Set aside. Mince the chicken breasts, add 4 cups of water and boil. Remove meat residue by filtering the stock through muslin. Stuff the prepared bird's nest into the breast cavity of the chicken, and sew the opening close with bamboo skewers. Place chicken and goji seeds into a double boiler. Add the stock and steam for about 1 hour. Season with salt to taste and serve.

Serves 4-6

The bird's nest is a top draw at any banquet and an exotic and highly prized addition to your festive menu. According to the culinary analects, a dish featuring bird's nest should have generous portions and clean, simple flavors. The poetry of this dish comes from its name 'Phoenix' which refers to the chicken and the 'swift,' of course, refers to the bird that spins the nests. —*H.K. & Pauline D. Loh*

TANDOORI LAMB CHOPS (BURRAH KABAB)

Suvir Saran & Hemant Mathur • Dévi • New York, NY

2 pounds rib lamb chops, cut 1 to 1 1/2 inches thick
1 tablespoon paprika
1/2 teaspoon cayenne pepper
1/4 teaspoon ground mace
1/4 teaspoon ground nutmeg
1 tablespoon garam masala
1 tablespoon toasted cumin seeds, coarsely ground, using mortar and pestle
8 medium garlic cloves, minced very finely or ground to a paste
3 inches fresh ginger, peeled and minced very finely or ground to paste
2 tablespoons green papaya paste (optional)
1/4 cup malt vinegar
juice of 1 lemon
1 teaspoon salt
3/4 cup yogurt, drained in a cheesecloth-lined strainer or a coffee filter for 2 hours
2 tablespoons canola oil
3 tablespoons melted butter

Cut three or four deep slashes in each of the chops. Mix all of the remaining ingredients except the oil and melted butter in a nonplastic bowl large enough to hold the chops. Add the chops and toss to coat in the marinade. Put the chops with the marinade in a large, resealable plastic bag and refrigerate overnight. Preheat the oven to 550° F or preheat the grill. Add the oil to the bag with the chops, reseal, and massage the bag between your hands to mix the oil. Remove the chops from the marinade. If roasting in the oven, put the chops in a single layer on a rack in a foil-lined baking pan and roast 20 minutes; remove from the oven and let rest 5 minutes, then turn the chops, drizzle with the butter and roast 10 more minutes. If grilling, grill 5 minutes each side. Let rest 5 minutes off the grill, then brush with the butter and grill 5 more minutes each side.

Serves 4

PHOTO: Tuck Loong

THE WARM FLAVORS OF GARLIC, CUMIN, NUTMEG AND MACE, BALANCED BY THE SHARPNESS OF VINEGAR AND LEMON RESULT IN AN EXQUISITE BALANCE. THE CHOPS NEED TO MARINATE OVERNIGHT TO ABSORB THE MARINADE. THE PAPAYA PASTE ACTS LIKE A TENDERIZER. BE SURE TO DRAIN THE YOGURT FOR AT LEAST 2 HOURS BEFORE USING OR THE LAMB WILL NEVER DEVELOP THAT SAVORY CRUST DURING COOKING. BURRAH LITERALLY MEANS "BIG" SO THIS IS A RECIPE FOR PEOPLE WHO LIKE BIG KABABS. THERE IS A MOSQUE IN OLD DELHI CALLED JAMA MASJID THAT IS THE LARGEST MOSQUE IN INDIA. THE STREETS AROUND IT ARE PEPPERED WITH STALLS SELLING STREET FOODS. ONE SUCH STALL IS KARIM'S, ONE OF MY FAVORITE PLACES TO TAKE FRIENDS AND ESPECIALLY FIRST TIME VISITORS TO INDIA. KARIM'S IS FAMOUS FOR MANY OF THEIR LAMB PREPARATIONS AND THIS IS ONE OF THEM. —*SUVIR SARAN & HEMANT MATHUR*

THAITANIC BEEF

Pathama Parikanont • Thep Phanom • San Francisco, CA

10 ounce ribeye beef
1 medium green bell pepper, cut into squares
2 garlic cloves, minced
2 tablespoons vegetable oil

Thaitanic Sauce
1 teaspoon green curry paste
1/4 teaspoon turmeric and white pepper
2 teaspoons good quality Thai fish sauce
1 teaspoon oyster sauce
1 teaspoon sugar
3 fresh kaffir lime leaves, sliced fine
1 lemon grass, white part only, sliced fine
1 1 inch knuckle of ginger, sliced fine
1-2 tablespoons coconut milk

Garnish
deep fried garlic slices
fresh basil

Cook the beef on a high heat broiler to medium rare, about 3-4 minutes on each side. Cut the beef into quarter inch strips, about 1 inch long. Cut the bell pepper into square inch pieces. Place the bell pepper on broiler to soften them about 4-5 minutes. Then, set the beef and bell pepper aside. In a wok or pan, over medium heat, heat the oil and stir fry the minced garlic until golden. Remove pan from heat and save some crisp garlic aside for garnishing. Add Thaitanic sauce at once and place the pan over medium high heat. Add beef and bell pepper and stir fry for 2-3 minutes. Add the coconut milk to deglaze the pan and to soften the flavor. Transfer to a serving dish. Garnish with crisp garlic and fresh basil.

Serves 2

YOU CAN ALSO REPLACE THE BEEF WITH PRAWNS, CHICKEN, SALMON, PORK OR TOFU. —*PATHA PARIKANONT*

ZIPPED UP BEEF WRAP *(KOREAN BULGOKI AND TOFU)*

Jason Ha & Sean Ahn • Zip Fusion Sushi • Los Angeles, CA*

Marinated Beef
3 pounds boneless beef shoulder, pre-sliced 1/8 inch thick or freeze for 1 hour until stiff before slicing by hand or with an electric meat slicer
1 small white onion, peeled, halved root to stem and sliced crosswise into 1/8 inch thick slices
1/2 ripe kiwi, peeled and ground or mashed
2 cups plus 1 tablespoon and 1 teaspoon of soy sauce
1 2/3 cup sugar
10 tablespoons mirin
2 teaspoons sesame oil
2 cups plus 1 tablespoon and 1 teaspoon of water
5 garlic cloves, peeled and crushed with the flat of a chef's knife
1 teaspoon freshly ground black pepper

Marinated Radish
1 1/4 cup sugar
1 1/4 cup mirin
1 1/4 cups unseasoned rice vinegar
1 daikon radish, peeled and very thinly sliced (1/16 inch to 1/8 inch thick)

Sesame Dressing (Goma Dressing)
1 cup Ponzu sauce
1/2 cup Asian sesame paste
cream or milk, to adjust consistency of dressing
2 blocks soft tofu, carefully sliced about 1/4 inch thick x 2 inches long
1 butter lettuce or red leaf lettuce, washed and dried
toasted sesame seeds

PHOTO: Apinun Pom Limkuln

(recipe continued on following page)

(recipe continued from previous page)

Beef: Mix ingredients and marinate beef. Cover and refrigerate for two hours or overnight.

Radish: Combine sugar, sake and vinegar. Place daikon radish slices in marinating liquid. Cover with plastic wrap and place in refrigerator for three hours. Lift the beef from its marinade, discarding the marinade. Place the beef in a 12-14 inch skillet over high heat, pan frying the beef in two batches until cooked thoroughly and until the liquid on the beef has nearly evaporated, approximately seven minutes.

Sesame Dressing (Goma Dressing): Combine Ponzu and sesame paste adding cream or milk to adjust consistency of dressing.

To Serve: Place the hot beef in the middle of a dish. Lay the lettuce leaves attractively next to the beef. Fold the marinated radish slices in half and slide them between thumb and forefinger to remove excess liquid. Arrange the folded radish slices along one side of the plate. Place the tofu slices along the other side of the plate in domino fashion. Lightly drizzle a zig-zag of the sesame dressing on top of the tofu. Lightly sprinkle the beef with toasted sesame seeds. The diner takes a lettuce leaf, unfolds a radish slice onto the middle of the leaf, places a piece of tofu on the radish and tops with a portion of the beef. Fold the lettuce leaf upwards in half and eat.

Serves 4-6

*Please see page 260 for a complete list of restaurant locations.

THIS BEAUTIFUL AND HEALTHY BEEF AND TOFU DISH MAKES A TASTY, DELIGHTFUL EXPERIENCE FOR DINERS OF ALL AGES BECAUSE IT IS EATEN AS A WRAP. THE KIWI IS A SECRET TO MAKE BEEF TENDER WHILE ADDING ONLY A SUBTLE FLAVOR. —*JASON HA & SEAN AHN*

PHOTO: Sharon Ackerman

RICE & NOODLES

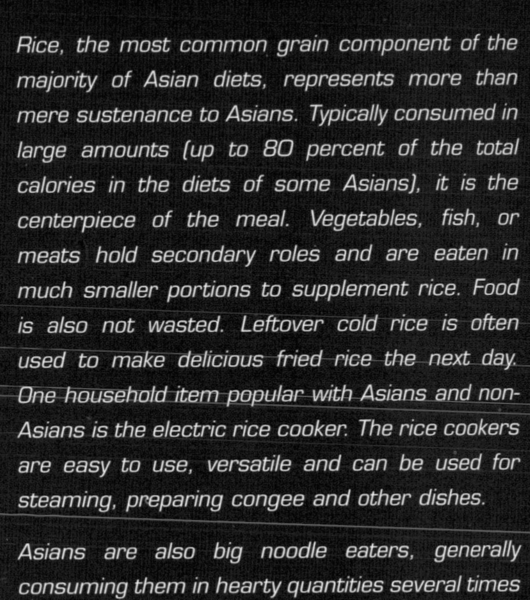

Rice, the most common grain component of the majority of Asian diets, represents more than mere sustenance to Asians. Typically consumed in large amounts (up to 80 percent of the total calories in the diets of some Asians), it is the centerpiece of the meal. Vegetables, fish, or meats hold secondary roles and are eaten in much smaller portions to supplement rice. Food is also not wasted. Leftover cold rice is often used to make delicious fried rice the next day. One household item popular with Asians and non-Asians is the electric rice cooker. The rice cookers are easy to use, versatile and can be used for steaming, preparing congee and other dishes.

Asians are also big noodle eaters, generally consuming them in hearty quantities several times a week. A variety of vegetables are mixed with small amounts of seafood, poultry or meat. Noodles come in all shapes, sizes, and thickness and while they are most often made from wheat, they are also made from rice, buckwheat, sweet potato, mung bean, soybeans and other grains, legumes, and vegetables. One ingenious creation made from rice is the distinctive dried rice paper rounds of Vietnam, cousins to the rice noodle. They serve as wrappers around a vegetable platter known as dia rau song composed of aromatic herbs, julienned cucumbers, carrots, bean sprouts, green onions, pickled shallots, a small bundle of rice vermicelli surrounding tiny bits of grilled poultry, seafood, or meat to form a package. This is the ideal example of combining small amounts of protein with generous portions of vegetables as recommended by the food pyramid.

AISHA NOODLES

Tommy Tang • Tommy Tang's • Los Angeles, CA

Noodles
4 ounces fresh noodles or dried Rad Na noodles (thick rice noodles) reconstituted and cooled
1 tablespoon olive oil
1/2 teaspoon Thai fish sauce seasoning
1 teaspoon sweet black bean sauce

Vegetables
1 tablespoon olive oil
1 teaspoon fresh garlic, chopped
2 teaspoons Chinese style fermented salted black beans
1/2 cup baby corn
1/4 cup straw mushrooms
1 1/2 cup Asian broccoli, cut into bite size pieces

Sauce
1 cup chicken or vegetable stock
1 tablespoon oyster sauce
1 tablespoon Thai fish sauce seasoning
2 teaspoons sugar
1 tablespoon rice vinegar
1/4 teaspoon ground white pepper
3 teaspoons tapioca flour or cornstarch in 3 tablespoons water
1 1/2 tablespoons chilies in vinegar, finely diced
1/2 teaspoon dried Kee Noo chili flakes

Place olive oil in a skillet over high heat. Add noodles and stir for a minute and add fish sauce, sweet black bean sauce and stir for 2 minutes. Remove and transfer to a serving plate. Hold warm. Combine olive oil, garlic and bean condiments in a skillet over medium heat and stir for a minute. Add baby corn, straw mushrooms and stir for a minute. Add broccoli and stir for a minute. Add chicken stock, oyster sauce, fish sauce, sugar, vinegar, white pepper, and bring sauce to a boil. Dissolve tapioca in the water and slowly add to the boiling sauce mixture stirring constantly to prevent sauce from becoming lumpy. Cook for 2 to 3 minutes or until sauce thickens. Toss reserved warm noodles with sauce and vegetable mixture and serve. Add diced chilies in vinegar and chili flakes as desired.

Serves 1

MyPyramid.gov

THIS IS MY DAUGHTER AISHA'S FAVORITE RICE NOODLE. WHEN WE GO OUT FOR LUNCH, HER SISTER CHYNA WILL ORDER HER PINK NOODLES, AISHA WILL ORDER THIS DISH AND I WILL ORDER WHATEVER MY HEART DESIRES. AISHA WILL ORDER CHICKEN NOODLES WITHOUT CHICKEN BUT ADD STRAW MUSHROOMS AND BABY CORN WITH NO MSG. GO FIGURE! THE SERVERS ALWAYS GET A HEADACHE.
—TOMMY TANG

BLACK PASTA WITH ROASTED GARLIC AND SUN DRIED TOMATO SAUCE

Tommy Tang • Tommy Tang's • Los Angeles, CA

Sauce
10 pieces sun dried tomatoes, soaked in 2 cups of water
12 garlic cloves, skins intact
8 whole shallots, skins intact
3 whole red bell pepper
1/2 teaspoon sea salt
3 tablespoons virgin olive oil
1/3 cup white wine
1 1/2 tablespoons Thai fish sauce

Pasta
12 ounces black squid ink pasta (spaghetti or linguine)
3 quarts boiling water
1 tablespoon sea salt

Garnish
3 tablespoons parsley, finely chopped
1 garlic clove, peeled and finely chopped
1 shallot, peeled and finely chopped

Soak sun dried tomatoes in 2 cups of water for 1 hour, reserve soaking water. Wrap garlic and shallots in aluminum foil and fold to cover (2-3 folds). Squeeze foil to make the packets airtight and place wrapped garlic and shallots onto a preheated grill or onto a burner with a wire rack over medium low heat. Grill garlic and shallots for 6 to 7 minutes and the red bell pepper for 9 to 10 minutes. Place grilled ingredients into a bowl and cover with plastic wrap. Allow them to sweat to facilitate the removal of the skins. Place skinned garlic and shallots into a food processor and chop coarsely, remove and set aside. Place skinned and seeded red bell peppers, drained sun dried tomatoes and salt into the same food processor and puree, remove and set aside. Place olive oil, chopped garlic and shallots into a large skillet over high heat and sauté for 2 minutes. Add white wine and simmer for 3 to 4 minutes. Add sun dried tomato, red bell pepper puree, and fish sauce. Stir and bring sauce to a boil. Add reserved water and bring sauce to a boil. Reduce heat to medium low and simmer for 7 to 8 minutes. While sauce is simmering, place water and salt into a stockpot over high heat and bring to boil. Add pasta and cook for 9 to 10 minutes, drain and transfer pasta to roasted garlic sauce and mix until pasta is thoroughly coated. Add chopped parsley and stir into pasta and transfer to a platter and serve.

Serves 4

MyPyramid.gov

If you've never cooked with sun dried tomatoes before, they come in different varieties. Please make sure to use the ones with less salt or without salt. — *Tommy Tang*

COOL SOBA NOODLES WITH WASABI, AVOCADO AND SALMON ROE

Jake Klein • Pulse • New York, NY

Avocado Sauce
1 ripe avocado
1 cup soy milk
1 bunch scallions, chopped
1/4 cup prepared wasabi
2 tablespoons mirin

Soba Noodles
1 pound of buckwheat soba noodles
1 cup of high quality soy sauce
1 cup sugar
1/2 cup mirin
1/2 cup sake
2 cups scallions, cut on the bias
3 tablespoons salmon roe
water for boiling noodles

Sauce: Bring a small pot of water to a boil. Add chopped scallions. When they turn bright green and slightly tender (about 30 seconds) remove immediately, placing them in ice water. In a blender, combine the avocado, soy milk, blanched scallions, wasabi and mirin. Puree on high until completely smooth. There should no longer be any flecks of green from the scallion. Depending on the ripeness of your avocado, you may need to add a little water to achieve the right consistency. It should be appear thick like reduced heavy cream.

Soba Noodles: Cook soba noodles until tender. If using dried noodles, this will take three to four minutes. Do not add any oil to the water. Once the noodles are cooked, submerge, and hold them in cold water for later use. Over very low heat combine your soy sauce, sugar, mirin and sake. Stirring frequently, allow the sugars to cook and caramelize. This process will take 30 to 45 minutes. Do not rush this. Soy sauce and sugar burn easily. Once the sugar is caramelized and the sauce is the consistency of maple syrup, remove from heat and allow to cool.

At the bottom of each of your serving bowls, pour about 1/4 cup of avocado sauce. Swirl them around in your hands to disperse the sauce evenly around the well of the bowl. Drain and pat dry the noodles. In a mixing bowl, combine your noodles, sweet soy sauce and one cup of the sliced scallions. Using a dinner fork, create six bundles of noodles and scallions. Place each bundle in the center of each bowl. Divide the remaining scallions and place on top of each noodle bundle. Top each bundle off with 1/2 tablespoon of salmon roe.

Serves 6

PHOTO: Julie Stapen

WHEN EATING THIS DISH, ENCOURAGE YOUR GUESTS TO MIX EVERYTHING TOGETHER. EACH COMPONENT IS NECESSARY TO ACHIEVE PROPER SEASONING. —*JAKE KLEIN*

CRAB MEAT FRIED RICE

Michael Huynh • Bao Noodles • New York, NY*

4 cups canned jumbo lump crab meat (Phillips brand is most shell-free)
5 tablespoons olive oil
1 cup shallots, thinly sliced
2 tablespoons garlic, chopped
6 cups cold cooked organic Jasmine rice
2 teaspoons freshly ground white pepper
1 teaspoon salt
1 tablespoon fish sauce
4 eggs, beaten
5 sprigs or 1 cup chopped coriander (cilantro) leaves

Heat 4 tablespoons of oil in a wok and sauté the shallots and garlic until golden brown. Add rice, pepper, salt and mix well. Sprinkle fish sauce over the rice and mix again. Push the rice aside, leaving space for frying the beaten egg. Pour the remaining oil into the wok and add the beaten egg. Cook until almost solid then quickly mix the rice into the egg, breaking up the omelet. Stir in the lump crab meat and cook until the crab meat is heated through. Garnish with coriander leaves.

Serves 4

*Please see page 260 for a complete list of restaurant locations.

SANUKI UDON RECIPES*

Osamu Miyoshi • Hinode • Sakaide City, Japan

Dashi (clear soup base)
1/2 ounce kombu seaweed (about 1 sheet)
1 ounce dried sardines, head and insides removed (Snap off head and base of fish, the belly section, which contains the intestinal track)
1 ounce dried bonito shavings
Place kombu seaweed and dried sardines in a pot and let it sit in 1 quart of water for 1 hour. Turn on the stove and once the water starts boiling add the dried bonito shavings. Boil for 5 minutes. Take off the stove and filter out the kombu seaweed, dried bonito and dried sardines from the dashi.

Kake Soup (for hot/cold noodles)
1 quart of dashi (clear soup base)
2 ounces Usukuchi soy sauce or light soy sauce
2/3 ounce sake
1 1/4 ounces mirin
Boil sake and mirin to burn out the alcohol. Add soy sauce. Add the mixture into dashi.

Tsuke Soup (for dipping, you can keep the soup in the refrigerator for 2 days)
1 quart soup base
1 3/4 ounces mirin
1/2 tablespoon brown crystal sugar
1 3/4 ounce Usukuchi soy sauce or light soy sauce
1 3/4 ounce Koikuchi soy sauce or dark soy sauce
2/3 ounce sake
Boil sake and mirin to burn out the alcohol. Add soy sauce, then add sugar. Add mixture into dashi.

Recommended ways to enjoy Sanuki Udon Noodles:
Shoyu, Sanuki with Light Soy Sauce: Splash cold water onto freshly cooked Sanuki to make the noodles firmer, and then sprinkle with a few drops of soy sauce. This is best enjoyed with ground daikon, sudachi or lemon. For additional spice, add diced scallions, ginger, tempura crumbs, sesame seeds and shichimi.
Bukkake, Sanuki with Rich "Dashi": Splash cold water onto freshly cooked Sanuki to make the noodles firmer, and then add in the dashi clear soup base. Top with diced scallions, ginger, tempura crumbs, sesame seeds and shichimi. (Bukkake is one of the most progressive ways to enjoy Sanuki. This recipe originated from Yudame, in which Sanuki was eaten from a sake cup.)

(recipe continued on following page)

(recipe continued from previous page)

Kake (3 Variations):

1. Atsu-Atsu (hot noodles in hot soup) Rinse freshly cooked Sanuki in cold water to firm noodles. Briefly return the Sanuki to hot water and place in a bowl filled with hot kake soup (see recipe below) and eat. Add variety with diced scallions, ginger, tempura crumbs, sesame seeds and shichimi.

2. Hiya-Atsu (cold noodles in hot soup) Similar to Atsu-Atsu, this time, the cold noodles are not rinsed but added directly to the hot kake soup. The unique texture of the noodles in Hiya-Atsu will be more pronounced than in Atsu-Atsu. Again, enjoy with diced scallions, ginger, tempura crumbs, sesame seeds and shichimi.

3. Hiya-Hiya (cold noodles in cold soup) Rinse freshly cooked Sanuki in cold water and then add the noodles to cold kake soup. The colder noodles will have a firm, enjoyable texture. This is very popular during hot summers. This dish can be enjoyed with diced scallions, ginger, tempura crumbs, sesame seeds and shichimi.

Kama-Age ("from the pot"): For some excitement, after the Sanuki is cooked, simply remove the noodles from the pot with chopsticks, dip them briefly in a cup of tsuke soup and enjoy. Do not rinse the noodles. Add diced scallions, ginger, tempura crumbs, sesame seeds and shichimi to the soup for extra flavor.

Kama-Tama ("pot and egg"): Similar to Kama-Age, however, instead of dipping the un-rinsed hot noodles into a cup of soup, place them in a bowl of soy sauce and a raw egg. Flavor with diced scallions, ginger, tempura crumbs, sesame seeds and shichimi.

*Sanuki Udon noodles can be purchased at most Japanese food stores.

SANUKI UDON IS A SPECIALTY NOODLE FROM KAGAWA, JAPAN. IN OUR AREA WE LOVE SANUKI UDON SO MUCH THAT IS ACCUSTOMED TO EAT IT ONCE A DAY. WE EAT SANUKI UDON OFTEN, IT IS HEALTHY BECAUSE IT DOES NOT INCLUDE ANY OIL. ENJOY SANUKI WITH ANY TOPPINGS YOU LIKE AS THE FLAVOR OF THE NOODLES WILL REFLECT THE TASTES OF THE COOK. —*OSAMU MIYOSHI*

SOBA NOODLES WITH PORK

Chris Behre • Cinch • Santa Monica, CA

1 pound braised pork belly, diced, about 4 ounces per person
4 tablespoons sesame oil
1 tablespoon fresh garlic, finely chopped
3 tablespoons shallots or white onion, finely chopped
1 teaspoon red chili flakes
2 ounces blanched fresh ginger, julienned
1/2 cup pork braising liquid
8 ounces shimiji mushrooms or similar Asian mushrooms
2 tablespoons soy sauce
2 tablespoons mirin
salt & pepper to taste

Vegetables
4 ounces snow peas, julienned
4 ounces snow pea tendrils
6 ounces bok choy, cleaned and cut into quarters
12 ounces fresh soba noodles (cook and then rest)

Garnish (optional)
4 ounces lotus chips, thinly sliced lotus root, (fried in oil till crispy remove excess grease with paper towel)
Kizami Nori, julienned, thinly cut sushi nori sheets
white sesame seeds (hulled)

Sauté garlic, shallots, pork belly and shimiji mushrooms with a little oil quickly in a wok until crispy. Add all the vegetables, blanched ginger and pork braising liquid. Season with mirin and soy sauce. Add the rest of the sesame oil and chili flakes. Toss the vegetables until they have a good color. Add the fresh cooked soba noodles coating them with the cooking sauce. Turn out into 4 bowls and garnish with deep fried lotus root chips, sesame seeds and nori julienne. Serve.

Serves 4

PHOTO: Martin Herbst

COOK IN A WOK OR A VERY HOT PAN. —*CHRIS BEHRE*

SOYBEAN MINTED FRIED RICE

Martin Yan • Yan Can • Santa Clara, CA*

1 1/4 cup thawed frozen shelled soybeans
1 tablespoon vegetable oil
3 garlic cloves, minced
4 cups cold cooked long-grain rice
2 tablespoons chicken broth
2 tablespoons oyster-flavored sauce
1 teaspoon soy sauce
1/4 teaspoon freshly ground white pepper
2 eggs, lightly beaten
3 tablespoons fresh mint, minced
2 teaspoons Furikake or shredded nori

Place a stir fry pan over high heat until hot. Add the oil, swirling to coat sides. Add the garlic and cook until fragrant, 10-15 seconds. Add the rice and cook, separating grains with the back of a wooden spoon. Add the soybeans and cook, stirring constantly, until the rice is heated through, 2 to 3 minutes. Add the broth, oyster-flavored sauce, soy sauce, and white pepper and stir to combine. Make a well in the center of rice. Add the eggs and gently stir eggs until they form soft curds, about 1 minute. Add the mint and mix eggs into the rice. Sprinkle with Furikake and serve.

Serves 4

NOTE: Soybeans can be purchased shelled and cooked in the frozen food section at Asian grocery stores. They are a rich source of protein and fiber.

*Please see page 260 for a complete list of restaurant locations.

SPICY SHRIMP AND SNAP PEA FRIED BROWN RICE WITH MANGO YOGURT

Ming Tsai • Blue Ginger • Wellesley, MA

1/2 cup (4 ounces) medium shrimp, cleaned and deveined
3/4 teaspoon Asian sesame oil
3/4 teaspoon cornstarch
3/4 teaspoon soy sauce
1 cup snap peas, ends trimmed (if needed), blanched in boiling water, shocked in ice water, drained, and cut on the bias
1/4 cup small red onion, cut into 1/4 inch dice
1/2 teaspoon red jalapeno,
stemmed and minced
1/3 teaspoon fresh ginger, peeled and minced
3/4 teaspoon sambal
1/2 cup (4 ounces) cooked day old brown rice
1/2 tablespoons grapeseed or canola oil
Kosher salt to taste
freshly ground black pepper to taste
1/2 cup mango, peeled and
cut into 1/2 inch dices
1/2 cup low fat plain yogurt
3/4 teaspoon cilantro, finely chopped
(may substitute with mint)
greens scallions for garnish

In a large bowl, combine the shrimp, sesame oil, cornstarch, and soy sauce and mix. Set aside for 10 minutes. Heat a wok or heavy sauté pan over high heat. Add the grapeseed oil and swirl to coat the pan. Add the shrimp and stir fry until just cooked through, about 2 to 3 minutes. Add the snap peas, onion, jalapeno, ginger, sambal, and the rice and toss to heat through. Season with salt and pepper and remove from heat. While the fried rice is cooking, in a bowl, combine the mango, yogurt and cilantro and set aside. To serve, mold rice in a small bowl and turn over on plate. Drizzle with mango yogurt and garnish with green scallions.

Serves 1

MyPyramid.gov

The first dish I ever cooked was fried rice when I was 10. Every Chinese Household has leftover rice so it's made frequently. Last year, our family converted to brown rice for health reasons but brown rice actually makes an excellent fried rice since it's a bit drier. For this dish, I chose shrimp—a great protein that is virtually fat free and raises good cholesterol. The mango yogurt sauce is inspired by Indian raita and a great way to add fruit and dairy to this dish. I love temperature contrast in dishes and this contributes a wonderful cooling element. —*Ming Tsai*

PHOTOS: Left, Stephanie Liu Jan;

SRI LANKAN SPICED RICE

Charmaine Solomon • Cookbook Author • Sydney, Australia

1 pound basmati or other long grain rice
2 tablespoons ghee (clarified butter)
1 large onion, finely sliced
4 whole cloves
1 quill cinnamon (about 3 inches long)
1 teaspoon ground turmeric
4 cups beef or chicken stock, or water and stock cubes
2 teaspoons salt
1/4 cup sultanas (golden raisins)
cooked peas, eggs and cashews for garnishing

If rice needs washing, wash in cold water and drain in a colander for at least 30 minutes. Heat stock to simmer and hold. Chose a heavy saucepan with a well fitting lid because it is important to keep the steam in so rice cooks perfectly. Heat ghee or butter and fry the onions until golden. Add whole spices and the rice. Fry over medium heat for 5 minutes, stirring with a metal spoon, until all the grains are coated with ghee. Add turmeric, hot stock and salt, and bring to the boil. Stir in sultanas. Reduce heat as low as it will go, cover the pot tightly, and allow rice to steam for 20 minutes without lifting lid or stirring. At the end of this time, turn off heat and allow rice to stand for another 5 minutes. Gently fork the grains so they are fluffy and separate. Using a metal spoon (a wooden spoon would crush the grains) transfer to a serving dish and garnish with egg slices, cooked peas and fried or toasted cashews. If you are not a curry lover, try serving this rice with roasts or grills. Or, for a vegetarian meal, a bowl of thick natural yogurt mixed with diced cucumbers and some fruit chutney.

Serves 4-6

Since I was born and lived almost half my life in Sri Lanka, I chose a Sri Lankan recipe to contribute. Rice being the staple food of Asia, it is appropriate to feature it in this gently spiced main dish which may be served with curries of fish, poultry, meat and vegetables, or simply with slices of hard boiled egg and fried or toasted cashew nuts as shown in the photograph. The flavors of cinnamon and cardamom lift it from the ordinary and represent the spice for which the island is famous. The botanical name of cinnamon is cinnamomum zeylanicum for it is where the best cinnamon grows and Sri Lanka was once known as Zeylan, then Ceylon. I implore those who decide to try this recipe to use a cinnamon quill and not ground cinnamon, because research reveals that much of what is labeled cinnamon is, in fact, cassia—a cousin but much coarser in flavor. —*Charmaine Solomon*

STICKY RICE OR SWEET RICE *(KAO NEAL)*

Penn Hongthong • Cookbook Author • Middle Island, NY

1 cup of rice per serving

Soak the rice in warm water at least 2 hours. Fill the pot with water up to 3 inches from the bottom and place on the stove over high heat. Make sure the rice does not touch the water when the steamer basket is inserted. Strain the rice in the steamer basket, rinse well, drain out the excess water, and place the basket on the steamer pot. Steam with a cover on high heat for 20 minutes until the rice is cooked. Take the basket off the pot, wet a wooden spoon and stir the rice for a minute to cool then transfer to a bamboo rice keeper.

To Reheat the Rice: Fill the pot with water up to 3 inches from bottom and place it on the stove over high heat. Wet the steamer basket, break the rice in small pieces, replace it in the basket, and steam until the rice is soft, about 10 minutes. When the rice is reheated, it cooks faster and tastes softer. The rice stays good in a room temperature for a couple of days, but must be reheated within 24 hours otherwise it will dry up. Place the cool leftover rice in a plastic bag and refrigerate until ready to reheat.

To pop the rice: Cooked dried rice can be fried and it will pop like rice cakes. Rice must be completely dried before frying. Dry the leftover cooked rice in the sun until completely dried, for 3 to 4 days. Fill a medium pot with oil 3 inches from the bottom. Turn the heat on high. Wait until the oil gets very hot. Add dried rice, the rice will pop in a second, stir constantly until golden brown. Scoop the rice out onto a large bowl with layers of paper towels to absorb the access oil. Sprinkle with salt and eat for snack.

PHOTO: Miles Harris

SINCE LAOTIANS EAT RICE WITH ALMOST EVERY MEAL, THE RICE IS PRESOAKED THE NIGHT BEFORE, COOKED FIRST THING IN THE MORNING, AND SHOULD SUFFICE FOR BREAKFAST AND LUNCH. BY NOON, ANOTHER BOWL SHOULD BE SOAKED FOR DINNER. AT DINNER, RICE MUST BE HOT FOR THE MOST IMPORTANT MEAL OF THE DAY. IN LAOS, EVERY NIGHT BEFORE I WENT TO BED, MY MOTHER TOLD ME TO "SOAK THE RICE." WHY COULDN'T I JUST COOK IT? I NEVER GOT THE EXPLANATION. ONE DAY I FORGOT TO SOAK THE RICE, SO I WET THE RICE AND STEAMED IT LIKE ALWAYS. MY MOTHER SOON NOTICED THAT THE RICE WASN'T COOKING. I HAVEN'T FORGOTTEN TO SOAK THE RICE SINCE! —*PENN HONGTHONG*

VEGETABLES

Throughout much of Asia, outdoor markets display a bountiful and glorious choice of greens. One all time favorite green among Asian chefs is water spinach or swamp cabbage called kangkung, a large pointed green leaf with long hollow stems that tastes like a cross between spinach and watercress. Like spinach and fresh pea shoots, kangkung has an affinity for a pungent garlic and fermented bean curd sauce.

Other greens and vegetables such as bamboo shoots (regarded as the queen of vegetables), crunchy fresh water chestnuts, bok choy (a green leaf Chinese cabbage), gai lan (Chinese broccoli), protein packed fresh mung bean sprouts, angled luffa (the warty-skinned bitter melon loaded with Chinese medicinal benefits), taro, daikon, and other hearty vegetables make up a major food group in the Asian diet. Often stir fried and paired with proteins or meat, the proportion is about three-fourths vegetables to no more than one-fourth meat or poultry. This ratio points out how a small amount of these high fat protein sources are used to flavor a bounty of low fat, vitamin and mineral laced vegetables.

Chefs are introducing various and slightly bitter flavors of Asian leafy greens such as mizuna and tatsoi to the western palate. These delicious vegetables are now appearing frequently in menus across America. Cooks in some countries, particularly in India and China, have developed varied, healthful, and tasty vegetarian diets that use herbs and spices rather than meats, poultry or seafood to flavor their dishes. Tofu (soybean curd) is commonly used as the protein base to create delicious vegetarian meals that deliver the necessary nutrients for a healthy lifestyle.

CALI CEVICHE "ARE YOU READY TO" ROLL

Luis Aguilar Jr. • El Barrio • Los Angeles, CA*

1 cucumber (English or hot house cucumbers are best)
1 haas avocado
2 sheets of Nori (Japanese seaweed wrappers)
sesame seeds
makisu (sushi rolling mat)
pickled ginger
wasabi paste, prepared
You will need a small bowl of water for moistening the fingers so the rice does not stick to them while preparing rolls. You can mix a little lemon juice or ginger juice in the water.

Ceviche
2 pounds shrimp, cleaned
1/4 pound onions, chopped
1 cup roasted red bell peppers, chopped
1/2 cup fresh squeezed lemon juice
1/2 cup fresh squeezed lime juice
1 hot pepper (chipotle), chopped

Vinegar Water Solution, Tezu
1 cup of water
2 tablespoons rice vinegar
1 teaspoon salt

Sticky Rice
2 cups raw rice, short or medium grain
2 cups and 2 tablespoons water
4 tablespoons rice vinegar
2 tablespoons and 1 teaspoon sugar
1 teaspoon salt

Cucumbers: Peel the cucumber and cut in half. Cut the cucumber around as a thin peel. It should be noted that this peel could be used as the wrapper instead of nori. For the filler, flatten, fold and stack the peel and cut in half. Re-stack and chop into fine strips. Set aside.
Avocado: Peel and pit the avocado. You can rub it with lemon juice to help preserve it. Cut the avocado in half and then into 1/4 inch thick strips.
Ceviche: Cut shrimp into pieces. Add remaining ingredients and marinate in the refrigerator for about 8 hours. Drain and put a little mayonnaise in the ceviche so it binds together.
Vinegar Water Solution, Tezu: Mix water, rice vinegar and salt together and set aside.
Sticky Rice: Wash the rice several times until the water is clear. Place it in a colander and drain for an hour. Transfer the rice to a heavy pot or electric rice cooker and add the measured water. Make sure there is a tight-fitting lid and bring to a boil. Simmer over low heat allowing the rice to steam for 15 minutes more with the cover on at all times. Remove from heat and remove the lid momentarily to stretch a clean tea towel over the pot and replace the cover. Let it remain covered and without heat to finish steaming for another 15 minutes. Meanwhile, mix the rice vinegar, sugar and salt together in a small saucepan. While stirring, heat the mixture until the sugar dissolves. Set aside the mixture to cool to room temperature. After the rice has steamed properly, take a wooden spatula or spoon and cut and fold the rice. Dampen a cloth using the pre-prepared Tezu and rub the

insides of a bowl. The traditional bowl to use is the flat-bottomed wooden sushi oke or hangiri. The wood absorbs excess moisture and the large surface allows the rice to cool more quickly and evenly. Put the hot rice into the bowl and quickly add the seasoned rice vinegar solution. Mix with the same cutting and folding motion. After mixing, fan the hot rice mixture in order to remove moisture as well as to cool it. This should take about 10 minutes. The result will be ideal sushi rice with a slightly chewy consistency and just a touch of stickiness. Place Nori on your preparation surface with the long side facing you. Dip your fingers a couple of times in the water bowl. Grab some rice and form into a ball just a bit larger than a baseball. Place the rice ball in the center of the Nori and re-moisten hands. Press and push the rice, spreading it with the thumbs and fingers to cover the Nori. Don't work it too much. Sprinkle sesame seeds on top. Flip the Nori over so that the Nori is now on the top.

Filling: Whatever filling you are using, leave a bit of room on the sides so the filling doesn't get squeezed out. Put the cucumber strips in to piles along the center line and short side of the Nori. There should be about 6 strips in each pile. Lay 3 avocado slices along the top of the cucumber pieces. Spread Ceviche over the top of the avocados. Roll the side nearest over the central ingredients and finish the roll such that the seam is on the bottom. Hold and tuck the ingredients with the fingers while using the thumbs to roll. Tear a sheet of plastic wrap about the same size as your sushi rolling mat. Place plastic wrap over the roll so approximately 1 inch extends onto the counter and the longer end is closer to you. Place the mat over the roll and plastic wrap. With both hands, press lightly on the sides to firm up the roll. There is no need to apply pressure to the top of the roll or to slide your hands along the mat. Slide the mat to one side and then the other to tap the two ends of the roll to make it neat. You are ready to cut the roll into 8 pieces. Place the tip of the knife into your water bowl and with the handle down, tap the end of the handle on the table such that the water flows over the entire blade. Remove the sushi rolling mat and with the plastic wrap still on, cut the roll in half. Cut each of the halves in half and again and one more time so that you have 8 pieces. Place the makisu over the roll again and press lightly to re-form the roll. Remove the mat and the plastic wrap and moisten hands once more to move the rolls to a serving plate.

Makes 4 to 5 rolls (32 to 40 pieces)

*Please check the website www.newasiancuisine.com for updated information.

Don't refrigerate the rice and it should be used within an hour after preparation. Keep the rice covered with a clean cloth and at room temperature until you are ready to make your rolls. It needs to be kept warm so it is pliable. I prefer to create reverse rolls where the rice is on the outside of the roll. Not only does this roll taste fresher, it also allows you to put more items in the roll. —*Luis Aguilar Jr.*

DRIED CURRY LEAVES CHUTNEY

Monica Bhide • Cookbook Author • Dunn Loring, VA

1 cup curry leaves
2 tablespoons sesame seeds
2 tablespoons roasted peanuts
1 teaspoon mango powder
1/2 teaspoon red chili powder
pinch of sugar
salt to taste

Place the curry leaves in a large skillet and dry roast over medium low heat till all the moisture dries out. The leaves will begin to darken. Pick one up and if they crumble easily between your fingers, they are ready. Let cool. In a blender, combine with all the other ingredients, grind to a fine powder. It may be slightly sticky due to the peanuts in the mix which is fine. Store refrigerated for up to a week in an airtight container.

Serves 1

Adapted from *The Spice is Right—Easy Indian Cooking for Today* by Callawind Publications

MY MOTHER-IN-LAW SUBMITTED THIS RECIPE TO A CONTEST IN MUMBAI AND WON THE FIRST PRIZE. SHE COMPETED WITH 80 WOMEN. THIS DRY CHUTNEY CAN BE USED AS A SPREAD FOR BREAD, SPRINKLED ON WARM RICE OR AS A TOPPING FOR WHIPPED SALTED YOGURT. *—MONICA BHIDE*

DUMPLINGS IN YOGURT STEW *(PUNJABI KADHI)*

Sanjeev Kapoor • Yellow Chilli • Uttar Pradesh, India*

Pakoras
3/4 cup flour (besan)
1 medium sized onion, finely chopped
1/2 cup fenugreek leaves (methi), chopped
1 inch piece ginger, grated
1 teaspoon carom seeds (ajwain)
1 teaspoon red chili powder
1/4 teaspoon baking powder
salt to taste
oil to deep fry

Kadhi
1 cup yogurt
1/4 cup flour (besan)
1 teaspoon turmeric powder
salt to taste
2 tablespoons oil
1/2 teaspoon fenugreek seeds (methi)
1/2 teaspoon cumin seeds
6 peppercorns
2 whole red chilies, broken into 2 pieces
1 medium sized onion, sliced (optional)
1/2 inch piece ginger, chopped
1 teaspoon red chili powder

Mix all the pakora ingredients, except oil, adding about half a cup of water. Heat sufficient oil in a kadai (you can also use a wok or a deep frying pan), drop small portions of the flour mixture and deep fry till golden brown. Drain onto an absorbent paper and keep aside. For kadhi, whisk yogurt well and mix flour. Blend thoroughly to ensure that there are no lumps. Add turmeric powder, salt and three cups of water. Heat oil in a kadai. Add fenugreek seeds, cumin seeds, peppercorns and red chilies. Stir fry for half a minute. Add sliced onions and chopped ginger and stir fry for a minute. Add yogurt mixture. Bring to a boil and simmer on low heat for about fifteen minutes, stirring occasionally. Add red chili powder and fried pakoras and continue to simmer for four to five minutes. Serve hot with steamed rice.

Serves 4

*Please see page 260 for a complete list of restaurant locations.

FISH MOUSSE STUFFED SHIITAKE MUSHROOMS

Larry Chu • Chef Chu's • Los Altos, CA

4 large Shiitake mushrooms (2 inches in diameter), lightly rinsed, stems removed
Chinese broccoli stalks

Mousse Filling
3 ounces sea bass or any white fish, boneless, skinless fillets, cut in 1 inch chunks
3 tablespoons water
1 tablespoon cornstarch
pinch of salt
pinch of white pepper
1 teaspoon dried tangerine peel, reconstituted, finely minced
1 teaspoon white part of green onion, minced

Sauce
1 teaspoon garlic, minced
1 teaspoon ginger, minced
1/2 small jalapeno, seeded, minced (optional)
1/2 cup chicken broth
1 tablespoon soy sauce
1/4 teaspoon sugar (to taste)
1 teaspoon cornstarch paste (1 teaspoon cornstarch and 1 teaspoon water)
1/2 stalk green onion, sliced

Line the edges of a rimmed heatproof plate with whole Chinese broccoli stalks arranged around the edge. Combine seasoning sauce ingredients in a bowl. To make mousse, place filling ingredients in a food processor. Process filling for about 1 minute until mixture becomes fluffy. Add green onions. Pulse a few times to incorporate them evenly into a mixture. To stuff mushrooms, place a rounded tablespoon of filling onto the bottom of each mushroom cap and divided evenly. Smooth the top with the spoon and place the stuffed caps in the center of the heatproof plate. To steam, bring water to a boil inside a steamer fitted with a rack. Place stuffed mushroom plate onto the rack. Cover and steam for 6 minutes and remove dish. To make the sauce, heat a small saucepan and add sauce ingredients. Bring to a boil. Thicken sauce with enough cornstarch paste to make a light consistency sauce. Stir in green onions. Spoon the sauce over stuffed mushrooms.

Serves 4

MyPyramid.gov

FOR A MILDER SAUCE, HEAT 1/4 CUP CHICKEN BROTH TO A BOIL, ADD A PINCH OF SALT AND WHITE PEPPER TO TASTE. SIMMER AND ADD ENOUGH CORNSTARCH PASTE (LESS THAN 1 TEASPOON) TO MAKE A LIGHTER SAUCE. SPOON THE SAUCE OVER THE MUSHROOMS TO GLAZE. —*LARRY CHU*

KOBACHA SQUASH CROQUETTE

Troy N. Thompson • Jer-ne Restaurant and Bar, The Ritz-Carlton • Marina del Rey, CA

1 small peeled and deseeded Kobacha squash
1/2 onion, finely diced
all purpose flour
2 large eggs
1/2 cup milk
2 cups Panko bread crumbs
1/2 ounce furikake (Japanese rice seasonings)
4 cups oil
salt and pepper

Cut up Kobacha squash and place on a microwavable plate and cover with plastic wrap so that it is airtight. Microwave on high for 3 to 4 minutes or until it is soft to the touch. Place it in a medium mixing bowl. Add salt and pepper and mash with a fork until the squash is the consistency of mashed potatoes. Cook the onion on low heat in a sauté pan until translucent and add to the squash. Let the onion and squash mixture come to room temperature. Separate the mixture into 4 equal parts and form small cakes by hand. Place the cakes on a plate and allow to firm in the freezer. Mix the eggs and milk together in a bowl. Put the flour and Panko in two separate bowls. Take the squash cakes from the freezer and dust each one in flour. Dip the cakes in the egg mixture. Then, coat the cakes in the Panko. When the cakes are coated, fry them in the oil at 365° F until golden brown. Remove from the oil. Let the excess oil drain off on a paper towel. Finish with furikake.

PHOTO: Ray Grefe

Serves 4

LEMON AND GARLIC SMOKED TOFU WRAPPERS WITH PINE NUTS

Alan Yu • Zengo • Washington, DC

4 ounces lemon garlic smoked tofu, small dice
1/4 cup carrots, small dice
1/4 cup water chestnuts
1/2 cup Shiitake mushrooms, small dice
1/4 cup baby zucchini, small dice
1/4 cup string beans, small dice
1 package of hydro bibb lettuce

Seasonings
2 tablespoons of chili bean sauce
1 tablespoon garlic, finely minced
1 tablespoon of chipotle in adobo sauce
1 tablespoon light soy sauce
3 tablespoons scallions, chopped
1 teaspoon of salt (to taste)
pinch of freshly grounded black pepper

Put peanut oil in a sauté pan over medium high heat, add garlic and cook until fragrant. Add all diced vegetables and cook for a few minutes. Add the rest of the seasonings. Serve in a bowl with lettuce leaves on the side to use as wrappers. The lettuce leaves should be filled with the cooked mélange and eaten out of the hand.

Serves 2

MIZUNA AND MUSHROOM OHITASHI

Yorinobu Yamasaki • Kai • New York, NY

Dashi Base
1 quart water
2 inch square dried kelp
1 ounce bonito flakes
cheesecloth
1 1/2 cup baby mizuna (Japanese mustard greens)

Ohitashi
5 caps Shiitake mushrooms, stems removed
5 caps, oyster mushrooms, stems removed
1/4 of a small 2 ounce package of enoki mushrooms, remove only base of stems
1/4 teaspoon salt
1/4 teaspoon soy sauce
1/2 teaspoon sake

Dashi: Add kelp to 1 quart water in a pot. Just before the water starts to boil, take out the kelp. After the water is boiling, add bonito flakes and remove from heat. Strain dashi with the cheesecloth into another pot. Bring 1 cup of dashi base, salt, soy sauce and sake to a boil.

Ohitashi: Blanch baby mizuna with lightly salted water, cool in ice water and drain. Slice Shiitake and oyster mushrooms. Then, boil all the mushrooms for 1 minute and drain. Combine mizuna and mushrooms with dashi. Chill for 1 hour in a refrigerator before serving.

Serves 2

PHOTOS: Left, Robert Epstein;

MUNG DAL *(LENTILS)*

Heather Carlucci-Rodriguez • Lassi • New York, NY

1/2 cup mung dal (lentils)
2 cups water
2 green Thai chilies, finely chopped
1 pinch turmeric
1/2 teaspoon salt
2 tablespoons cilantro, finely chopped
1 tablespoon canola oil
1/2 teaspoon cumin seeds
1 small red onion, diced small
1/2 tablespoon fresh ginger, grated
1/2 tablespoon coriander, ground
1/2 teaspoon ground cumin
1/8 teaspoon paprika

Combine dal, water, chilies, turmeric and salt. Bring to a boil. Cook cumin seeds in canola oil until seeds sizzle. Caramelize onions in oil with cumin seeds. Add ginger and cook until soft. Add coriander, cumin and paprika and cook through. Pour over dal and stir. Add cilantro.

Serves 8

MUSHROOM CILANTRO MASALA

J.K. Paul • Maurya • Beverly Hills, CA

1 pound fresh button mushrooms
2 1/2 ounces cilantro
1/2 cup canola oil
8 ounces onions
1 ounce ginger
2 jalapenos
1 ounce ginger paste
1 ounce garlic paste
1/4 ounce red chili powder
1 pound tomatoes
1 ounce red bell peppers
1/4 ounce Indian spice mix (garam masala)
salt to taste

Clean, wash and chop cilantro. Peel, wash and chop onions. Scrape, wash and julienne cut ginger. Remove stems, wash, slit, deseed and chop jalapenos. Slice 1 1/2 ounces of tomato and blanch. Peel and chop rest of the tomatoes. Remove stem, wash and cut bell peppers into halves. Remove the white teeth and seeds and dice. Slice off earthy base of the stalks of the mushrooms and wash in cold water just prior to cooking. Heat oil in kadai (a typical Indian iron pan) or in any cooking pan. Add onions and sauté over medium heat until light brown. Add ginger paste, garlic paste and sauté for a minute. Add julienned ginger and dissolve red chili powder in 2 tablespoons water. Stir for another minute. Add chopped tomatoes and sauté for 8 to 10 minutes until the fat leaves the mixture. Add mushrooms, bring to a boil and simmer until the liquid has evaporated. Add bell peppers and stir for a minute. Adjust the seasoning. Add sliced tomatoes and cilantro and stir gently for another minute. Sprinkle spice mix and stir. Remove and place on a dish and serve with rice or any Indian bread as a vegetarian entrée.

Serves 4

PHOTO: Martin Jansche

This colorful mushroom and cilantro combination cooked with fresh herbs is a vegetarian delicacy. It is prepared without pounded spices and fenugreek, which is significant in traditional Kadai cooking. —*J.K. Paul*

SAAG *(SPINACH)*

Salim Mohmed & Santok Singh • Gaylord India Restaurant • Sausalito, CA*

2 ten ounce bags of spinach, trimmed and washed
2 teaspoons vegetable oil
1/2 teaspoon cumin seeds
10 garlic cloves, thinly sliced
2 dried red chilies
salt to taste

Heat the vegetable oil over medium heat in a non-stick pan. Add cumin seeds and stir for 5-10 seconds. Add garlic and fry until soft. Add chilies and cook for another 3 seconds. Add the spinach, toss or mix well until spinach is wilted. Season with salt.

Serves 6

*Please see page 260 for a complete list of restaurant locations.

SAIGON ROLL

Kimmy Tang • Michelia • Los Angeles, CA

4 pieces shrimp, peeled
1 stalk green onion
1/2 pound jicama, finely julienned
1/4 pound cucumber, finely julienned
1/8 pound pickled carrot, finely julienned
1/4 pound mix baby green lettuce
1 slice ginger
8 pieces mint leaves
4 sheets of 12 inch round rice paper
3 1/4 cup water
1 teaspoon oil

Dipping Sauce (Nuoc Cham)
1 tablespoon sugar
1 tablespoon rice vinegar
2 tablespoons water
1 teaspoon fish sauce
1 garlic clove, finely chopped
1 small fresh red chili, minced

Divide the baby green lettuce, jicama, cucumber, pickled carrots, mint leaves, onion and cucumbers in 4 portions. Use a sauté pan and heat up with oil and ginger. Stir until fragrant and then add shrimp. Stir frequently until shrimps turn pink and are cooked. Set aside until they cool down, then slice each shrimp in half lengthwise. Heat water in a pot. Take rice paper and soak it in hot water. Remove quickly and lay it on the tabletop. Each rice paper sheet is good for one roll. Spread one portion of the vegetable mixture on the sheet of rice paper and add 2 sliced shrimp pieces over the mixture and roll it. Cut each roll in two and serve cold with dipping sauce (see below).

Dipping Sauce: Mix all the ingredients listed above until the sugar dissolves. Put in a small bowl and serve on the side.

Serves 4

SHAAM SAVERA

Sanjeev Kapoor • Yellow Chilli •
Uttar Pradesh, India*

Kofta
2 medium bundles of spinach
2 green chilies, finely chopped
6-8 garlic cloves, finely chopped
3 tablespoons cornstarch
salt to taste
4 ounces Indian farm cheese (paneer), grated
oil to deep fry

Tomato Gravy
3 tablespoons butter
6 cloves
4 green cardamoms
1 bay leaf
2 teaspoons ginger paste
2 teaspoons garlic paste
2 green chilies, finely chopped
2 cups tomato puree
1 tablespoon red chili powder
1/2 teaspoon garam masala powder
salt to taste
3 tablespoons sugar or honey
1/2 teaspoon dry fenugreek leaves
1 cup fresh cream

Clean, trim and wash spinach in plenty of running water. Blanch in boiling hot water for 2 to 3 minutes and refresh in cold water. Squeeze out water and chop finely. Mix the spinach, green chilies, garlic, cornstarch and salt to taste. Divide into twelve equal portions. Add salt to taste to grated cheese and mash well. Divide into twelve equal balls. Take spinach portions, flatten it on your palm and stuff cheese balls in it. Shape into a ball. Heat sufficient oil in a kadai or fry pan and deep fry balls in moderately hot oil for five minutes. Drain onto a paper towel and keep aside. For gravy, heat butter in a pan, add cloves, green cardamoms and bay leaf. When they crackle, add ginger paste, garlic paste and green chilies. Cook for two minutes. Add tomato puree, red chili powder, garam masala powder, salt and one cup of water. Bring it to a boil, reduce heat and simmer for ten minutes. Add sugar or honey. Crush the dry fenugreek leaves and add it to the gravy. Stir in fresh cream. Serve koftas halved and placed on a bed of tomato gravy.

Serves 4

*Please see page 260 for a complete list of restaurant locations.

BEFORE PROCEEDING WITH ALL THE KOFTAS, DEEP FRY ONE AND CHECK IF THEY BREAK. IF THEY BREAK, ADD SOME MORE CORNSTARCH IN SPINACH MIXTURE AND THEN DEEP FRY IN HOT OIL. —*SANJEEV KAPOOR*

SHIITAKE MUSHROOMS STUFFED WITH TOFU

Mari Fujii • Fushiki-An • Kamakura, Japan

8 large fresh Shiitake mushroom caps (each about 3 inches in diameter)
1 block tofu, silken if available
2 tablespoons mirin
2 tablespoons soy sauce
2 tablespoons white sesame seeds, roasted
1/2 teaspoon salt
all-purpose flour for dusting
sesame oil for frying
4 shiso leaves, finely shredded (optional)

Wrap the tofu in a paper towel, place a plate on top and refrigerate for 30 minutes to remove excess moisture. In a saucepan, mix the mirin and soy sauce, boil for 1-2 minutes, then set aside. Grind the sesame seeds, then blend with tofu and salt, using a food processor. Evenly dust the undersides of the Shiitake caps with flour. Fill the Shiitake caps with a generous quantity of tofu mixture, then fry both sides in sesame oil over medium heat for 5-6 minutes. Add the mirin and soy sauce mixture to the pan. Turn the heat to low and cook, shaking the pan occasionally until the liquid evaporates. Arrange the Shiitake on a serving plate, garnish with the shredded shiso leaves.

Serves 8

NOTE: 4 tablespoons of teriyaki sauce can be substituted for the mirin and soy sauce.

In temple cuisine, vegetable ingredients are sometimes used to imitate shellfish or seafood. This fun dish uses Shiitake mushrooms and tofu to imitate the abalone. —*Mari Fujii*

PHOTO: Left, Sanjeev Kapoor;

SPICED AUBERGINE MASH

Vikram Garg • IndeBleu • Washington, DC

16 ounces eggplant, about 4 units
2 ounces olive oil
1/4 teaspoon cumin seeds
2 garlic cloves, minced
1/2 inch ginger, minced
2 shallots, sliced
1/4 teaspoon turmeric powder
1/2 teaspoon sweet paprika powder
1 Roma tomato, diced
1/2 teaspoon sea salt
1 ounce cilantro, chopped

Cut eggplant length wise in half and roast in a oven at 500° F. Scoop the pulp and puree. Heat oil and add cumin seeds. When it starts to crackle, add shallots, ginger and garlic. Sauté until transparent. Add turmeric, paprika and sauté for 30 seconds. Add eggplant, salt and cilantro. Sauté until it starts to leave the side of the pan.

Serves 4

SPINACH BREAD *(PALAK PARATHA)*

Heather Carlucci-Rodriguez • Lassi • New York, NY

1 pound 4 ounces Chapatti flour
(Durham wheat flour—also called Atta flour)
1/4 ounce Kosher salt
3 cups fresh spinach leaves

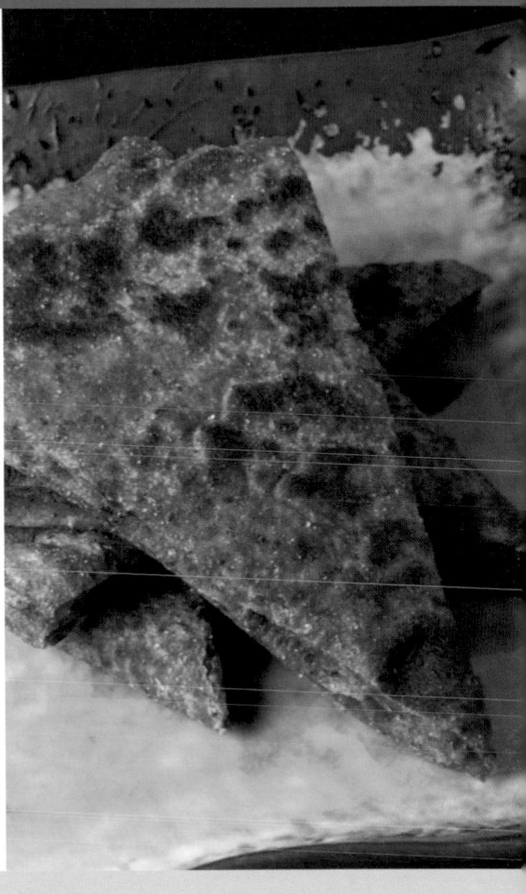

Puree spinach leaves in blender with 1/4 cup water until smooth and liquid. Combine flour and salt thoroughly. Add pureed spinach a little at a time and slowly incorporate with your hands until you have bread dough consistency. Place in an oiled bowl and cover with a damp cloth. Refrigerate for at least an hour. Divide dough into eight equal portions and place on oiled surface. Place well seasoned skillet on medium heat. Meanwhile, roll out one portion of paratha dough 1/8 inch thick. Brush with oil and lay oiled side down on hot skillet. Cook until brown. Brush upside of paratha with oil and turn over with wide spatula. Let brown and flip again to assure even cooking. Remove from skillet, brush with butter and fold in half. Repeat with rest of portioned dough. Serve parathas warm.

Serves 8

PHOTO: Martin Jansche

STIR FRY WATER SPINACH WITH FRESH PRAWNS

Toni Robertson • Silks at The Mandarin Oriental Hotel • San Francisco, CA

1/2 pound fresh water prawns, peeled and deveined
1 tablespoon peanut oil
2 cloves garlic, chopped
2 long red fresno chilies, sliced
1 tablespoon shrimp paste
1 cup tomato, diced
1 pound water spinach (kangkung), washed and drained well, chop and use stems as well as leaves
1/2 teaspoon salt
2 tablespoons tamarind paste

Heat the oil in a wok until very hot. Stir in the shrimp paste and tamarind paste and once it sizzles, add in the garlic and sauté until fragrant. Stir in the prawns and continue to sauté for approximately 1 minute. Add in the remaining ingredients and stir fry over high heat for 3-5 minutes. Serve the stir fry immediately over brown rice.

Serves 8

THIS DISH IS VERY LOW IN FAT AND VERY HEALTHY. BURMESE CUISINE DRAWS ON ITS CHINESE AND INDIAN INFLUENCES, AND THESE ARE EVIDENT IN THIS DISH WITH ITS UNIQUE BLEND OF WATER SPINACH, AND THE SHRIMP AND TAMARIND PASTES. —*TONI ROBERTSON*

SUMMER VEGETABLE TOFU

Toshi Kihara • Hamasaku • Los Angeles, CA

Soybean Tofu
1 tablespoon soybean puree
1 cup soy milk
1 tablespoon nigari*

Pumpkin Tofu
2 tablespoons pumpkin puree
1 cup soy milk
1 tablespoon nigari*

Onion Tofu
2 tablespoons Maui onion puree
1 cup soy milk
1 tablespoon nigari*
**Nigari is a tofu coagulant and can be bought from a Japanese tofu specialty store.*

Bonito Stock
3 cups bottled water
2 ounces dried seaweed
1 cup dried bonito

Basil Ponzu Sauce
3 cups bonito stock
3 cups rice vinegar
1 cup mirin vinegar
1 cup light colored soy sauce, low sodium
1 cup dried bonito
2 ounces chopped Japanese sweet basil

Daikon Garnish
1/2 cup daikon, julienned
1/4 cup carrots, julienned
1 cup kaiware daikon
1/4 cup chives

Soybean Tofu: Boil approximately 10 soybeans. When soft, put in food processor and puree. Add soy milk and puree further. Add nigari and mix. Put in a Chinese porcelain spoon, place in steamer basket and steam for five minutes. Refrigerate.
Pumpkin Tofu: Boil pumpkin or use canned. When soft, put in food processor and puree. Add soy milk and puree further. Add nigari and mix. Put in a Chinese porcelain spoon, place in steamer basket and steam for five minutes. Refrigerate.
Onion Tofu: Boil chopped Maui onion until soft. When soft, put in a food processor and puree. Add soy milk and puree further. Add nigari and mix very well. Put in a Chinese porcelain spoon, place in steamer basket and steam for five minutes. Refrigerate.
Bonito Stock: Boil 3 cups bottled water and add 2 ounces dried seaweed in the boiling water. Boil for 10 minutes. Remove seaweed. Add 1 cup dried bonito in water, boil for 5 minutes. Place paper towel over bowl. Drain over bowl to strain water of dried bonito and any seaweed remains. Discard bonito and seaweed.
Ponzu Sauce: Take the bonito stock you have just prepared and combine with mirin vinegar and soy sauce. Place on medium flame until it boils slowly for approximately 7 minutes. Add the additional 1 cup dried bonito and bring back to a boil. Drain through paper towel into the bowl. Add chopped basil to liquid and marinate for 24 hours. Strain through towel once more for pure Ponzu sauce.
Daikon Garnish: Combine all daikon and carrots together. Drizzle basil Ponzu on plate to create artistic effect. Then, place each type of tofu on plate. Arrange the daikon salad on each tofu. Drizzle additional basil ponzu over tofu and daikon garnish.

PHOTO: Ray Grefe

Serves 4

MyPyramid.gov

TOFU MUSHROOM GALORE IN LEMON GINGER SAUCE

Sue Lee • Korean Chef • New York, NY

3 1/2 ounces firm tofu, cut into squares (see dimensions below)
cornstarch or potato starch for dusting
1/2 cup oyster mushrooms, cut into long thin slices
1/2 cup Shiitake mushrooms, cut into long thin slices
1/4 cup abalone mushrooms, cut into long thin slices
1/4 cup button mushrooms, cut into thin slices
5 carrots, thinly sliced
6 eggplant, thinly sliced
4 zucchini, thinly sliced
5 leaves Napa cabbage, shredded
cooking oil for frying

Sauce
1/2 cup Asian pear, small dices
1/2 cup orange, small dices
3 tablespoons onions, small dices
3 tablespoons ginger paste (blended ginger)
1/2 tablespoon sesame oil
1/4 cup water
2 tablespoons brown sugar
6 tablespoons soy sauce
1 tablespoon sake
1/4 piece lemon for juice
1 tablespoon potato starch

Cut the hard tofu into 1 inch x 1 inch squares and 1/2 inch in depth. Coat the tofu squares with starch. Deep fry the tofu squares for about 3 to 4 minutes until they are golden brown. Drain excess oil. In a wok, sauté the fried tofu with all the vegetables and mushrooms for about 2 minutes. In a separate saucepan, mix all the sauce ingredients and cook on a low flame for about 10 minutes. Pour the cooked sauce on the tofu, mushrooms and vegetables. Add the potato starch and let it simmer for 3 minutes.

Serves 2

TOFU PÂTE

Hiroshi Noguchi • Renaissance Orlando Resort at Marriott • Orlando, FL

8 ounces fish fillets, tilapia or sole

Tofu Mousse
6 ounces soft tofu
3 medium size scallops
dash of soy sauce
1 tablespoon cornstarch
dash of salt and pepper
8 ounces water
1/2 teaspoon dashi powder
1 egg
dash of mirin

Brush soy sauce on the fish fillets and grill. Squeeze water out of tofu and place in food processor. Add scallops and mix. Add dashi, salt, soy sauce, mirin, cornstarch, pepper, water, and egg. Mix until consistency is smooth and thick. Place 1/3 of mousse in terrine. Lay grilled fish into terrine on top of the first layer of mousse. Top grilled fish with remaining 1/3 of mousse and spread evenly to complete a smooth top layer. Cover the third layer of fish with the last third of mousse. Steam for 15 minutes. Put weight on the cover of terrine while the tofu pâte cools off.

Serves 4

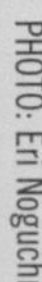

VEGETABLE SUSHI RISOTTO

Toshi Kihara • Hamasaku • Los Angeles, CA

Risotto
4 yasukouchi tomatoes (available from a Japanese farm in Carlsbad/Oceanside area)
2 pickled Japanese eggplant (not too sweet. not too salty)
8 snowpeas
1 Japanese cucumber, very finely julienned
1 medium avocado, chopped in chunks
1 tablespoon yellow corn
1 piece Tokyo green onion, very finely julienned
2 ounces sushi rice

Black Olive Soy Sauce
1 ounce black olives
1 large or 4 small cloves garlic
1 cup soy sauce, low sodium
1/4 cup balsamic vinegar
Oba (shiso leaf) and Italian parsley for garnish

Sushi Rice
1/3 cup sugar
2 small pieces dried seaweed
1 1/3 cup rice vinegar
1 cup cooked sushi rice
1/8 cup sushi-zu

Pickled Eggplant
1 cup rice vinegar
1/2 cup sugar
1 ounce ginger, grated
1 piece dried seaweed

Sushi Rice: Combine vinegar, sugar, dried seaweed. Cook rice, add sushi-zu when cooked and mix together.

Pickled Eggplant: Combine all the ingredients. Add diced eggplant. Make sure they are about half the size of your thumb. Marinate at least overnight for sweet and 1 day for a more sour taste.

Black Olive Soy Sauce: Combine black olives, soy sauce, garlic and balsamic vinegar in a food processor. Puree until thoroughly combined.

Tomato Cup: Boil water. Place tomatoes in water and remove immediately. Peel and cut top off of tomato to create a cup. Remove seeds.

Snow Peas: Boil snow peas with little salt to accentuate green color, about 5 minutes.

Risotto: Over the plate, drizzle black olive soy sauce. Combine sushi rice, corn, avocado, and snowpeas. Place in tomato cups and pickled eggplant on top. Drizzle additional black olive soy sauce over tomatoes with rice and vegetable mixture and eggplant. Garnish with oba and Italian parsley.

Serves 4

MyPyramid.gov

PHOTO: June Miller Richards

VEGETARIAN DUMPLINGS

Frank Yang • Din Tai Fung Dumpling House • Arcadia, CA*

2 cups of hot water dough (see recipe below)
1/3 pound of Napa or Chinese cabbage
1 box of bean curd
3 dried black mushrooms, soaked until soft, stems removed
1 bundle of bean thread or vermicelli, soaked until soft

Seasonings
1 teaspoon salt
1 teaspoon sugar
1/8 teaspoon pepper
1 tablespoon vegetable oil
3 tablespoons sesame oil

Hot Water Dough: Add 1/4 cup of boiling water to 2 cups of flour. Then, add 1/4 cup of cold water. Knead dough.

Stuffing: Remove leaves from Napa cabbage, rinse, blanch until soft. Remove and squeeze out excessive water. Chop finely. Cut soaked bean thread into small sections. Finely chop mushrooms. Chop the bean curd into small pieces. Combine all ingredients in a big bowl, add all seasoning. Stir to mix well. Divide dough into small balls. Roll each ball into a circle. Place a little stuffing in the center of each dough circle, fold over, press edges tightly to seal, steam in steamer on medium for 10 minutes. Remove and serve.

Serves 4

*Please see page 260 for a complete list of restaurant locations.

WARM TOFU WITH SAIKYO MISO, ROASTED CASHEWS AND CHILI

Jake Klein • Pulse • New York, NY

1 box Japanese firm tofu
1/4 saikyo miso (sweet)
1/3 cup water
1 teaspoon toasted sesame oil
1 egg yolk
1/4 cup roasted cashews, chopped
4 teaspoons of thinly sliced scallion rings, green part only
1 teaspoon sliced red chili

PHOTO: Julie Stapen

Tofu: Cut tofu into 6 equal sized pieces. You can do this by slicing the block in half lengthwise once, and slicing it again into thirds, width wise. Place your 6 pieces of tofu in a steamer basket to heat.

Miso Sauce: Over a double boiler, in a non-reactive bowl, whisk the miso, water, egg yolk and sesame oil together. Continue to whisk until the mixture has thickened to the consistency of reduced heavy cream. This should take about 10 minutes. The sauce should be rich, creamy and salty sweet. In the center of each plate, place one block of warm tofu. Spoon approximately 1 tablespoon of sauce directly over the top of the block. Allow to drip down the sides. Sprinkle with 3/4 tablespoon of toasted cashews, a pinch of sliced scallions and 2 or 3 rings of red chili. Serve immediately.

Serves 6

DESSERTS

One of the highlights of the outdoor marketplaces throughout Asia is the profusion of colorful fresh fruits: juicy mangoes, bananas of different shapes and sizes, spiky rambutans, plump pomelos, five-sided starfruits, stinky durians, fuzzy kiwifruits, leathery-skinned lychees, longan, refreshing watermelon, and the stunning sphere-shaped dragon fruit— a brilliant magenta-red outer skin covering the white flesh flecked with tiny black kiwi-like seeds. The fruits are eaten as is, some crushed into juice, combined with vegetables in a salad, or mixed with small amounts of meat and a lot of vegetables in stir fries or curries.

Most Asian desserts are low in fat and refined sugar, including sweet-sour dried plums; strips of candied coconut, pineapple, or mango; fresh coconut juice; or freshly squeezed papaya, watermelon, or sugarcane juice. Adzuki beans, lentils, mung beans, tapioca pearls, rice, and/or corn, steeped in sugar syrup and served beneath a mound of shaved ice, sometimes drizzled with condensed or coconut milk are popular in the Philippines (halo-halo), Singapore and Malaysia (kacang), Taiwan and Korea. These are more often eaten as a snack than to end a meal.

ALMOND TOFU WITH KIWI IN ROCK SUGAR SYRUP

Pichet Ong • P*ONG • New York, NY

Almond Tofu Base
1 tablespoon gelatin powder
1 1/2 cup almond milk
(available in health food stores)
1 1/2 cup soy milk
1/2 cup sugar
1 teaspoon almond oil
pinch of salt

Kiwi in Rock Sugar Syrup
4 ripe kiwis (mix green and gold kiwis
if in season)
1/4 cup Chinese yellow rock sugar (2 ounces)
1/2 cup water

Sprinkle gelatin over almond milk in a large cup and let sit for a minute. In the meantime, bring soy milk and sugar to a scald in a saucepan, stirring until the sugar is dissolved. Remove from heat and whisk in the gelatin and almond milk mixture. Add almond extract and stir to blend. Pour into 8 glasses or molds and refrigerate until firm, at least 3 hours. Bring sugar and water to a boil. Let sit until all the sugar melts. In the meantime, peel and cut kiwis in half. Cut each half into 4 wedges and place in a bowl. Pour the sugar syrup mixture onto the kiwis and refrigerate the mixture completely before use.

Assembly: For each portion, serve almond tofu with 4 pieces of kiwi and about 4 tablespoons of syrup.

Serves 8

MyPyramid.gov

Recipe adapted from *An Exotic Finish* by Pichet Ong (Morrow-Harper Collins, 2007)

This is my take on what is arguably the most popular dessert among Chinese restaurants around the world. Often made with milk, the "tofu" in the name is given to the dish because of the tofu-like consistency and color of the pudding, which has just enough gelatin to enable it to set. In this version, however, soy milk and almond milk are used instead of dairy, making it a true tofu dessert. Typically almond tofu is served with canned fruit cocktail. I prefer to serve mine with mild flavored tropical fruits, such as kiwi, just simply macerated in Chinese yellow rock sugar syrup, which is believed to contain health enhancing properties that also help sooth the throat. —*Pichet Ong*

AVOCADO MOUSSE WITH LYCHEE SORBET

Rodelio Aglibot • Yi Cuisine • Los Angeles, CA

Raspberry Sauce
1 cup raspberries
1/4 cup sugar
1/3 cup water

Lychee Sorbet
1 can (15 ounces) lychees

Mousse
1/3 cup sugar
2 cups heavy whipping cream
3 ripe avocados
2 tablespoons instant gelatin
1/2 cup warm water

Garnish
mint sprigs

Raspberry Sauce: Combine the berries, sugar and water. Puree and strain.
Lychee Sorbet: Puree the lychees with syrup in a food processor. Freeze in an ice cream maker. Spoon into a glass container. Cover and freeze.
Mousse: Dissolve the gelatin in the warm water. In a food processor, puree the avocado until smooth. Slowly add the gelatin mix and blend until incorporated. Add the avocado puree to the sweetened whip cream mixture, gently folding until blended. Chill in the refrigerator until the mousse sets, about 35 to 40 minutes. For each serving, spoon the raspberry sauce into the bottom of a large bowl. Place a small scoop of lychee sorbet on top of the sauce. Fill the frozen avocado shells with the mousse to resemble uncut avocados and place on top of the sorbet. Garnish with mint.

Serves 4

NOTE: An ice cream maker is needed for this recipe.

MAKE THE MOUSSE JUST BEFORE SERVING. IT WILL DARKEN IF LEFT TO STAND. —*RODELIO AGLIBOT*

PHOTOS: Left, Martin Jansche;

CARDAMOM APRICOTS FILLED WITH CREAM AND PISTACHIOS

Carol Selva Rajah • Chef, South East Asian Cuisine• Sydney, Australia

1 cup whole dried apricots, cut in half
3 cups water
1 cup sugar
4 cardamom pods, pounded slightly to release aromas
1 tablespoon fresh lime juice
1 1/2 cups thickly whipped cream
1/2 cup finely chopped unsalted pistachios

Soak apricots in warm water for 2 hours to soften. Drain and slice across to make two halves. Combine sugar, water, cardamom and lime juice and boil until syrupy on high heat. Keep stirring so that it will not caramelize. Remove from heat. Pass through a fine sieve to remove cardamom and let cool. Whip the cream, then fold crushed pistachios into the cream, arrange half the apricots halves in a single layer and fill each one with cream mixture. Drizzle syrup and sprinkle remaining pistachio on top as garnish. Serve chilled.

Serves 6

NOTE: The apricots and the syrup can be prepared ahead but assembled with cream and nuts just before serving.

MyPyramid.gov

THIS IS A TURKISH RECIPE THAT FOUND ITS WAY INTO MALAYSIA, PROBABLY THROUGH NORTH INDIA, REMINDING US OF THE MIDDLE EASTERN INFLUENCES THAT ARE PART OF INDIA'S HERITAGE. —*CAROL SELVA RAJAH*

CHINESE RESTAURANT WALNUT COOKIES

Pichet Ong • P*ONG • New York, NY

2 cups walnut halves
1 1/3 cups all-purpose flour
1 teaspoon baking powder
1 teaspoon baking soda
1/2 teaspoon salt
1 cup unsalted butter, chilled and cut into 1 inch cubes
1/3 cup sugar
1/3 cup light brown sugar
1 egg
1 1/2 teaspoons vanilla extract

Preheat the oven to 300° F. Put the walnuts on a baking sheet and transfer to the oven. Toast for ten minutes, stirring the walnuts halfway through. Remove from the oven and cool completely. Meanwhile, sift the flour, baking powder, baking soda and salt together in a medium mixing bowl. Put the butter, sugars, and 1/2 cup walnuts in the bowl of an electric mixer fitted with the paddle attachment. Cream on medium speed, scraping down the sides of the bowl as necessary, until the walnuts break up and the mixture is light and fluffy, about 5 minutes. With the mixer running, add the eggs, one at a time and then add the vanilla. When fully incorporated, scrape down the bowl and add the flour mixture and mix on low speed just until you don't see any traces of flour. Cover and refrigerate for at least four hours and up to three days. When ready to bake, preheat the oven to 325° F, and line two baking sheets with parchment paper. Using a 1 inch diameter ice cream scoop or measuring spoon, scoop the dough into balls and place 2 inches apart on the baking sheets. Use your palm to slightly flatten each ball and gently press a walnut half into the center of each cookie. Bake until lightly golden brown, 8 to 10 minutes. Cool on a wire rack and serve.

Makes 3 dozen

Recipe adapted from *An Exotic Finish* by Pichet Ong (Morrow-Harper Collins, 2007)

PHOTO: Martin Jansche

CREAMING THE BUTTER WITH SOME WALNUTS RESULTS IN MORE AROMATIC COOKIES. IF YOU DON'T HAVE A STANDING MIXER, YOU CAN ALSO DO THIS BY HAND WITH A WOODEN SPOON. CRUSH THE NUTS A LITTLE FIRST, THEN CREAM VIGOROUSLY. BEFORE FORTUNE COOKIES SOARED IN POPULARITY IN THE 1950'S, EGG-GLAZED ALMOND COOKIES CAME WITH THE CHECK AT MANY CHINESE RESTAURANTS. THIS IS MY TAKE ON THAT CLASSIC COOKIE. WALNUTS ARE THE PREFERRED NUT IN CHINESE COOKING, BOTH BECAUSE THEY ARE PERCEIVED TO BE CLASSIER THAN ALMONDS AND BECAUSE THEY ARE GOOD FOR YOU. UNLIKE THEIR HARD, CRUNCHY ANCESTORS, THESE COOKIES CRUMBLE IN YOUR MOUTH. —*PICHET ONG*

CHOCOLATE BEIGNETS WITH CARAMELIZED BANANAS AND VANILLA ICE CREAM

Michelle Myers • Sona • Los Angeles, CA

Chocolate Beignets
3 cups flour
1/2 cup sugar
2/3 cup cocoa powder
1/2 teaspoon salt
2 cups carbonated water
1/2 cup melted butter
5 eggs

Tahitian Vanilla Bean Ice Cream
1 liter half and half (1/2 liter milk with 1/2 liter of cream)
1 1/4 cups sugar
10 egg yolks
1 Tahitian vanilla bean

Caramelized Bananas
8 Ecuadorian bananas, peeled, split in half length wise
1 tablespoon whole butter
4 ounces rum
1 cup brown sugar

Chocolate Ganache
1 pound of bittersweet chocolate, chopped
1/3 cup of butter
12 ounces of heavy cream
1/4 cup powdered sugar
1 quart vegetable oil

Chocolate Beignets: With an electric mixer, combine flour, sugar, cocoa, salt and then add water. Mix in eggs one at a time and mix until well combined.

Tahitian Vanilla Bean Ice Cream: Bring half and half, sugar and the vanilla bean to a boil in a heavy saucepan. Cover and steep for 20 minutes. Bring back to a boil and in a separate bowl, mix the egg yolks and remaining sugar. Pour 1/4 of the warm liquid into the yolks, whisk and return to the saucepan. Cook over medium heat, stirring constantly until a thin custard forms or coats the back of a wooden spoon. Strain, chill and freeze in an ice cream machine.

Caramelized Bananas: Melt butter in large sauté pan, when it begins to "sizzle" add the bananas and lower heat. When bananas begin to brown at the edges, remove pan from burner, add the rum, carefully return pan to burner and allow the rum to flame. Remove bananas from the pan to a warm plate. Add brown sugar to rum and stir until smooth. Return bananas and coat with sugar sauce.

Chocolate Ganache: Combine butter and chocolate in a bowl. Bring the cream to a boil and pour over the butter and chocolate. Let sit for two minutes. Mix until smooth. Chill and roll into 1 inch balls and freeze. Heat one quart of vegetable oil to 375° F. Drop the ganache ball into the batter using a fork, coat well. Then, drop the ganache batter combination into the hot oil for 1 to 1 1/2 minutes. Drain the beignets on paper towels. Serve with chocolate sauce, caramelized bananas, vanilla ice cream and dust with powdered sugar.

Serves 8

CHOCOLATE CHICORY BOMBÉ WITH RASPBERRY COMPOTE

Jehangir Mehta • Aix • New York, NY

20 egg yolks
1 cup sugar
1/3 cup corn syrup
1 cup bittersweet chocolate, melted, held warm
2 tablespoons, chicory powder
1 quart heavy cream, whipped (measure before whipping)
1/2 teaspoon cinnamon
1/2 teaspoon star anise
1 cup bittersweet chocolate,
grated to form flakes

Raspberry Compote
1 pint raspberries
1/2 cup sugar
zest of 2 limes

Beat yolks in an upright mixer at medium speed. In a saucepot, cook sugar and corn syrup on medium heat until large bubbles appear. Add the chicory powder, cinnamon and star anise to the boiling syrup. Turn mixer to high speed and add the cooked sugar slowly to the bowl while the mixer is on. When sugar syrup has been added, return mixer to slow speed and add melted chocolate. When chocolate is completely incorporated, turn off mixer and remove bowl from stand. Using a rubber spatula check the edges of the bowl to make sure that all ingredients are completely combined, then gently fold in the whipped cream. Pour this mixture in 6 half round molds and freeze. Once frozen, remove from molds and place in back of the freezer on a sheet pan lined with paper. Just before serving, liberally sprinkle with the chocolate flakes.

Raspberry Compote: Heat skillet, add the raspberries, sugar and zest. Toss for 30 seconds and remove. To serve, place the chocolate bombés on a plate and drizzle with warm raspberry compote around the dish.

Serves 6

CRISPY COCONUT RICE PUDDING, GREEN TEA ICE CREAM AND MANGO COULIS

Michael Laiskonis • Le Bernardin • New York, NY

Coconut Rice Pudding
1/2 cup coconut milk
3/4 cup whole milk
1/4 cup water
1 stalk lemon grass, thinly sliced
1 tablespoon ginger, peeled and chopped
1/2 vanilla bean, split and scraped
3/4 cup short grain sushi rice
water, as needed
1/4 cup plus 2 tablespoons granulated sugar
2 tablespoons dried mango, finely chopped
6 sheets feuille de brick*
butter, melted or clarified butter as needed

Green Tea Ice Cream
1 cup heavy cream
1 cup whole milk
1 tablespoon non fat dry milk powder
2 teaspoons Matcha green tea powder (available in health food stores)
1/2 cup plus 2 tablespoons granulated sugar
4 large egg yolks

Mango Coulis
1 ripe mango, peeled
1/4 cup water
2 tablespoons granulated sugar
1/2 teaspoon lime juice

Assembly
butter, melted or clarified
confectioner's sugar

PHOTO: Martin Jansche

(recipe continued on following page)

(recipe continued from previous page)

Coconut Rice Pudding: In a saucepan, combine coconut milk, whole milk, water, lemon grass, ginger and vanilla. Bring to a boil. Remove from heat, cover and allow to infuse for 15 minutes. Meanwhile, place rice in a second saucepan, with cold water to cover. Bring to a boil, drain and reserve. Strain coconut milk infusion through a fine mesh sieve. Combine with the rice in a saucepan and gently bring to a boil. Reduce heat to lowest setting, cover and cook for 30 to 40 minutes, or until rice is tender. Remove from heat and allow to cool. Add sugar and chopped mango. Transfer to the refrigerator to chill thoroughly. Brush a sheet of feuille de brick with melted or clarified butter. Place about 1/4 cup of the coconut rice pudding onto the bottom third of the sheet and roll tightly, folding in the sides. The roll should measure about 8 inches long by 3/4 inch in diameter. Repeat with the remaining filling and sheets. Chill and reserve until assembly.

Green Tea Ice Cream: In a non-reactive pan, whisk together cream, milk and milk powder. Bring to a boil over high heat. Combine green tea powder, sugar and whisk into egg yolks. Temper hot cream into yolk mixture. Return to medium-low heat and cook just until mixture is slightly thickened, stirring constantly. Remove from heat and strain through a fine mesh sieve. Chill in ice water and then process into a ice cream maker according to manufacturer's instructions. Store in freezer until assembly.

Mango Coulis: Combine all ingredients in a blender and puree until smooth.

Assembly: In a large sauté pan over low heat, carefully fry rice pudding rolls in melted or clarified butter until lightly browned on all sides. Remove from heat and transfer to a paper towel to absorb excess fat. Trim ends off of each roll and slice into quarters. Dust with confectioner's sugar and arrange on a plate. Garnish with green tea ice cream and mango coulis. Serve immediately.

Serves 1

*Feuille de brick is a thin pastry dough originating in North America. It is somewhat like phyllo, but studier and more flexible, allowing one to pan fry the coconut rice pudding. Feuille de brick is available in gourmet and specialty markets.

I developed this recipe several years ago working with a Japanese chef, Takashi Yagihashi, one of the most influential mentors I've been lucky to work with. This dessert meets our goal of combining Asian ingredients with Western cooking techniques and presenting a classic idea in a new, refreshing way. —*Michael Laiskonis*

FENNEL BRITTLE WITH MANGO LASSI

Jehangir Mehta • Aix • New York, NY

Fennel Brittle
1 cup fennel seeds
1/4 cup sugar
cooking oil spray

Mango Lassi
1 cup mango puree
3/4 cup yogurt
1/2 teaspoon amchoor (dried mango) powder

Fennel Brittle: In a small heavy bottom saucepot, caramelize the sugar and add the fennel seeds and stir. Remove and place on parchment paper, which is sprayed with cooking oil. Roll as thin as possible. Once it is cool, break into bite size portions.

Mango Lassi: Place in a blender and blend for 30 seconds and chill. Pour into a glass to serve.

Serves 10

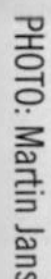

GINGER-APPLE TART TATIN

Philippe Chin • CuiZine • Aiken, SC

2 large Granny Smith apples
3/4 cup sugar
3 tablespoons butter
1/4 cup water
4 circles of puff pastry, 4 1/2 inch diameter
1 tablespoon ginger, chopped

In a saucepan, cook butter and sugar until mixture turns light brown in color. Whisk in water and add ginger. Divide the caramel equally in four 4 1/2 inch tartelette molds. Peel, core and halve apples. With the side down, cut the apples lengthwise into thin slices. Fan apple slices in the caramel molds. Place pastry on top of apples and punch in holes to allow the steam to evaporate. Preheat oven to 375° F and bake the tarts for 15 minutes or until golden brown. Remove the tarts from the molds while still warm by turning them upside down onto the serving plates.

Serves 4

GINGER CRÈME BRULÈE

Wolfgang Puck • Spago • Beverly Hills, CA*

3 cups heavy cream
1/3 cup granulated sugar for the custard, plus 1/2 cup for the topping
3 thin slices ginger root
6 egg yolks

Combine the cream, the 1/3 cup sugar, and the ginger root in a medium saucepan and bring to a simmer. Remove from the heat, cover, and let steep for 15 minutes. Meanwhile, preheat the oven to 300° F with the rack in the center. Place six 1/2 cup ramekins or four 1 cup ramekins in a baking dish that is at least 1/2 inch deeper than ramekins. Beat the egg yolks in a medium-size bowl. Whisking the egg yolk mixture continuously, slowly pour in the hot cream. Strain through a fine strainer into a bowl and discard the ginger slices. Fill the ramekins to the top with the custard. Fill the baking dish with enough hot water to 2/3 of the way up the sides of the ramekins. Cover loosely with foil and place in the oven. Bake 40 to 45 minutes, until the custards have set but have not browned. They should jiggle slightly. Remove the ramekins from the baking dish and chill for at least 2 hours or for up to 2 days. Shortly before serving, make the caramel topping. Sprinkle half the remaining sugar (1/4 cup) over the custards in an even layer. Ignite a kitchen torch and move flame back and forth over the sugar until it melts and forms a glossy deep-brown caramel. Repeat the process with the remaining 1/4 cup sugar. Do not let the caramelized crème brulee sit for more than an hour.

Serves 4-6

*Please see page 260 for a complete list of restaurant locations.

Recipe courtesy of Wolfgang Puck, *Wolfgang Puck Makes it Easy*, Rutledge Hill Press, 2004

Here's another Asian twist on a classic French dessert. In any given restaurant, crème brulee will always top the list of favorite desserts. Literally "burnt cream", this preparation conceals creamy vanilla custard beneath a translucent, amber brittle topping of caramelized sugar. The custard's simplicity allows for seemingly endless variation. It can be infused with spices like cinnamon, or with violet or rose petals; it can be fortified with espresso or butterscotch or chocolate. — *Wolfgang Puck*

JAMUN WITH STEWED STRAWBERRIES AND BALSAMIC VINEGAR

Jehangir Mehta • Aix • New York, NY

Syrup
5 cups water
1 1/2 cups sugar
15 cardamom pods, crushed

Dough for Jamun
1 cup milk powder
2 tablespoons all purpose flour
3/4 teaspoon baking powder
1/4 teaspoon salt
2 ounces milk
1 tablespoon condensed milk
cooking oil for frying Jamun

Stewed Strawberries
1/2 cup balsamic vinegar
1 pint fresh small strawberries, cleaned

Mix all the dry ingredients together. Whisk the milk and condensed milk together. Then, slowly pour over dry ingredients in a food processor to form the dough. Make balls the size of small marbles. In a medium saucepot, warm 2 inches of oil to 230° F. Add the balls and fry them till golden brown. Place in syrup and refrigerate. Reduce the strawberries to puree with the balsamic to a very thick syrup consistency over a medium flame in a saucepot. Add the fresh strawberries in the syrup and stew for approx 7 to 10 minutes over a low flame. Switch off. Cool and refrigerate. Place 2 jamuns on a plate, drizzle strawberry sauce around the plate and place 1 tablespoon of strawberries on the side.

Serves 6

JER-NE'S TOFU FROZEN CREAMS IN MINI CONES

Troy N. Thompson • Jer-ne Restaurant and Bar, The Ritz-Carlton •
Marina del Rey, CA

Mango
12 ounces extra soft tofu
22 ounces fresh ripe mango
6 ounces sugar
1 cup unsweetened soy milk
1/2 fresh squeezed lemon juice

Kiwi
12 ounces extra soft tofu
22 ounces kiwi, peeled
12 ounces sugar

Raspberry
12 ounces extra soft tofu
22 ounces raspberry
12 ounces sugar

Yogurt
12 ounces extra soft tofu
16 ounces yogurt, plain
8 ounces sugar
1 cup unsweetened soy milk
1 piece vanilla bean, scraped
1/2 fresh squeezed lemon juice

Chocolate
12 ounces extra soft tofu
8 ounces dark chocolate
8 ounces sugar
1 1/2 cup soy milk

Cones
1/2 pound powdered sugar
4 2/3 ounces all purpose flour
5 1/2 ounces egg whites
5 1/2 ounces butter, melted
pinch of lemon zest

Chocolate Cream: Heat milk with sugar and pour over chocolate. Puree with tofu.
All Other Creams: Put the ingredients of cream in a blender. Purée till smooth. Freeze in an ice cream freezer till firm. Scoop and serve.
Cones: In an electric mixer, sift dry ingredients, add butter and add egg whites at the same time on full speed in the mixer. Spread on a sheet in a very thin fan shape. Bake in an oven at 350° F till golden brown. Roll into tiny cones while warm and let cool. Scoop frozen creams into cones and serve.

PHOTO: Martin Jansche

MyPyramid.gov

MANGO CHEESECAKE

Surbhi Sahni • Dévi • New York, NY

Crust

2 1/2 cups all-purpose flour
2/3 cup confectioner's sugar
1 1/2 sticks cold unsalted butter
2 tablespoons ice cold water
1 1/2 cups slivered almonds
1/2 cup plus 2 tablespoons clarified butter, melted

Mango Cheesecake Filling

3/4 pound cream cheese, cut into cubes and softened
1/4 cup plus 2 tablespoons sugar
3 eggs
1 3/4 cup (15 ounces) mango puree
2 teaspoons lime juice

Passion Fruit-Mango Sauce

2 tablespoons sugar
1 tablespoon water
3/4 teaspoon corn syrup
2 tablespoons unsalted butter
1/4 cup passion fruit puree
(available in specialty food stores and online)
1/4 cup mango puree

Assembly

individual mango cheesecakes
1/2 cup sugar
Passion Fruit-Mango Sauce
2 fresh mangos, peeled and julienned

Crust: Preheat the oven to 350° F. Grease a 9 x 18 inch baking sheet and set aside. Place the flour and sugar in a food processor and pulse to combine well. Add the butter and pulse until it has a breadcrumb consistency. Then, add the water and pulse for 4 short bursts. Flatten the mixture onto the greased baking sheet and cool in the refrigerator for 10 minutes. Bake for 10 minutes, then turn the baking sheet 180° F and bake for an additional 10 minutes. Cool on a rack. Place the crust in a food processor and process into fine crumbs. Add the almonds and pulse in 4 short bursts. Add 1/2 cup of butter and pulse in 6 short bursts. At this point the mixture should have a breadcrumb consistency and should come together easily when handled. Take the 9 individual cylinder molds (3 inches high and 2 inches in diameter; with no base) and cover one end with aluminum foil so that the foil completely covers the outside of the cylinder. Place on a baking sheet, foil side down. Brush the inside of the mold with melted butter including the foil bottom. Put in a tablespoon of the above prepared crust in each, press it down to flatten it evenly at the bottom and chill in the refrigerator for 10 minutes. Bake at 350° F until the crust has a deep golden brown color, about 15 minutes. Remove from the oven and cool completely before adding the filling.

Mango Cheesecake Filling: Preheat the oven to 300° F. Place the cream cheese in a food processor and blend until smooth. Add sugar and blend until smooth. Be sure to scrape down the sides with a spatula. Add eggs and pulse until well blended. Pour the puree and the lime juice into this mixture and blend for 3 minutes. Divide the mixture equally among the molds. Take a deep baking pan and place the filled molds in the pan. Add cold water in the pan so that the water level reaches 3/4 the height of the molds. Place the pan in the oven and bake for 45 minutes. Carefully turn the pan 180° F and bake for another 20 minutes. At this point, turn off the oven and leave the cheesecakes inside the oven for about 30 minutes. Remove molds from the pan and cool to room temperature. When the molds are cool, remove the foil and cover the bottom of each mold with plastic wrap. Chill overnight before use

Passion Fruit-Mango Sauce: Put sugar, water and corn syrup in a pan and caramelize over a low flame until golden brown, about 5 minutes. Add butter immediately. After the butter melts halfway, add the puree and cook for another minute or so until smooth. Cool the sauce and serve it at room temperature.

Assembly: Take the cheesecakes and run a small knife around the edge of the mold to loosen them. Carefully push the cheesecake down so that the cheesecake stands on the crust base. Sprinkle the top of each cake evenly with 1 1/2 teaspoons of sugar and burn it with a propane or butane torch. Circulate the torch for even coloring. Once the sugar melts, bubbles and turns to a golden color, allow to cool for about a minute before serving. To serve, place cheesecake in the middle of each plate; drizzle 2 tablespoons of sauce around it and put some julienned mango in a heap on the side. Serve immediately.

Serves 9

NOTE: The mango puree used in this recipe is imported from India and available in any Indian grocery store. It is pre-sweetened. If you choose to use any other puree you may have to add sugar to taste.

PHOTO: Battman Studios

THESE SMALL CHEESECAKES SHOULD BE MADE ONE DAY BEFORE SERVING. THIS RECIPE MAKES 9 INDIVIDUAL SERVINGS AND AS IT IS A FRAGILE CHEESECAKE, I WOULD NOT RECOMMEND CONVERTING IT INTO ONE LARGE CAKE. THE LEFTOVERS OF THE CRUST CAN BE USED AS A BASE FOR OTHER CHEESECAKES. THE CRUST CAN BE MADE IN ADVANCE AND STORED IN THE REFRIGERATOR FOR UP TO TWO WEEKS. PRIOR TO USE, LEAVE THE CRUST OUT FOR ABOUT TWO HOURS OR MICROWAVE THE QUANTITY NEEDED TO SOFTEN THE BUTTER BEFORE USE. —*SURBHI SAHNI*

ORANGE KUMQUAT SORBET

James McDevitt • Restaurant Budo • Napa, CA

1 pound kumquats
2 cups water
1 cup sugar
3 cups orange or tangerine juice

Simmer kumquats, water and 1/2 cup sugar for 20 minutes. Drain and chill. When cool, scoop out the pulp and seeds of kumquats. Discard. Puree kumquats, remaining sugar and orange juice together. Strain and freeze in an ice cream machine.

Makes about 1 quart

PANDAN INFUSED MANGO YOGURT PANNA COTTA

Arnold Eric Wong • EOS •
San Francisco, CA*

6 ounces low fat yogurt
8 ounces heavy cream
4 ounces mango puree
1/2 cup sugar
2 pandan leaves, chopped
4 gelatin leaves

In a saucepan, heat the cream and bring it to a simmer. Add the pandan leaves and steep for 15 minutes. Remove from heat, strain and discard the leaves. In a small bowl, with a little water, soak the gelatin leaves. Whisk the gelatin into the infused cream. The cream should not be above 120° F , as the strength of the gelatin will be affected. Also, never boil the gelatin. In a separate bowl, whisk the yogurt, sugar and mango puree till smooth. Combine the infused cream and the yogurt mango mixture. Whisk well and pour into four greased ramekins. Chill in the refrigerator for a minimum of six hours or overnight. To unmold, quickly place the ramekins into a hot water bath and turn out onto a serving dish. Garnish with fresh Asian fruits.

Serves 4

PHOTOS: Ray Grefe

Please see page 260 for a complete list of restaurant locations.

Pandan is a leaf used throughout Thailand, Indonesia and Malaysia. It is used to perfume rice when steamed, and is added to curries and wrapped around candies. In this recipe, it will almost lend a vanilla like flavor when steeped in the cream. —*Arnold Eric Wong*

PERSIMMON AND OLIVE OIL CAKE

Pichet Ong • P*ONG • New York, NY

Cake

14 ounces all purpose flour
1/2 ounce baking powder
1 teaspoon salt
18 1/2 ounces sugar and 1 cup additional for lining molds
7 ounces almond flour
9 eggs
zest of 2 oranges
1 teaspoon vanilla extract
8 ounces extra virgin olive oil and 1 cup additional for lining molds
4 ripe fuyu persimmons
2/3 ounces raw sugar

Brush cake mold with additional olive oil and line with additional sugar. Set aside until use. Sift together flour, almond flour and baking powder. Trim off skin of persimmon and cut each half into 8 wedges. In a mixer, beat eggs at medium speed with orange zest until frothy, 1 minute. Add sugar and salt and beat at high speed until ribbon stage, about 5 minutes. Add vanilla and beat for another minute. Whisk in dry ingredients at low speed until incorporated. Take some of batter to make a liaison with oil. Fold into rest of batter, making sure that there aren't any lumps. Fill cake mold with cake batter and place 3 wedges of persimmon in the center. Use remaining additional olive oil to brush the top of persimmon. Sprinkle the top of persimmon wedges with a pinch of raw sugar. Bake in preheated 350° F oven until tester comes out clean in the center, about 12 minutes. Let cool slightly before unmolding.

Serves 20

ROASTED BANANA BOAT WITH WALNUT CARAMEL SAUCE

Khai Duong • Ana Mandara • San Francisco, CA

1 whole ripe banana
2 ounces heart of palm sugar
1 tablespoon water
1 tablespoon coconut milk
1/5 teaspoon lemon juice
1/2 ounce walnuts, chopped

Preheat oven to 350° F. In a small saucepan, combine the heart of palm sugar, water and lemon juice. Bring to boil over medium heat. Continue to boil, swirling the pan a few times, until the mixture is colored brown and is syrupy, then add coconut milk, chopped walnuts and cook for 2 minutes. Reduce the heat to low and keep warm. Bake the whole unpeeled banana in the oven at 350° F for 10 minutes. To serve, put the roasted banana in a long plate, split the banana length-wise, open as a pocket. Spoon walnut caramel sauce on top of the roasted banana and serve.

MyPyramid.gov

Serves 1

PHOTO: Ray Grefe

IF YOU WISH, YOU CAN SPRINKLE POWDER SUGAR ON TOP OF THE ROASTED BANANA FOR GARNISH OR SERVE WITH A SCOOP OF ICE CREAM. —*KHAI DUONG*

SESAME BALLS

Pichet Ong • P*ONG • New York, NY

Sesame Ball Dough
2 cups sugar
1 tablespoon salt
1 1/2 teaspoons baking soda
5 1/4 ounces of taro, generously peeled and cut into 1/2 inch slices crosswise
one 1-pound bag glutinous rice flour
grapeseed, corn, or canola oil for deep-frying
1 cup white sesame seeds

Date Filling
1 pound dried dates
1/2 cup maltose sugar
1 teaspoon cinnamon
1 teaspoon salt

To prepare date filling, puree all ingredients in a food processor until smooth, scraping the bowl as necessary. Refrigerate until use. Put the sugar, salt, and baking soda in the bowl of an electric mixer. Mix well and set aside. Prepare a steamer with the water at a rolling boil. Add the taro and steam until very soft, about 10 minutes. It should be soft enough so that if poked with a knife, it will fall apart. Immediately transfer the taro to the electric mixer bowl with the sugar mixture and beat with the paddle attachment on medium speed until the sugar dissolves and the mixture is pasty. Meanwhile, bring 1 cup water to a boil. Turn the mixer speed to low and add the glutinous rice flour. When the mixture is crumbly, add the boiling water all at once. Continue beating the dough until it is soft and only slightly sticky. Squeeze the dough into a ball, wrap in plastic wrap, and then refrigerate until completely cooled. When cool, shape the dough into a log 1 inch in diameter and cut the log into 2 inch lengths. Flatten each piece of dough with your palm into a circle, 4 inches in diameter and 1/4 inch thick. Put 1 tablespoon of the date filling

SESAME BALLS ARE CLASSIC DIM SUM—UNADULTERATED AND OH-SO-GOOD. IN THE YUM CHA (DIM SUM) CULTURE, THESE STICKY-SWEET TREATS ARE EATEN BETWEEN SAVORY BITES THROUGHOUT THE MEAL. TRADITIONALLY, THE DOUGH IS MADE ONLY WITH GLUTINOUS RICE FLOUR, WHICH IS QUITE STICKY AND WILL LEAVE YOU SEARCHING FOR A TOOTHPICK. I'VE ADDED TARO TO MAKE THE DOUGH TENDERER, TASTIER AND A LOVELY SHADE OF LAVENDER. THE CONTRAST BETWEEN THE CRISP SESAME SEED COATING AND SOFT CHEWY DOUGH IS

into the center of a circle, then bring the edges together and pinch shut. Pinch off the excess dough at the two end points then roll the filled dumpling into a ball. Repeat with the remaining dough circles and filling. Fill a deep, heavy saucepan (at least 6 inches wide) with oil to a depth of at least 4 inches. Bring to 300° F. Fill a shallow dish with water. Roll sesame balls in the water, just enough to moisten then roll in the sesame seeds. Using a slotted spoon, carefully lower half of the coated balls into the oil and cook until they float, about 5 minutes. Do not disturb the balls at all when they cook. Carefully remove from oil and drain on paper towels. Repeat with the remaining balls. Serve immediately or at room temperature.

Makes about two dozen 2 inch balls

NOTE: Recipe for fortune cookies (featured in photo here) is on page 242

Recipe adapted from *An Exotic Finish* by Pichet Ong (Morrow-Harper Collins, 2007)

PHOTO: Martin Jansche

Remarkable. I have also substituted flavorful dates for the traditional lotus seed or red bean fillings. In Chinese cooking, sesame seeds are never deeply browned—their white color symbolizes purity. Be sure to start with untoasted white sesame seeds to achieve a light golden color when the balls are done. Most fried desserts are best eaten right away, but these stay delicious and crisp even at room temperature. —*Pichet Ong*

SOY MILK JELLY WITH STRAWBERRY SAUCE

Mari Fujii • Fushiki-An • Kamakura, Japan

4 teaspoons agar-agar powder
3 1/3 cups soy milk
4 tablespoons maple syrup

Sauce
1/2 cup strawberries
2 tablespoons lemon juice
2 tablespoons maple syrup

To make the sauce, place the strawberries in a small saucepan. Mash and stir over low heat for 5-6 minutes. Remove from heat and leave to cool. Blend the strawberries, lemon juice, and maple syrup in a food processor. Combine the agar-agar and soy milk in a saucepan, and mix well. When the agar-agar is completely dissolved, mix in the maple syrup. Place over heat, bring to a boil then, remove from heat. When the soy milk has cooled, pour into cups or molds, and refrigerate until set. Serve the jellies in individual dishes, dressed with the sauce.

Serves 8

THIS RECIPE USES AGAR-AGAR, A FORM OF GELATIN DERIVED FROM SEAWEED, WHICH IS FULL OF HEALTHY FIBER. IT IS OFTEN USED IN ASIAN DESSERTS. —*MARII FUJI*

SOY MILK MOUSSE WITH BLUEBERRY SAUCE

Mari Fujii • Fushiki-An • Kamakura, Japan

2 tablespoons plain yogurt, unsweetened type
2 tablespoons lemon juice
6 tablespoons soy milk
1 block firm tofu
3/4 cup bananas, peeled

Sauce
1/2 cup dried blueberries
3/4 cup and 2 tablespoons soy milk
2 tablespoons lemon juice
2 tablespoons maple syrup

In a food processor, blend the yogurt, lemon juice, soy milk, tofu and bananas for 2-3 minutes, until thick and smooth. To make the sauce, combine the blueberries, soy milk, lemon juice and maple syrup in a saucepan, bring to a boil, then cook on low heat for about 30 minutes. Serve the mousse in individual dishes, topped with the sauce.

Serves 4

Blueberry sauce adds sweetness to this smooth, tasty dessert. —*Mari Fujii*

PHOTOS: Koji Iwamoto

VIETNAMESE COFFEE FORTUNE COOKIES

Pichet Ong • P*ONG • New York, NY

1/2 pound unsalted butter at room temperature
1 teaspoon salt
5 tablespoons condensed milk
1 3/4 ounces Vietnamese coffee powder
9 ounces all purpose flour
3/4 ounce milk powder
7 ounces confectioner's sugar
5 1/2 ounces egg whites

With the paddle attachment in an electric mixer, cream butter, condensed milk, salt and coffee powder just until combined, about 3 minutes. In the meantime, sift together confectioner's sugar, flour and milk powder. Add sifted dry ingredients to the butter mixture and mix to combine, scraping the bowl as necessary. With the mixer at low speed, slowly add in egg whites and mix until incorporated. Scrape the bottom of bowl again and mix well. Chill batter with plastic wrap covering directly on surface for at least 1 hour before use. Spread batter onto silicone baking liner using a stencil with 4 inch round circles. Bake in preheated 350° F oven until done with surface dry to the touch, about 5 minutes. Place fortune paper in middle of each circle, fold in half and then bring the 2 points together with the seam on the broad side. Lay into a ridged tuile pan to cool. It is imperative that the cookie is folded when hot otherwise the cookie will break.

Makes approximately 50 cookies

Recipe adapted from *An Exotic Finish* by Pichet Ong (Morrow-Harper Collins, 2007)

I HAD THE OPPORTUNITY TO OPEN JEAN GEORGES' CHINESE RESTAURANT, 66, WHERE I DEVELOPED HOMEMADE FORTUNE COOKIES TO SERVE TO GUESTS UPON RECEIVING THE CHECK. I HAD SO MUCH FUN WITH THEM THAT A VARIETY OF FLAVORS WERE DEVELOPED, INCLUDING GREEN TEA, TARO, SESAME, CHOCOLATE AND VIETNAMESE COFFEE. —*PICHET ONG*

WARM SPICED BANANAS *(KOLAK PISANG)*

Yono Purnomo • Yono's Restaurant • Albany, NY

4 ripe bananas, peeled, then split lengthwise, then in half to make quarters
4 scoops of vanilla ice cream
1 fresh orange
4 tablespoons coconut milk
3 ounces palm sugar or light brown sugar
4 tablespoons butter
2 pandan leaves, or 1 vanilla bean
1 cup orange juice
juice of 2 fresh limes
1 1/2 ounces banana liqueur
1 1/2 ounces orange liqueur

Heat pan on low heat. Grate the orange peel from the fresh orange into the pan. Add the butter and sugar and pandan leaf or vanilla bean. Cook until the sugar caramelizes. Remove pan at least 6 inches from burner, then flambé with the liqueur until the mixture is boiling. Then, add the orange juice, coconut milk and bananas. Continue cooking until liquid has been reduced by a third, has thickened and the bananas are fork tender. Place a scoop of ice cream an each plate, place four banana slices around each scoop then, spoon sauce over the top.

Serves 4

NOTE: Flambé with caution. Briefly touch the edge of the pan to the burner and then remove from burner again until the flame in the pan subsides.

PHOTO: Martin Jansche

MyPyramid.gov

ASIAN COCKTAILS

Medical studies concur that a moderate amount of alcohol consumption is beneficial to one's health.

Sake is the national beverage of Japan. It is made from fermented rice wine and has been around for 6800 years. Sake, like green tea, has the enzyme polyphenol, which is associated with the prevention of cancer and heart disease. It is also rich in amino acids. Unlike wine, sake does not have sulfites that cause asthma-like symptoms, which is a benefit for those allergic to sulfites.

Soju is an ancient Korean liquor distilled from sweet potatoes and grains, such as rice and barley. Technically a white spirit, soju is markedly less potent than other distilled spirits. At 20-24% alcohol by volume, soju contains roughly half of the alcohol content of vodka or gin.

We hope you like the wonderful ways our chefs have used sake, soju, beer and other beverages to create delicious Asian inspired cocktails for you to enjoy!

THE ASIAN COCKTAIL BAR

Glassware:

cordial
flute
heatproof mug
highball
margarita
martini
pint
pitcher
red wine
rocks
snifter
white wine

Bar Tools:

bar spoon
blender
channel knife
cirtrus juicer
cocktail shaker
corkscrew
double jiggler
muddler
strainer

Garnishes:

Asian pear
dragon fruit
guava
kiwi
kumquat
lemon grass
lychees
mango
pineapple spears
star fruit

ASIAN PEAR SOOTHER

Simpson Wong • Jefferson Grill • New York, NY*

1 ounce vodka
1 ounce pear brandy
1 ounce pear nectar
1/2 ounce Cointreau
dash of lime juice

Stir all ingredients together with ice and strain into a chilled martini glass. Garnish with a slice of Asian pear with the point side in the drink

Serves 1

*Please see page 260 for a complete list of restaurant locations.

THE ASIAN PEAR SHOULD BE PIE SLICED FROM STEM TO BASE INTO 10 TO 12 PIECES. THEN, SLICED PART WAY ON THE DIAGONAL FROM TOP OF BULB TOWARDS BASE SO THAT THE TOP OF THE PEAR WILL PLUNGE INTO THE DRINK. —*SIMPSON WONG*

BONSAI BERRY

Chris Johnson • Bao 111 •
New York, NY*

fresh blackberries
orange cubes
2 ounces sake
1 1/2 ounce Tequila
1/2 ounce fresh lime juice
splash of Casis

Take three black berries, five small pieces of orange and muddle in a mixing glass. Add sake and shake. Add Tequila and a squeeze of fresh lime. Shake with ice. Pour into a martini glass and garnish with a lemon twist.

Serves 1

*Please see page 260 for a complete list of restaurant locations.

BUDDHISM IN RIO *(GREEN TEA CAPARINA)*

Chris Johnson • Bao 111 •
New York, NY*

fresh mint, approximately 10 leaves
3 lime wedges
2 teaspoons of sugar
1 1/2 ounce Zen liquor
1 1/2 ounce Cacacha
splash of fresh lime juice

Take fresh mint and lime wedges and muddle with sugar in a mixing glass. Add Zen green tea liquor. Add Cacacha and fresh lime juice. Add ice and shake. Pour into glass with ice and garnish with a lime wheel.

Serves 1

CALAMANSI COLLINS

Simpson Wong • Jefferson Grill • New York, NY

2 ounces gin
1 ounce calamasi juice
3/4 ounce lemon juice
1/2 ounce lime juice
club soda

Stir all ingredients together with ice and strain into a tall Collins glass. Top off with club soda.

Serves 1

POMEGRANATE COLLINS

Simpson Wong • Jefferson Grill • New York, NY*

2 ounces vodka
1 ounce Cointreau
1/2 ounce pomegranate juice
1/2 ounce calamansi juice
1/4 ounce Yuzu juice
a few pomegranate seeds

Shake all ingredients together with ice and strain into a chilled martini glass. Garnish with a few pomegranate seeds.

Serves 1

*Please see page 260 for a complete list of restaurant locations.

Calamansi is a Southeast Asian citrus, similar to a small, very tart lime. These are available fresh in large Asian markets in the U.S. If unavailable, a suitable substitute would be to combine 2/3 fresh lime juice with 1/3 fresh tangerine juice and a few drops of lemon. —*Simpson Wong*

CITRINE

Litty Mathews & Melkon Khosrovian • Modern Spirits Vodka • Monrovia, CA

1 1/2 ounces Modern Spirits Candied Ginger Vodka
1 ounce lemon grass-infused simple syrup
3 ounces club soda
generous squeeze of lime
lemon grass for garnish

Serve over ice in a tall glass and garnish with lime and lemon grass.

Serves 1

GINGER COSMOPOLITAN

Bill Tocantins • Gingerita • Santa Monica, CA

1 1/2 ounces vodka
large splash of Gingerita
cranberry juice
lime wedge

Chill vodka and Gingerita in an ice shaker. Add cranberry juice until pink. Shake and strain into a martini glass. Garnish with lime.

Serves 1

GINGER LEMONADE

Bill Tocantins • Gingerita • Santa Monica, CA

one tall glass of iced lemonade
shot of Gingerita
lime wedge

Add one shot of Gingerita to the glass of lemonade. Shake or stir. Garnish with a lime wedge.

Serves 1

GINGER MARGARITA

Bill Tocantins • Gingerita • Santa Monica, CA

2 ounces Tequila
2 ounces Cuervo's Margarita Mix
2 ounces Gingerita
1 cup ice

Blend and garnish with lime.

Serves 1

I CREATED GINGERITA, A FRESH GINGER JUICE CONCOCTION, WHILE WORKING IN ASIAN AND INDIAN RESTAURANTS WHERE DRIED GINGER IS COMMONLY USED. THIS DERIVES FROM EARLY TIMES, WHEN IT TOOK MONTHS TO TRANSPORT GINGER BY SHIP FROM INDIA TO EUROPE. OTHER THAN IN TEA, GINGER HAS SELDOM BEEN USED IN ASIAN BEVERAGES—DISTILLED SPIRITS ARE ALMOST NON-EXISTENT. NOW, CHEFS AND HOME COOKS CAN GET FRESH GINGER FLAVOR IN DRINKS AND DISHES. —*BILL TOCANTINS*

GINGER PUNCH

Bill Tocantins • Gingerita • Santa Monica, CA

1 quart sparkling water or club soda
1 cup Gingerita
5 mint sprigs for garnish
ice

Fill a glass pitcher with ice. Add sparkling water or club soda. Add one cup of Gingerita. Finely chop 5 large sprigs of mint. Mix thoroughly. Fill glass with ice and pour.

Serves 6

GINGER STAR

Litty Mathews & Melkon Khosrovian • Modern Spirits Vodka • Monrovia, CA

1 1/2 ounces Modern Spirits Candied Ginger Vodka
3 ounces sweetened, cold chrysanthemum tea
star fruit, sliced thin

Combine ingredients. Decorate a short glass with thin slices of star fruit. Serve over ice.

Serves 1

GINGER TOM

Jamie Terrell • Global Brand Ambassador, V&S Plymouth Ltd. • London, England

1 3/4 ounces Plymouth Gin
3/4 ounce ginger syrup
3/4 ounce fresh lime juice
splash of sugar syrup
sparkling mineral water
1 sprig of mint
lime wedge

Build ingredients over ice into a Collins glass and top with sparkling water. Stir to chill. Garnish with a lime wedge and a mint sprig.

Serves 1

INDIAN SUMMER

Jamie Terrell • Global Brand Ambassador, V&S Plymouth Ltd. • London, England

1 1/4 ounces Plymouth Gin
1 bar spoon Rose Water
5 fresh raspberries
1 3/4 ounces cranberry juice
dash of gomme*
1 rose petal for garnish

Shake ingredients with ice and strain over crushed ice in a highball glass. Garnish with raspberries and a rose petal.

Serves 1

*A type of syrup used to sweeten cocktails (non-alcoholic).

INTI

Paul Tanguay • Beverage Director, Sushi Samba • New York, NY

1/3 of a kiwi, peeled
1/2 bar spoon of sugar
1/2 ounce Bacardi Light
1 ounce Bacardi Lemon
1/2 ounce Triple Sec
1 ounce lychee puree
1/2 ounce pineapple juice

Muddle kiwi with sugar. Add Bacardi, Triple Sec, lychee puree and pineapple juice. Serve in highball glass over ice.

Serves 1

PHOTO: Bill Durgin

JEFFERSON GRILL BLOODY MARY

Simpson Wong • Jefferson Grill • New York, NY*

6 ounces fresh tomato juice
1 1/2 ounces premium vodka
1 stalk lemon grass, lime wedge, cucumber wheel for garnish
Dash of each of the following to taste:
lemon juice, fresh grated horseradish, grated fresh ginger, wasabi powder, tabasco, worchester sauce, sea salt, freshly ground black pepper and celery salt

Toss all ingredients over ice and pour into a highball glass. Garnish with a stalk of lemon grass, lime wedge and cucumber wheel.

Serves 1

*Please see page 260 for a complete list of restaurant locations.

KUMQUAT MOJITO

Chris Johnson • Bao 111 •
New York, NY

4 kumquats
fresh mint, approximately 10 leaves
1 teaspoon sugar
2 ounces white rum
1/2 ounce fresh lime juice
splash mango juice

Muddle 3 kumquats and mint in a glass with a teaspoon of sugar. Add ice to a mixing glass. Add rum, fresh limejuice and mango juice. Shake well. Pour into a Collins glass. Top with soda water. Garnish with kumquat and mint.

Serves 1

The muddled fruit serves as an easy substitute to infusing your own sake. —*Chris Johnson*

MANDARIN DELIGHT

Sean Beck • Sommelier/Beverage
Director, Backstreet Café •
Houston, TX

1 3/4 ounces Mandarin vodka
1/2 ounce white cranberry juice
1/2 ounce tangerine juice
splash of lime juice
1 orange or tangerine slice
a few dried cranberries

Shake well over ice and serve in a martini glass straight up. Garnish with an orange or tangerine slice and drop a few dried cranberries into the glass.

Serves 1

MELANCIA

Paul Tanguay • Beverage Director, Sushi Samba • New York, NY

1 1/2 ounces vodka
1 ounce soju
7 pieces of watermelon
6 mint leaves
1 ounce lime juice
2 flat bar spoons of sugar

Muddle watermelon, mint and sugar. Add remaining ingredients. Shake. Serve in a wine glass.

Serves 1

PHOTO: This page, Bill Durgin

MOTHER-IN-LAW'S TONGUE

(THERE'S NOTHING SHARPER!)

Robert Gadsby, • Noe Restaurant, Omni Hotel • Los Angeles, CA

3 cardamom pods
1 cup half & half
1/2 cup sugar
zest of 1/2 orange
1 cup freshly squeezed orange juice, strained
1/4 cup crème fraîche
1/2 cup ice
2 shots (4 ounces) Mandarin vodka

In a small skillet over high heat, toast cardamom pods until they begin to color and are fragrant, about five minutes. Using a mortar and pestle or the back of a knife and crack open the pods and roughly chop or bruise them. Place the cardamom, half & half, sugar and zest in a small saucepan and bring to a simmer over medium-high heat, stirring until the sugar dissolves. Strain the mixture into a bowl and let cool to room temperature. Place the milk mixture, orange juice, crème fraîche and vodka, along with ice, into a blender and blend until smooth. Serve immediately.

Serves 2

PEAR ANISE COOLER

Khai Duong • Ana Mandara • San Francisco, CA

1 star anise
1/4 Asian pear
1 bar spoon honey
1 1/2 ounces pear liquor
5 ounces light beer
3 thin slices Asian pear for garnish

In a shaker, add star anise, Asian pear and honey. Muddle completely. Fill with ice and add pear liquor. Shake and strain into a tall glass. Fill glass halfway with ice. Top with a light beer and garnish with a slice of Asian pear.

Serves 1

GROWING UP IN VIETNAM, WE WOULD MIX FRUIT AND ICE COLD BEER FOR A REFRESHING DRINK DURING THE HOT STEAMY SUMMERS. —*KHAI DUONG*

PURE PASSION

Chris Johnson • Bao 111 • New York, NY

2 to 3 passion fruits
1 ounce fresh ripe mango
fresh orange juice
fresh limes
2 ounces vodka
1 orange slice for garnish

Take whole passion fruits and cut in half. Through a strainer, remove seeds and set aside juice. Taste the juice. Balance with a little bit of fresh orange juice and fresh lime. Orange juice will smooth out the tartness and the lime will brighten the flavors. The total amount of juice should yield about 2 ounces. Muddle chunks of mango with sugar. Place juice in a shaker and add vodka. Shake well and pour into a martini glass. Garnish with an orange slice.

Serves 1

WHEN USING FRESH PASSION FRUIT, IT IS ALWAYS BETTER TO CREATE A BASE FIRST. EACH ONE HAS A DIFFERENT SWEETNESS AND TARTNESS THAT NEEDS TO BE ADJUSTED IN ORDER TO ACHIEVE THE PERFECT COCKTAIL. —*CHRIS JOHNSON*

SAKE JULEP

Chris Johnson • Bao 111 • New York, NY

1 ripe peach
fresh mint, approximately 10 leaves
1/2 teaspoon of sugar
1 1/2 ounces of sake
1 ounce vodka
1 1/2 ounces fresh lime juice mix
splash of tonic
1 lime wheel for garnish

Place mint in the bottom of the glass. Add 1/2 teaspoon of sugar and muddle the mint. Take half of the ripe peach and cut into small pieces. Add the peaches and muddle again. Pour the sake over this mixture. Shake. Add vodka and fresh lime juice. Shake with ice. Pour over ice in a Collins glass. Top with tonic and garnish with a lime wheel and/or a peach slice.

Serves 1

SHO-ZEN

Paul Tanguay • Beverage Director, Sushi Samba • New York, NY

2 ounces soju
1 ounce Zen green tea liqueur
1/2 ounce pineapple juice
1/2 ounce lime juice
2 shiso leaves
1 flat bar spoon of sugar
1 slice star fruit for garnish

Muddle sugar and shiso. Add remaining ingredients. Shake. Serve in a rock glass with star fruit garnish

Serves 1

PHOTO: Left, ; Jennifer Pottheiser;

SPICY GINGER CHU-HI

Paul Tanguay • Beverage Director, Sushi Samba • New York, NY

2 pinches of fresh ginger
2 level bar spoons of sugar
2 ounces soju
1/2 ounce Bacardi Razz
1 ounce guava
1/2 ounce lime juice

Muddle together the soju, Bacardi Razz, guava and lime juice. Add the pinches of ginger and sugar. Shake and strain. Serve in a martini glass.

Serves 1

SUMMERTIME

Chris Johnson • Bao 111 • New York, NY

fresh strawberries and kiwi
sugar
2 ounces sake
splash of Triple Sec
1 ounce champagne

Muddle one slice of kiwi and one strawberry with sugar. Add sake and shake. Add Triple Sec and ice. Shake again. Pour with ice into a glass, top with champagne. Garnish with kiwi and strawberries.

Serves 1

THAI LADY

Jamie Terrell • Global Brand Ambassador, V&S Plymouth Ltd. • London, England

1 1/2 parts Plymouth Gin
1/2 part Cointreau
1 part fresh lemon juice
1/2 part lemon grass syrup

Lemon Grass Syrup
1/2 liter of simple syrup
4 lemon grass stalks, chopped

Mix and shake all ingredients and serve. ***Lemon Grass Syrup:*** Blend simple syrup with lemon grass stalks in a food processor. Sieve into container. Can store tightly sealed in the refrigerator for up to one month.

Serves 1

YUZU COSMOPOLITAN

Simpson Wong • Jefferson Grill • New York, NY*

2 ounces vodka
1 ounce Cointreau
1 ounce plum wine
1/2 ounce Yuzu*
1 ounce lime juice
1 lime wheel for garnish

Shake all ingredients together with ice. Strain into a chilled martini glass and garnish with a fresh lime wheel.

Serves 1

*Yuzu is a Japanese citrus fruit similar to a bitter lime. Good quality bottled yuzu juice is available at many Asian supermarkets.

*Please see page 260 for a complete list of restaurant locations.

PHOTOS: Far left, Bill Durgin;

CELEBRITY CHEFS' RESTAURANTS

**Please check the website www.newasiancuisine.com for updated information*

ARIZONA

Roy's Desert Ridge
Roy Yamaguchi
5350 East Marriott Drive
Phoenix, AZ 85054
(480) 419-7697
www.roysrestaurants.com

Roy's Scottsdale
Roy Yamaguchi
7001 North Scottsdale Road
Scottsdale, AZ 85253
(480) 905-1155
www.roysrestaurants.com

CALIFORNIA

Ahi Sushi
Jimmy Wu
12915 Ventura Boulevard
Studio City, CA 91604
(818) 981-0277
www.ahisushi.com

Amuse Café
Brooke Williamson & Nick Roberts
796 Main Street
Venice, CA 90291
(310) 450-1956
www.amusecafe.com

Ana Mandara
Khai Duong
891 Beach Street
San Francisco, CA 94109
(415) 771-6800
www.anamandara.com

Asian Pearl
Michael Au & Tony Su
3288 Pierce Street
#A-118
Richmond, CA 94084
(510) 559-7888

Bacar
Arnold Eric Wong
448 Brennan Street
San Francisco, CA 94107
(415) 904-4100
www.bacarsf.com

Beechwood
Brooke Williamson & Nick Roberts
822 Washington Boulevard
Venice, CA 90292
(310) 448-8884
www.beechwoodrestaurant.com

Blowfish Sushi To Die For
Ritsuo Tsuchida
2170 Bryant Street
San Francisco, CA 94110
(415) 285-3848
www.blowfishsushi.com

Blowfish Sushi To Die For
Ritsuo Tsuchida
355 Santana Row,
Suite 1010
San Jose, CA 95128
(408) 345-3848
www.blowfishsushi.com

Blowfish Sushi To Die For
Ritsuo Tsuchida
9229 Sunset Boulevard
West Hollywood, CA 90069
(310) 887-3848
www.blowfishsushi.com

Chef Chu's
Larry Chu
1067 North San Antonio Road
Los Altos, CA 94022
(650) 948-2696
www.chefchu.com

Chinois
Wolfgang Puck
2709 Main Street
Santa Monica, CA 90405
(310) 392-9025
www.wolfgangpuck.com

Cinch
Chris Behre
1519 Wilshire Boulevard
Santa Monica, CA 90403
(310) 395-4139
www.cinchrestaurant.com

Din Tai Fung Dumpling House
Frank Yang
1108 South Baldwin Avenue
Arcadia, CA 91007
(626) 574-7068

El Barrio
*Luis Aguilar Jr.**
Los Angeles, CA

EOS
Arnold Eric Wong
901 Cole Street
San Francisco, CA 94117
(415) 566-3036
www.eossf.com

Gaylord India Restaurant
Salim Mohmed & Santok Singh
1706 El Camino Real
Menlo Park, CA 94027
(650) 326-8761
www.gaylords.com

Gaylord India Restaurant
Salim Mohmed & Santok Singh
1501 14th Street
Sacramento, CA 95814
(916) 441-6700
www.gaylords.com

Gaylord India Restaurant
Salim Mohmed & Santok Singh
201 Bridgeway
Sausalito, CA 94965
(415) 339-0172
www.gaylords.com

Hamasuku
Toshi Kihara
11043 Santa Monica Boulevard
Los Angeles, CA 90025
(310) 479-7636
www.hamasakula.com

Jer-ne Restaurant and Bar at The Ritz-Carlton
Troy N. Thompson
4375 Admiralty Way
Marina del Rey, CA 90292
(310) 574-4333
www.troynthompson.com

Maurya
J.K. Paul
151 South Doheny Drive
Beverly Hills, CA 90211
(310) 786-7858
www.mauryabeverlyhills.com

Michelia
Kimmy Tang
8738 West Third Street
Los Angeles, CA 90048
(310) 276-8288
www.micheliabistro.com

New Canton Restaurant
Michael Au & Tony Su
2523 Broadway
Sacramento, CA 95818
(916) 739-8888

Nobu Malibu
Nobu Matsuhisa
3835 Cross Creek Road
#18A
Malibu, CA 90265
(310) 317-9140
www.noburestaurants.com

Noe Restaurant at Omni Hotel
Robert Gadsby
251 South Olive Street,
3rd Floor
Los Angeles, CA 90012
(213) 617-3300
www.omnihotels.com

Norman's
Norman Van Aken
8570 Sunset Boulevard
West Hollywood, CA 90069
(310) 657-2400
www.normans.com

Postrio
Wolfgang Puck
545 Post Street
San Francisco, CA 94102
(415) 776-7825
www.wolfgangpuck.com

Restaurant Budo
James McDevitt
1650 Soscol Avenue
Napa, CA 94559
(707) 224-2330
www.restaurantbudo.com

Roy's LaJolla
Roy Yamaguchi
8670 Genesee Avenue
San Diego, CA 92122
(858) 455-1616
www.roysrestaurants.com

Roy's Los Angeles
Roy Yamaguchi
800 South Figueroa Street
Los Angeles, CA 90017
(213) 488-4994
www.roysrestaurants.com

Roy's Newport Beach
Roy Yamaguchi
453 Newport Center Drive
Newport Beach, CA 92660
(949) 640-7697
www.roysrestaurants.com

Roy's Pebble Beach at The Inn at Spanish Bay
Roy Yamaguchi
2700 Seventeen Mile Drive
Pebble Beach, CA 93953
(831) 647-7500
www.roysrestaurants.com

Roy's Rancho Mirage
Roy Yamaguchi
71959 Highway 111
Rancho Mirage, CA 92270
(760) 340-9044
www.roysrestaurants.com

Roy's San Francisco
Roy Yamaguchi
575 Mission Street
San Francisco, CA 94109
(415) 777-0277
www.roysrestaurants.com

Roy's Woodland Hills
Roy Yamaguchi
6363 Topanga Canyon Boulevard
Woodland Hills, CA 91367
(818) 888-4801
www.roysrestaurants.com

Silks at The Mandarin Oriental Hotel
Toni Robertson
222 Sansome Street, 2nd Floor
San Francisco, CA 94104
(415) 276-9600
www.mandarinoriental.com

Sino Restaurant & Lounge
Chris Yeo
377 Santana Row, Suite 1000
San Jose, CA 95128
(408) 247-8880
www.sinorestaurant.com

Sona
David Myers & Michelle Myers
401 North La Cienega Boulevard
Los Angeles, CA 90048
(310) 659-7708
www.sonarestaurant.com

Spago
Wolfgang Puck
176 North Canon Drive
Beverly Hills, CA 90210
(310) 385-0880
www.wolfgangpuck.com

Spago
Wolfgang Puck
265 Lytton Avenue
Palo Alto, CA 94301
(650) 833-1000
www.wolfgangpuck.com

Straits Café
Chris Yeo
3300 Geary Boulevard
San Francisco, CA 94118
(415) 668-1783
www.straitsrestaurants.com

Straits Restaurant
Chris Yeo
333 Santana Row, #1100
San Jose, CA 95128
(408) 246-6320
www.straitsrestaurants.com

Straits Restaurant
Chris Yeo
3295 El Camino
Palo Alto, CA 94306
(650) 494-7168
www.straitsrestaurants.com

Straits Restaurant
Chris Yeo
1100 Burlingame Avenue
Burlingame, CA 94010
(650) 373-7883
www.straitsrestaurants.com

Thep Phanom
Pathama Parikanont
400 Waller Street
San Francisco, CA 94117
(415) 431-2526
www.thepphanom.com

Tommy Tang's
Tommy Tang
7313 Melrose Avenue
Los Angeles, CA 90046
(323) 937-5733
www.tommytangs.com

Vert
Wolfgang Puck
6801 Hollywood Boulevard, 4th Floor
Hollywood, CA 90028
(323) 491-1300
www.wolfgangpuck.com

X'otik Kitchen
Stoney Chen
6121 Washington Boulevard
Culver City, CA 90232
(310) 280-3961
www.xotikkitchen.com

Yan Can
Martin Yan
3927 Rivermark Plaza
Santa Clara, CA 95054
(408) 748-3355
www.yancancook.com

Yan Can
Martin Yan
35 Crescent Drive
Pleasant Hill, CA 94523
(925) 827-4133
www.yancancook.com

Yan Can
Martin Yan
179 Ranch Drive
Milpitas, CA 95035
(408) 945-1733
www.yancancook.com

Yi Cuisine
Rodelio Aglibot
7910 West 3rd Street
Los Angeles, CA 90048
(323) 658-8028
www.yicuisine.com

Zip Fusion Sushi
Jason Ha & Sean Ahn
744 East 3rd Street
Los Angeles, CA 90013
(213) 680-3770
www.zipfusion.com

Zip Fusion Sushi
Jason Ha & Sean Ahn
11301 West Olympic Boulevard, Suite 116
Los Angeles, CA 90064
(310) 575-3636
www.zipfusion.com

COLORADO

Olives
Todd English
315 East Dean Street
Aspen, CO 81611
(970) 920-3300
www.toddenglish.com

CONNECTICUT

Tuscany
Todd English
1 Mohegan Sun Boulevard
Uncasville, CT 06382
(860) 862-3238
www.toddenglish.com

FLORIDA

Blue Zoo, Walt Disney World at Dolphin Hotel
Todd English
1500 Epcot Resorts Boulevard
Lake Buena Vista, FL 32830
(407) 934-1111
www.toddenglish.com

Nobu Miami Beach
Nobu Matsuhisa
1901 Collins Avenue
Miami Beach, Fl 33139
(305) 695-3232
www.noburestaurants.com

Norman's
Norman Van Aken
21 Almeria Avenue
Coral Gables, Fl 33134
(305) 446-6767
www.normans.com

Norman's
Norman Van Aken
4012 Central Florida Parkway
Orlando, Fl 32837
(407) 393-4333
www.normans.com

Renaissance Orlando Resort at Marriott
Hiroshi Noguchi
6677 Sea Harbor Drive
Orlando, Fl 32821
(407) 351-5555
www.marriott.com

Roy's Bonita Springs
Roy Yamaguchi
26831 South Bay Drive, Suite 100, Bonita Bay Promenade
Bonita Springs, FL 34134
(239) 498-7697
www.roysrestaurants.com

Roy's Jacksonville Beach
Roy Yamaguchi
2400-101 South 3rd Street
Jacksonville, FL 32250
(904) 241-7697
www.roysrestaurants.com

Roy's Orlando
Roy Yamaguchi
7760 West Sand Lake Road
Orlando, FL 32819
(407) 352-4844
www.roysrestaurants.com

Roy's Tampa
Roy Yamaguchi
4342 West Boy Scout Boulevard
Tampa, FL 33607
(813) 873-7697
www.roysrestaurants.com

Sushi Samba Dromo
Paul Tanguay & Michael Cressotti
600 Lincoln Road
Miami Beach, FL 33139
(305) 673-5337
www.sushisamba.com

Wish at The Hotel
Michael Bloise
801 Collins Avenue
Miami Beach, FL 33139
(305) 531-2222
www.wishrestaurant.com

GEORGIA

Pastel on Central
Philippe Chin
2120 Central Avenue
Augusta, GA 30904
(706) 731-9094
www.pasteloncentral.com

Roy's Atlanta
Roy Yamaguchi
3475 Piedmont Road North East
Atlanta, GA 30305
(404) 231-3232
www.roysrestaurants.com

HAWAII

Roy's Honolulu
Roy Yamaguchi
6600 Kalanianaole Highway
Honolulu, HI 96825
(808) 396-7697
www.roysrestaurants.com

Roy's Kahana Bar & Grill
Roy Yamaguchi
4405 Honoapiilani Highway
Lahaina, HI 96761
(808) 669-6999
www.roysrestaurants.com

Roy's Kihei
Roy Yamaguchi
303 Piikea Avenue, Building 1
Kihei, HI 96753
(808) 891-1120
www.roysrestaurants.com

Roy's Ko' Olina
Roy Yamaguchi
92-1220 Aliinui Drive
Kapolei, HI 96707
(808) 676-7697
www.roysrestaurants.com

Roy's Poipu Bar & Grill
Roy Yamaguchi
2360 Kiahuna Plantation Drive
Koloa, HI 96756
(808) 742-5000
www.roysrestaurants.com

Roy's Waikoloa Bar & Grill
Roy Yamaguchi
250 Waikoloa Beach Drive
Waikoloa, HI 96738
(808) 886-4321
www.roysrestaurants.com

Spago at The Four Seasons Resort Maui
Wolfgang Puck
3900 Wailea Alanui Drive
Wailea Alanui, HI 96753
(808) 879-2999
www.wolfgangpuck.com

ILLINOIS

Roy's Chicago
Roy Yamaguchi
720 North State Street
Chicago, IL 60610
(312) 787-7599
www.roysrestaurants.com

Sushi Samba Rio
Paul Tanguay & Michael Cressotti
504 North Wells
Chicago, IL 60610
(312) 595-2300
www.sushisamba.com

Vong Thai Kitchen
Jean-Georges Vongerichten
6 West Hubbard Street
Chicago, IL 60610
(312) 644-8664
www.jean-georges.com

KENTUCKY

Asiatique
Peng S. Looi
1767 Bardstown Road
Louisville, KY 40205
(502) 451-2749
www.asiatique.bigstep.com

August Moon Chinese Bistro
Peng S. Looi
2269 Lexington Road
Louisville, KY 40206
(502) 456-6569
www.augustmoonbistro.com

MASSACHUSETTS

Blue Ginger
Ming Tsai
583 Washington Street
Wellesley, MA 02482
(781) 283-5790
www.ming.com/blueginger/

Bonfire at The Boston Park Plaza Hotel
Todd English
50 Park Plaza
Boston, MA 02116
(617) 262-3473
www.toddenglish.com

Elephant Walk
Longteine & Nadsa de Monteiro
900 Beacon Street
Boston, MA 02215
(617) 247-1500
www.elephantwalk.com

Elephant Walk
Longteine & Nadsa de Monteiro
2067 Massachusetts Avenue
Cambridge, MA 02140
(617) 492-6900
www.elephantwalk.com

Figs
Todd English
42 Charles Street
Boston, MA 02114
(617) 742-3447
www.toddenglish.com

Figs
Todd English
67 Main Street
Charlestown, MA 02129
(617) 242-2229
www.toddenglish.com

Figs
Todd English
92 Central Street
Wellesley, MA 02181
(781) 237-5788
www.toddenglish.com

Kingfish Hall
Todd English
188 Faneuil Hall Marketplace,
SouthMarket Building
Boston, MA 02109
(617) 523-8862
www.toddenglish.com

Olives
Todd English
10 City Square
Charlestown, MA 02129
(617) 242-1999
www.toddenglish.com

MARYLAND

Roy's Baltimore
Roy Yamaguchi
720 B Aliceanna Street
Baltimore, MD 21202
(410) 659-0099
www.roysrestaurants.com

MINNESOTA

20-21
Wolfgang Puck
Walker Art Center,
1750 Hennepin Avenue
Minneapolis, MN 55403
(612) 253-3410
www.wolfgangpuck.com

NEVADA

Bar & Grill at MGM Grand
Wolfgang Puck
3799 Las Vegas Boulevard South
Las Vegas, NV 89119
(702) 891-3000
www.wolfgangpuck.com

Chinois at The Forum Shops at Caesars
Wolfgang Puck
3500 Las Vegas Boulevard South, Suite L-3
Las Vegas, NV 89109
(702) 737-9700
www.wolfgangpuck.com

Nobu Las Vegas
Nobu Matsuhisa
4455 Paradise Road
Las Vegas, NV 89109
(702) 693-5090
www.noburestaurants.com

Okada at Wynn Las Vegas
Takashi Yagihashi
3131 Las Vegas Boulevard South
Las Vegas, NV 89109
(702) 770-7000
www.wynnlasvegas.com

Olives at Bellagio Hotel
Todd English
3600 Las Vegas Boulevard South
Las Vegas, NV 89109
(702) 693-8181
www.toddenglish.com

Postrio
Wolfgang Puck
3377 Las Vegas Boulevard
Las Vegas, NV 89109
(702) 796-1110
www.wolfgangpuck.com

Prime Steakhouse at Bellagio Hotel
Jean-Georges Vongerichten
3600 Las Vegas Boulevard South
Las Vegas, NV 89109
(702) 693-7223
www.jean-georges.com

Red 8 at Wynn Las Vegas
Hisham Johari
3131 Las Vegas Boulevard South
Las Vegas, NV 89109
(702) 770-7000
www.wynnlasvegas.com

Roy's Las Vegas
Roy Yamaguchi
620 East Flamingo Road
Las Vegas, NV 89119
(702) 691-2053
www.roysrestaurants.com

Roy's Summerlin
Roy Yamaguchi
8701 West Charleston Boulevard
Las Vegas, NV 89117
(702) 838-3620
www.roysrestaurants.com

Spago at The Forum Shops At Caesars
Wolfgang Puck
3500 Las Vegas Boulevard, South
Las Vegas, NV 89109
(702) 369-0360
www.wolfgangpuck.com

Trattoria Del Lupo at Mandalay Bay Resort & Casino
Wolfgang Puck
3950 Las Vegas Boulevard South
Las Vegas, NV 89119
(702) 740-5522
www.wolfgangpuck.com

Wing Lei at Wynn Las Vegas
Richard Chen
3131 Las Vegas Boulevard South
Las Vegas, NV 89109
(702) 770-7000
www.wynnlasvegas.com

NEW YORK

66
Jean-Georges Vongerichten
241 Church Street
New York, NY 10013
(212) 925-0202
www.jean-georges.com

Annisa
Anita Lo
13 Barrow Street
New York, NY 10014
(212) 741-6699
www.annisarestaurant.com

Asiate at The Mandarin Oriental
Noriyuki Sugie
80 Columbus Circle at 60th Street
New York, NY 10023
(212) 805-8880
www.mandarinoriental.com

Bao 111
Chris Johnson & Michael Huynh
111 Avenue C
New York, NY 10009
(212) 254 -7773
www.bao111.com

Bao Noodles
Chris Johnson & Michael Huynh
391 2nd Avenue
New York, NY 10010
(212) 725-7770
www.baonoodles.com

Café Asean
Simpson Wong
117 West 10th Street
New York, NY 10011
(212) 633-0348

Devi
Hemant Mathur, Surbhi Sahni, Suvir Saran
8 East 18th Street
New York, NY 10003
(212) 691-1300
www.deviny c.com

English Italian
Todd English
622 Third Avenue
New York, NY 10017
(212) 404-1700
www.toddenglish.com

Figs LaGuardia
Todd English
LaGuardia Airport, Central Terminal Building
Flushing, NY 11371
(718) 446-7600
www.toddenglish.com

Geisha
Kazuo Yoshida
33 East 61st Street
New York, NY 10021
(212) 813-1112
www.geisharestaurant.com

Hurapan Kitchen
Taweewat Hurapan
235 East 4th Street
New York, NY 10009
(646) 313-1987

Jean Georges at Trump International Hotel and Tower
Jean-Georges Vongerichten
1 Central Park West
New York, NY 10023
(212) 299-3900
www.jean-georges.com

Jefferson Grill
Simpson Wong
121 West 10th Street
New York, NY 10011
(212) 255-3333

JoJo
Jean-Georges Vongerichten
160 East 64th Street
New York, NY 10021
(212) 223-5656
www.jean-georges.com

Kai
Yorinobu Yamasaki
822 Madison Avenue
New York, NY 10021
(212) 988-7277
www.itoen.com/kai/index.cfm

Kittichai
Ian Chalermkittichai
60 Thompson Street
New York, NY 10014
(212) 219-2000
www.kittichairestaurant.com

Kuma Inn
King Phojanakong
113 Ludlow Street, 2nd Floor
New York, NY 10002
(212) 353-8866
www.kumainn.com

Land Thai Kitchen
David Bank
450 Amsterdam Avenue
New York, NY 10024
(212) 501-8121
www.landthaikitchen.com

Lassi
Heather Carlucci-Rodriguez
28 Greenwich Avenue
New York, NY 10011
(212) 675-2688

Le Bernardin
Michael Laiskonis
155 West 51st Street, The Equitable Building
New York, NY 10019
(212) 554-1515
www.le-bernardin.com

Les Halles
Anthony Bourdain
411 Park Avenue South
New York, NY 10016
(212) 679-4111
www.leshalles.net

Mercer Kitchen
Jean-Georges Vongerichten
99 Prince Street
New York, NY 10012
(212) 966-5454
www.jean-georges.com

Momofuku Noodle Bar
David Chang
163 First Avenue
New York, NY 10003
(212) 475-7899

Morimoto
Masaharu Morimoto
88 10th Avenue
New York, NY 10011
(212) 989-8883
www.chefmorimoto.com

Nobu Fifty Seven
Nobu Matsuhisa
40 West 57th Street
New York, NY 10019
(212) 757-3000
www.noburestaurants.com

Nobu New York
Nobu Matsuhisa
105 Hudson Street
New York, NY 10013
(212) 219-0500
www.noburestaurants.com

Nobu Next Door
Nobu Matsuhisa, Shin Tsujimura
105 Hudson Street
New York, NY 10013
(212) 334-4445
www.noburestaurants.com

Olives
Todd English
201 Park Avenue South
New York, NY 10003
(212) 353-8345
www.toddenglish.com

Partistry
Jehangir Mehta
7 East 35th Street, Suite 6E
New York, NY 10016
(800) 939-2990
www.partistry.com

Peacock Alley at The Waldorf=Astoria Hotel
Cedric Tovar
301 Park Avenue
New York, NY 10022
(212) 355-3000
www.hilton.com

P*Ong
Pichet Ong*
New York, NY

Pulse
Jake Klein
45 Rockefeller Plaza
New York, NY 10111
(212) 218-8600
www.thesportsclubla.com

Roy's New York at Marriott Financial Center Hotel
Roy Yamaguchi
130 Washington Street
New York, NY 10006
(212) 266-6262
www.roysrestaurants.com

Spice Market
Jean-Georges Vongerichten
403 West 13th Street
New York, NY 10014
(212) 675-2322
www.jean-georges.com

Sushi Samba droMo
Paul Tanguay & Michael Cressotti
245 Park Avenue South
New York, NY 10003
(212) 475-9377
www.sushisamba.com

Sushi Samba droMo
Paul Tanguay & Michael Cressotti
87 7th Avenue South
New York, NY 10014
(212) 691-7885
www.sushisamba.com

V Steakhouse
Jean-Georges Vongerichten
10 Columbus Circle, 4th Floor
New York, NY 10019
(212) 823-9500
www.jean-georges.com

Vong
Jean-Georges Vongerichten
200 East 54th Street
New York, NY 10022
(212) 486-9592
www.jean-georges.com

Yono's Restaurant
Yono Purnomo
25 Chapel Street
Albany, NY 12210
(518) 436-7747
www.yonosrestaurant.com

Zocalo
Julian Medina
Grand Central Terminal
New York, NY 10017
(212) 687-5666
www.zocalo.us

Zocalo
Julian Medina
174 East 82nd Street
New York, NY 10028
(212) 717-7772
www.zocalo.us

PENNSYLVANIA

Morimoto
Masaharu Morimoto
723 Chestnut Street
Philadelphia, PA 19106
(215) 413-9070
www.chefmorimoto.com

Roy's Philadelphia
Roy Yamaguchi
124-34 South 15th Street
Philadelphia, PA 19102
(215) 988-1814
www.roysrestaurants.com

Susanna Foo Chinese Cuisine
Susanna Foo
1512 Walnut Street
Philadelphia, PA 19103
(215) 545-2666
www.susannafoo.com

SOUTH CAROLINA

CuiZine
Philippe Chin
100 Laurens Street
Aiken, SC 29801
(803) 664-1234
www.cuizinerestaurant.com

TEXAS

Bistro 88
Jeff Liu
2712 Bee Caves Road
Austin, TX 78746
(512) 328-8888
www.bistro88.com

Houston Backstreet Café
Sean Beck
1103 South Shepherd Drive
Houston, TX 77019
(713) 521-2239

Nobu Dallas
Nobu Matsuhisa
400 Crescent Court
Dallas, TX 75201
(214) 252-7000
www.noburestaurants.com

Roy's Austin
Roy Yamaguchi
340 East 2nd Street
Austin, TX 78701
(512) 391-1500
www.roysrestaurants.com

Roy's Plano
Roy Yamaguchi
2840 Dallas Parkway
Plano, TX 75093
(972) 473-6263
www.roysrestaurants.com

WASHINGTON

Fish Club at Seattle Marriott Waterfront
Todd English
2100 Alaskan Way
Seattle, WA 98121
(206) 256-1040
www.fishclubseattle.com

Wild Ginger
Nathan Uy
1401 Third Avenue
Seattle, WA 98101
(206) 623-4450
www.wildginger.net

WASHINGTON DC

IndeBleu
Vikram Garg
707 G Street
Washington, DC 20001
(202) 333-2538
www.bleu.com/indebleu

Olives at World Center Building
Todd English
1600 K Street
Washington, DC 20006
(202) 452-1866
www.toddenglish.com

TenPenh
Cliff Wharton
1001 Pennsylvania Avenue
Washington, DC 20004
(202) 393-4500
www.tenpenh.com

Zengo
Alan Yu
781 7th Street
North West
Washington, DC 20001
(202) 393-2929

INTERNATIONAL LOCATIONS

AUSTRALIA

Grange Restaurant at Hilton Adelaide
Cheong Liew
233 Victoria Square
Adelaide, 5000
Australia
(+61) 8-82172000
www.hilton.com

CANADA

Lee Restaurant
Susur Lee
603 King Street West
Toronto, ON, M5V 1M5
Canada
(416) 504-7867
www.susur.com

Susur Restaurant
Susur Lee
601 King Street West
Toronto, ON, M5V 1M5
Canada
(416) 603-2205
www.susur.com

CHINA

Din Tai Fung
Frank Yang
Site 8, Whampoa Garden, Hunghom
Kowloon, Hong Kong
China
(+852) 2330-4886

Din Tai Fung
Frank Yang
19 Shui Cheng Road
Shanghai
China
(+86) 21- 6208-2488

Din Tai Fung
Frank Yang
168 Dong Bei Street,
Ping Jiang Qu
Suzhou, Jiangsu
China
(+86) 512-6753-1760

JG, Three on the Bund
Jean-Georges Vongerichten
No.3 The Bund, 4th Floor
3 Zhong Shan Dong Yi Road, Shanghai
China
(+86) 21-6321-7733
www.jean-georges.com

T'ang Court at Langham Hotel Hong Kong
Wai-Keung Kwong
8 Peking Road,
Tsimshatsui
Kowloon, Hong Kong
China
(+852) 2375-1133
www.langhamhotels.com

Vong at The Mandarin Oriental Hotel
Jean-Georges Vongerichten
5 Connaught Road
Central
Hong Kong
China
(+852) 2522-0111
www.jean-georges.com

FRANCE

Market
Jean-Georges Vongerichten
15 Avenue Matignon
75008 Paris
France
(+33) 1-56-43-40-90
www.jean-georges.com

GERMANY

Cocoon Club
Mario Lohninger
Carl-benz-strasse 21
60386 Frankfurt am Main
Germany
(+49) 69-900 200
www.cocoonclub.net

GUAM

Roy's Restaurant at Hilton Guam Resort & Spa
Roy Yamaguchi
202 Hilton Road
Tumon Bay
Guam 96913
(+671) 646-1835
www.roysrestaurants.com

INDIA

Yellow Chilli
Sanjeev Kapoor
J-56, Sector 18, Noida
Noida, Uttar Pradesh,
India
(+91) 120-2517543
www.sanjeevkapoor.com

IRELAND

Cafe Paul Rankin
Paul Rankin
Dundrum Town Centre
Dublin
Ireland
(+353) 1-2963105
www.rankingroup.co.uk

ITALY

Nobu Milan
Nobu Matsuhisa
Alia SRL, Via Manzoni 31
Milano, 20121
Italy
(+39) 2-723-18465
www.noburestaurants.com

JAPAN

Din Tai Fung at J-railway Nagoya Station, Takashimaya Department Store
Frank Yang
B-2F, 1-1-4 Mei-eki
Nakamura-Ku,
Nagoya City
Japan
(+81) 52-566-8196

Din Tai Fung at Karetta
Frank Yang
Shiodome Br. B-2F, 1-8-2
Higashi-Shinbashi,
Minato-Ku, Tokyo
Japan
(+81) 3-5537-2081

Din Tai Fung at Takashimaya Department Store
Frank Yang
Shinjiku Br. 10F, 5-24-2
Sendagaya,
Shibuya-Ku, Tokyo
Japan
(+81) 3-5361-1381

Din Tai Fung at Takashimaya Department Store
Frank Yang
Yokoyama Br. 6F, 1-6-31
Minami-saiwai
Nishi-Ku, Yokohama
Japan
(+81) 45-321-0036

Din Tai Fung at Takashimaya Department Store
Frank Yang
Kyoto Br. 3F, Nishiiru-Shinmachi, Kawaramachi
Shijo-Dori
Shimogyo-Ku, Kyoto City
Japan
(+81) 75-252-7992

Din Tai Fung at Tamagawa Takashimaya Shopping Center
Frank Yang
Minami-Kan 9F, 3-17-1
Tamagawa
Setagaya-Ku, Tokyo
Japan
(+81) 3-5797-3273

Din Tai Fung at Tsuruya Department Store
Frank Yang
Tsuruya Hyakaten 7F,
6-1 Tedori-Honmachi
Kumamoto City
Japan
(+81) 96-211-0667

Fushiki-An
Mari Fujii
3-12-25, Inamura-gasaki
Kamakura, Kanagawa
Japan
(+81) 467- 243462
http://fmari28.ld.infoseek.co.jp/fushikian.htm

Hinode
Osamu Miyoshi
1-8-5, Fujimi-cho
Sakaide City
Japan
(+81) 8-7746-3882
www.hinode.net

Mandarin Oriental, Tokyo
Hide Yamamoto
2-1-1 Nihonbashi
Muromachi, Chuo-ku
Tokyo 103-8328
Japan
(+81) 3-3270-8800
www.mandarinoriental.com

Nobu Tokyo
Nobu Matsuhisa
6-10-17 Minami
Aoyama, Minato-ku,
Tokyo 107-0062
Japan
(+81) 3-5467-0022
www.noburestaurants.com

Olives
Todd English
5F West Walk, Roppongi Hills
Minato-Ku, Tokyo,
1060032
Japan
(+81) 3-5413-9571
www.toddenglish.com

Roy's Café
Roy Yamaguchi
2F Mori Tower - Atago
Green Hills 2F
2-5-1 Atago Minato-ku,
Tokyo 105-6202
Japan
(+81) 3-5733-3400
www.roysrestaurants.com

Roy's Tokyo Bar & Grill
Roy Yamaguchi
5F West Walk in
Roppongi Hills
6-10-1 Roppongi
Minato-ku, Tokyo
106-0032
Japan
(+81) 3-5475-8181
www.roysrestaurants.com

SINGAPORE

Din Tai Fung
Frank Yang
290 Orchard Road
Singapore
(+65) 6836-8336

Hua Ting at Orchard Hotel Singapore
Kwok Chan
442 Orchard Road
Singapore, 238879
Singapore
(+65) 6734-3880
www.orchardhotel.com.sg

SOUTH KOREA

Wooreega
An Jung-Hyun
93-14 Samdo Building,
behind the M-net building
in Cheongdam-dong
Seoul
South Korea
(+82) 2-3442-2288

TAIWAN

Din Tai Fung
Frank Yang
218 Chung Hsiao East
Road
Section 4, Taipei
Taiwan
(+886) 2-2721-7890

Din Tai Fung
Frank Yang
194 Xin Yi Road
Section 2, Taipei
Taiwan
(+886) 2- 2321 8928

Tien Hsiang Lo at The Landis Taipei Hotel
Hsiu-Pao Tseng
41 Min Chuan East Road
Section 2, Taipei
Taiwan 104
(+886) 2-2597-1234
www.landistpe.com.tw

THAILAND

Baan Rim Naam at The Oriental
Vichit Mukura
48 Oriental Avenue
Bangkok, 10500
Thailand
(+66) 2659- 9000
www.mandarinoriental.com

THE BAHAMAS

Dune at the Ocean Club
Jean-Georges Vongerichten
Paradise Island
Nassau
The Bahamas
(+242) 363-2501
www.jean-georges.com

UNITED ARAB EMIRATES

Khazana Restaurant
Sanjeev Kapoor
Al Nasr Leisureland
Karama, Dubai
United Arab Emirates
(+971) 4-3360061
www.sanjeevkapoor.com

UNITED KINGDOM

Cafe Paul Rankin
Paul Rankin
Fountain Street
Belfast
United Kingdom
(+44) 28-9031-5090
www.rankingroup.co.uk

Cafe Paul Rankin
Paul Rankin
Arthur Street
Belfast
United Kingdom
(+44) 28-9031-0108
www.rankingroup.co.uk

Cafe Paul Rankin
Paul Rankin
Castlecourt Shopping
Center
Belfast
United Kingdom
(+44) 28-9024-8411
www.rankingroup.co.uk

Cafe Paul Rankin
Paul Rankin
Belfast International
Airport
(Departures Lounge)
Antrim
United Kingdom
(+44) 28-9445-4992
www.rankingroup.co.uk

Cafe Paul Rankin
Paul Rankin
High Street Mall
Portadown
United Kingdom
(+44) 28-3839-8818
www.rankingroup.co.uk

Cafe Paul Rankin
Paul Rankin
Junction One
International Outlet
Center
Antrim
United Kingdom
(+44) 28-9446-0370
www.rankingroup.co.uk

Cafe Paul Rankin
Paul Rankin
Bow Street
Lisburn
United Kingdom
(+44) 28-9262-9045
www.rankingroup.co.uk

Cafe Paul Rankin
Paul Rankin
Lisburn Road
Belfast
United Kingdom
(+44) 28-9066-8350
www.rankingroup.co.uk

Cayenne
Paul Rankin
7 Ascot House,
Shaftesbury Square
Belfast, BT2 7DB
United Kingdom
(+44) 28- 9033-1532
www.rankingroup.co.uk

Nobu Berkeley
Nobu Matsuhisa
15 Berkeley Street
London, W1J 8DY
United Kingdom
(+44) 20-7290-9222
www.noburestaurants.com

Nobu London
Nobu Matsuhisa
19 Old Park Lane
London, W1K 1LB
United Kingdom
(+44) 20-7447-4747
www.noburestaurants.com

Rain City
Paul Rankin
33-35 Malone Road
Belfast, BT9 6RU
United Kingdom
(+44) 28-9068-2929
www.rankingroup.co.uk

Roscoff Brasserie
Paul Rankin
7-11 Linenhall Street
Belfast, BT2 8AA
United Kingdom
(+44) 28-9031-1150
www.rankingroup.co.uk

Ubon by Nobu
Nobu Matsuhisa
34 Westferry Circus,
Canary Wharf
London, E14 8RR
United Kingdom
(+44) 20-7719-7800
www.noburestaurants.com

Zuma
Ricardo Zarate
5 Raphael Street
Knightsbridge, SW7 1DL
United Kingdom
(+44) 20-7584-1010

VIETNAM

Le Beaulieu & The Spices Garden at Hotel Sofitel Metropole Hanoi
Didier Corlou
15 Ngo Quyen Street
Hanoi
Vietnam
(+84) 4-8266919
www.sofitel.com

TRACK YOUR CULINARY ADVENTURES

NEW ASIAN CUISINE encourages you to visit the restaurants of the participating chefs, who have made this book possible. Document your visit in this section, and soon you will have a book filled with wonderful memories. This is your passport to fabulous eating around the world.

Dining Passport

Visit us online at **www.newasiancuisine.com** to find out about upcoming events and activities related to our chefs, including openings of new restaurants. Sign up for a free subscription of our newsletter for more cooking tips, interviews with chefs, and to be among the first to know about new cookbook releases, special events, culinary classes and chef tours.

Visit www.DiscoverHongKong.com and watch for news about *Gourmet Paradise*.

RESTAURANT

City

Date of Visit

Company

Favorite Dish

Journal

Autograph

RESTAURANT

City

Date of Visit

Company

Favorite Dish

Journal

Autograph

RESTAURANT

City

Date of Visit

Company

Favorite Dish

Journal

Autograph

RESTAURANT

City

Date of Visit

Company

Favorite Dish

Journal

Autograph

RESTAURANT

City

Date of Visit

Company

Favorite Dish

Journal

Autograph

RESTAURANT

City

Date of Visit

Company

Favorite Dish

Journal

Autograph

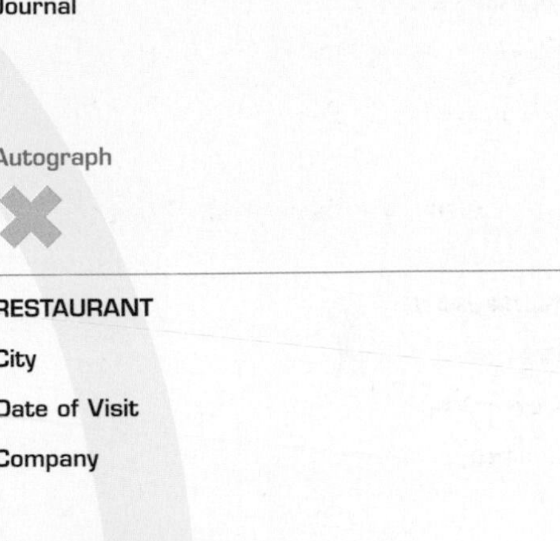

RESTAURANT

City

Date of Visit

Company

Favorite Dish

Journal

Autograph

RESTAURANT

City

Date of Visit

Company

Favorite Dish

Journal

Autograph

RESTAURANT

City

Date of Visit

Company

Favorite Dish

Journal

Autograph

RESTAURANT

City

Date of Visit

Company

Favorite Dish

Journal

Autograph

RESTAURANT

City

Date of Visit

Company

Favorite Dish

Journal

Autograph

✖

RESTAURANT

City

Date of Visit

Company

Favorite Dish

Journal

Autograph

✖

RESTAURANT

City

Date of Visit

Company

Favorite Dish

Journal

Autograph

✖

RESTAURANT

City

Date of Visit

Company

Favorite Dish

Journal

Autograph

✖

RESTAURANT

City

Date of Visit

Company

Favorite Dish

Journal

Autograph

✖

RESTAURANT

City

Date of Visit

Company

Favorite Dish

Journal

Autograph

✖

RESTAURANT

City

Date of Visit

Company

Favorite Dish

Journal

Autograph

RESTAURANT

City

Date of Visit

Company

Favorite Dish

Journal

Autograph

RESTAURANT

City

Date of Visit

Company

Favorite Dish

Journal

Autograph

RESTAURANT

City

Date of Visit

Company

Favorite Dish

Journal

Autograph

RESTAURANT

City

Date of Visit

Company

Favorite Dish

Journal

Autograph

RESTAURANT

City

Date of Visit

Company

Favorite Dish

Journal

Autograph

RESTAURANT

City

Date of Visit

Company

Favorite Dish

Journal

Autograph

✖

RESTAURANT

City

Date of Visit

Company

Favorite Dish

Journal

Autograph

✖

RESTAURANT

City

Date of Visit

Company

Favorite Dish

Journal

Autograph

✖

RESTAURANT

City

Date of Visit

Company

Favorite Dish

Journal

Autograph

✖

RESTAURANT

City

Date of Visit

Company

Favorite Dish

Journal

Autograph

✖

RESTAURANT

City

Date of Visit

Company

Favorite Dish

Journal

Autograph

✖

RESTAURANT

City

Date of Visit

Company

Favorite Dish

Journal

Autograph

RESTAURANT

City

Date of Visit

Company

Favorite Dish

Journal

Autograph

RESTAURANT

City

Date of Visit

Company

Favorite Dish

Journal

Autograph

RESTAURANT

City

Date of Visit

Company

Favorite Dish

Journal

Autograph

RESTAURANT

City

Date of Visit

Company

Favorite Dish

Journal

Autograph

RESTAURANT

City

Date of Visit

Company

Favorite Dish

Journal

Autograph

RESTAURANT

City

Date of Visit

Company

Favorite Dish

Journal

Autograph

RESTAURANT

City

Date of Visit

Company

Favorite Dish

Journal

Autograph

RESTAURANT

City

Date of Visit

Company

Favorite Dish

Journal

Autograph

RESTAURANT

City

Date of Visit

Company

Favorite Dish

Journal

Autograph

RESTAURANT

City

Date of Visit

Company

Favorite Dish

Journal

Autograph

RESTAURANT

City

Date of Visit

Company

Favorite Dish

Journal

Autograph

RESTAURANT

City

Date of Visit

Company

Favorite Dish

Journal

Autograph

RESTAURANT

City

Date of Visit

Company

Favorite Dish

Journal

Autograph

RESTAURANT

City

Date of Visit

Company

Favorite Dish

Journal

Autograph

RESTAURANT

City

Date of Visit

Company

Favorite Dish

Journal

Autograph

RESTAURANT

City

Date of Visit

Company

Favorite Dish

Journal

Autograph

RESTAURANT

City

Date of Visit

Company

Favorite Dish

Journal

Autograph

RESTAURANT

City

Date of Visit

Company

Favorite Dish

Journal

Autograph

✖

RESTAURANT

City

Date of Visit

Company

Favorite Dish

Journal

Autograph

✖

RESTAURANT

City

Date of Visit

Company

Favorite Dish

Journal

Autograph

✖

RESTAURANT

City

Date of Visit

Company

Favorite Dish

Journal

Autograph

✖

RESTAURANT

City

Date of Visit

Company

Favorite Dish

Journal

Autograph

✖

RESTAURANT

City

Date of Visit

Company

Favorite Dish

Journal

Autograph

✖

RESTAURANT

City

Date of Visit

Company

Favorite Dish

Journal

Autograph

RESTAURANT

City

Date of Visit

Company

Favorite Dish

Journal

Autograph

RESTAURANT

City

Date of Visit

Company

Favorite Dish

Journal

Autograph

RESTAURANT

City

Date of Visit

Company

Favorite Dish

Journal

Autograph

RESTAURANT

City

Date of Visit

Company

Favorite Dish

Journal

Autograph

RESTAURANT

City

Date of Visit

Company

Favorite Dish

Journal

Autograph

RESTAURANT
City
Date of Visit
Company

Favorite Dish

Journal

Autograph
✖

RESTAURANT
City
Date of Visit
Company

Favorite Dish

Journal

Autograph
✖

RESTAURANT
City
Date of Visit
Company

Favorite Dish

Journal

Autograph
✖

RESTAURANT
City
Date of Visit
Company

Favorite Dish

Journal

Autograph
✖

RESTAURANT
City
Date of Visit
Company

Favorite Dish

Journal

Autograph
✖

RESTAURANT
City
Date of Visit
Company

Favorite Dish

Journal

Autograph
✖

RESTAURANT
City
Date of Visit
Company

Favorite Dish

Journal

Autograph

RESTAURANT
City
Date of Visit
Company

Favorite Dish

Journal

Autograph

RESTAURANT
City
Date of Visit
Company

Favorite Dish

Journal

Autograph

RESTAURANT
City
Date of Visit
Company

Favorite Dish

Journal

Autograph

RESTAURANT
City
Date of Visit
Company

Favorite Dish

Journal

Autograph

RESTAURANT
City
Date of Visit
Company

Favorite Dish

Journal

Autograph

INDEX BY CHEF

INDEX BY RECIPE

ASIAN COCKTAILS 244-259

DESSERTS 216-243

FISH & SEAFOOD 74-135

MEAT & POULTRY 136-175

RICE & NOODLES 176-189

SALADS 42-61

SMALL PLATES 20-41

RECIPE CARDS

NEW ASIAN CUISINE

JASMINE BROWN RICE TABOULEH

PREMIUM QUALITY ROXY®

INGREDIENTS:

FOR RICE
2 cups **CHIMES GARDEN** Organic Jasmine Brown Rice
3 cups mushroom or vegetable stock, hot
1 sheet kombu (kelp)
1/4 cup olive oil
4 shallots, minced
1 inch piece fresh ginger, crushed
1/2 teaspoon salt

FOR GARNISH
1/2 cup parsley, minced
1/2 cup cilantro, minced
1/4 cup spearmint, minced
2 tablespoons lemon grass, ground
1 cup cucumber, small diced
1 cup tomato, small diced
1/2 cup green mango, small diced
1/4 cup scallions, minced
1/4 celery, small diced

FOR DRESSING
1 tablespoon soy sauce
1 tablespoon dark sesame oil
3 tablespoons peanut oil
1 teaspoon lime juice
1 teaspoon lemon juice
1 teaspoon tamarind paste, strained
1/4 teaspoon freshly ground black pepper
salt to taste

NEW ASIAN CUISINE

WOK-FRIED DICED RIBEYE STEAK WITH BULL HEAD BBQ SAUCE

INGREDIENTS:

10 ounce ribeye steak
1 clove garlic, minced
1 whole medium green bell pepper, cut into 1 inch triangles
1 whole medium red bell pepper, cut into 1 inch triangles
2 stalks celery, bias cut into 1 inch slices
3 ounces fresh mushrooms, cut into big pieces
3 ounces oyster mushrooms, cut into big pieces
1 1/2 ounces pineapple (fresh or canned) chopped
1 ounce butter

FOR SEASONING
1 teaspoon sugar
1 tablespoon **BULL HEAD®** BBQ Sauce
(a distinctive Asian sauce made from soy bean oil, garlic, shallots, chilies, spice and dried seafood)
1 teaspoon fish sauce

NEW ASIAN CUISINE

FRESH TOMATO BAKED ABALONE

PREMIUM QUALITY ROXY®

INGREDIENTS:

8 ounce can fresh **ROXY® BRAND** Whole Mexican Red Abalone
8 medium fresh tomatoes
1 teaspoon fresh ginger, minced
1 teaspoon chopped onion
1 cup tomato paste
2 tablespoons vegetable oil
2 tablespoons unrefined sugar
1 teaspoon table salt
1 tablespoon cornstarch
3 cups of water

NOTE: Fresh abalone, as opposed to the dried version which is typically extremely pricey, is easy to cook, very tender, and much less expensive. It is a good source of Vitamin E, Thiamin, Vitamin B12, Iron, Magnesium, Phosphorus, and protein. Whole abalones are considered a deluxe Chinese banquet essential.

NEW ASIAN CUISINE

METHOD:

Put kombu into hot vegetable stock and boil for 15 minutes then drain and discard kombu. Sweat shallots and ginger in olive oil, add brown rice, stir to combine. Add hot stock and stir only a couple times to combine. Cover and place in oven for 20 minutes. When rice is cooked, remove and spread in thin layer on sheet pan to cool. Reserve for later use.

Prep all garnish as described. Set aside for later use. Prepare dressing by combining all ingredients in bowl and mix together. In a large bowl fluff together cool rice and all of the garnish ingredients.

Drizzle prepared dressing into rice and garnish mixture. Lightly and gently toss to combine— DO NOT STIR. Serve cool in large bowl or on a platter.

Serves 10

CHEF: Professor Michael Pardus, *The Culinary Institute of America/Hyde Park, NY*

www.newasiancuisine.com www.roxytrading.com

NEW ASIAN CUISINE

METHOD:

Heat saucepan with a dab of butter, fry whole piece of steak until rare (half done).

Dice meat into 1/2 inch cubes.

Use fat in saucepan to fry the mushrooms until almost soft and set aside.

Heat the wok until hot, put in remaining butter and then add garlic. Quickly put all chopped red and green bell pepper, celery, and mushroom pieces, and mix well with spatula; then add in steak cubes.

Add the seasoning directly into wok, mix well with all ingredients and serve hot.

Serves 6

CHEF: Tony Su, *New Canton Seafood Restaurant/Sacramento, CA*

www.newasiancuisine.com www.roxytrading.com

NEW ASIAN CUISINE

METHOD:

After opening, drain water from can. Put abalone, ginger, onion and sugar in wok and cook at medium heat for 30 minutes.

Peel tomato skin after boiling them a few seconds to soften their skin. Skin can be left on if it's not too thick to preserve the vitamins in it. Cut a hole in top center of the tomato large enough to insert the abalone.

Fry minced ginger in oil until brown; add tomato paste, sugar, salt, cornstarch and stir to make paste. Pour paste over tomatoes that are stuffed with abalone and heat in oven for 10 minutes in medium high heat.

Sprinkle chopped green onions and serve.

Serves 8

CHEF: Michael Au, *Asian Pearl/Richmond, CA*

www.newasiancuisine.com www.roxytrading.com

NEW ASIAN CUISINE

THAI STYLE RED CURRY CHICKEN WITH JASMINE RICE

INGREDIENTS:

2 cups **WANG DERM BRAND™** Thai Jasmine Rice
1 cup thinly sliced chicken breast
1 1/2 cups **CHAO KOH™** Coconut Milk
1/2 cup sliced bamboo shoots
3 kaffir lime leaves
1/2 cup basil
2 tablespoons vegetable oil
2 1/2 tablespoons fish sauce
1 teaspoon palm sugar
1 tablespoon **MAE PLOY™** Red Curry Paste
2 sliced red hot chili peppers

NEW ASIAN CUISINE

SEASONED FRIED CHICKEN WINGS WITH SWEET CHILI SAUCE

INGREDIENTS:

1 pound chicken wings
1/8 cup black pepper
1/3 cup cilantro root
1/3 cup finely chopped fresh garlic
1/2 cup soy sauce
1/2 cup whole Thai Basil leaves
1 tablespoon salt
1 cup all purpose flour
frying oil
1 cup **MAE PLOY™** Sweet Chili Sauce for dipping

METHOD:

Mix seasonings together in large bowl, add chicken wings and toss to coat with seasonings. Allow to marinate for 30 minutes. Roll wings in flour, shake off excess flour and deep fry in hot oil until brown, turning occasionally.

Serve with MAE PLOY™ Sweet Chili Sauce.

Serves 4

NEW ASIAN CUISINE

TAMARIND AND SOY SAUCE CHICKEN

INGREDIENTS:

4 tablespoons **PEARL RIVER BRIDGE®** Premium Light Soy Sauce
2 tablespoons **PEARL RIVER BRIDGE®** Mushroom Flavored Superior Dark Soy Sauce
2 tablespoons tamarind concentrate
3 slices peeled ginger
3 pieces star anise
4 tablespoons brown sugar
2 tablespoons **PEARL RIVER BRIDGE®** cooking wine
1 stalk lemon grass, chopped into 1/2 inch lengths

FOR MEAT & SALAD
4 fresh chicken breasts, skin removed, washed and dried
2 tablespoons olive oil
salt and pepper (to taste)
1 cup organic field mix
2 tablespoons balsamic vinegar

NOTE: Pearl River Bridge soy sauces are brewed naturally and traditionally with high quality soy beans. They have no MSG, preservatives or other artificial coloring. They are lower in sodium than most other brands as well.

METHOD:

Heat oil in frying pan. Add Red Curry Paste and fry until fragrant. Add chicken and sauté to coat with sauce. Add coconut milk and bring to boil. Cook coconut mixture briefly until it begins to thicken. Add bamboo shoots. Add fish sauce and palm sugar to taste. Add Thai basil, kaffir lime leaves, and sliced chilies. Remove from heat and serve with steamed rice.

For steamed WANG DERM BRAND™ Thai Jasmine Rice:

Rice cooker: Rinse rice with water and drain. Add rice and 2 cups of water, start cooker.

Stove top: Rinse rice with water and drain. Without covering the saucepan, add rice and 3 cups of water over medium heat. Simmer until water is absorbed and rice grains are tender. Remove from heat. Stir and cover for 5 minutes before serving.

Serves 2-3

NOTE:

Asian meals are often served with rice and vegetables. This chicken wing dish is spicy and delicious, and best served with steamed WANG DERM BRAND™ Thai Jasmine Rice, with sliced raw peeled cucumber as a side dish.

METHOD:

Mix marinade in a large bowl with chicken pieces and refrigerate at least 4 hours (can be overnight); make sure the meat is well covered by laying flat.

Heat olive oil in a large saucepan over medium heat and brown chicken for about 3 minutes on each side. Cook meat in a pre heated 350° F oven for another seven minutes and remove.

In a deeper saucepan, bring marinade and balsamic vinegar to a simmer. Season with salt and pepper, if desired. Strain marinade with a fine mesh. When liquid is cool, emulsify with olive oil in a food processor till liquid is slightly thickened.

Serve roasted chicken over organic mix and drizzle with vinaigrette.

Serves 4

CHEF: Peng S. Looi, *Asiatique and August Moon Chinese Bistro/Louisville, KY*

RECIPE CARDS

NEW ASIAN CUISINE

CRAB MEAT FRITTATA WITH HEIRLOOM TOMATO AND OPAL BASIL

INGREDIENTS:

1 cup **PHILLIPS™** Crab Meat (any grade)
2 tablespoons extra virgin olive oil, divided
1 1/2 tablespoons butter, divided
1/4 cup shallots, diced
1/4 cup jalapeño pepper, julienned (optional)
1 cup heirloom tomato, peeled, seeded and diced
8 large eggs
salt and pepper to taste
4 stalks opal basil, cut into 1 inch lengths
Thai sweet chili sauce

NOTE: Phillips Crab Meat is premium quality ready-to-eat pasteurized crab meat that requires no picking of shells. Crab meat is high in protein, rich in Selenium, and a good source of Magnesium and Vitamin B6.

NEW ASIAN CUISINE

CRAB MEAT SPRING ROLLS WITH SHIITAKE MUSHROOMS AND NUOC NAM SAUCE

Phillips™
FOODS, INC.

INGREDIENTS:

1 pound **PHILLIPS™** Crab Meat (any grade)
20 chives, about 2 bunches
frying oil
1 tablespoon garlic, chopped
2 tablespoons shallot, chopped
1 cup Shiitake mushroom caps, chopped
1 teaspoon sea salt
1 tablespoon sugar
1 tablespoon fish sauce (nuoc nam)
freshly ground pepper
20 rice paper sheets or spring roll wrappers
1 bunch fresh mint for garnish

FOR NUOC NAM DIPPING SAUCE
1 teaspoon Asian chili paste, or 3 fresh red chilies, chopped
1 teaspoon Vietnamese chili garlic sauce
3 cloves garlic, finely chopped
1/4 cup sugar
3 tablespoons fresh lime juice
1 tablespoon vinegar
3 tablespoons fish sauce (nuoc nam)
1/2 cup water
1/2 teaspoon salt

NEW ASIAN CUISINE

ROAST DUCK & GOLD KIWIFRUIT

INGREDIENTS:

1 Chinese-style roast duck (buy from a Chinese Barbeque store)
4 **ZESPRI™ GOLD** Kiwifruit
1/2 cup roasted, salted cashew nuts, chopped
1 pack of bamboo skewers
watercress, to garnish

METHOD:

Take the duck meat from the bone, discarding any fat, and slice the meat into bite-size pieces.

Slice kiwifruit into halves and spoon out into large chunks, roughly the same size as the pieces of duck.

Spear the fruit and pieces of duck onto skewers.

Put the skewers on a platter, sprinkle with the chopped nuts, and garnish the dish with watercress.

Serves 4

METHOD:

Preheat oven to 400° F. Heat 1 tablespoon of olive oil and 1/2 tablespoon of butter in a large heavy base frying pan. Add shallots and cook until caramelized. Add jalapeño and tomatoes and cook for another 2 to 3 minutes and set aside. Lightly whisk eggs in a bowl and stir in the tomato mixture. Season to taste with salt and pepper. Melt 1 tablespoon of butter with 1 tablespoon of olive oil over high heat until it becomes foamy. Add in the egg mixture. Sprinkle in the crab meat and basil and reduce heat. Using a spatula, draw the mixture from the pan's edge slowly to the center, forming large curds and distributing the ingredients evenly. Cook over low heat until almost set. Transfer the pan to the preheated oven and bake at 400° F until the frittata is cooked. Remove the frittata onto a warm plate. Serve with Thai sweet chili sauce and either crusty sourdough bread or steamed Jasmine rice.

Serves 4

CHEF: Simpson Wong, *Jefferson Grill/New York, NY*

METHOD:

Poach the chives and let them cool. Heat the oil in the wok and sauté the garlic and shallot until fragrant. Add the Shiitake mushrooms, salt, sugar, fish sauce and pepper, and cook for 2 minutes. Add the crab meat and cook for 2 minutes. Let cool.

Cut the rice paper sheets or spring roll wrappers in 5 inch x 5 inch squares. Put a spoon of crab meat mixture in the middle of each sheet and wrap tightly. Tie each with a stem of chive. Fry the pockets in hot oil until they are crispy. Combine all the ingredients of nuoc nam dipping sauce at once and mix well. Serve the spring rolls hot with the nuoc nam dipping sauce. Garnish with fresh mint.

Makes 20 pieces

CHEF: Michael Huynh, *Bao Noodles/New York, NY*

NOTE:

ZESPRI™ GOLD Kiwifruit is New Zealand's new national treasure. It has a pleasant tropical sweet flavor and is packed with Vitamin C, Vitamin E, Potassium and fiber.

BOOKMARKS

NEW ASIAN CUISINE

Eat more
varieties of vegetables

Choose more dark green
and yellow/orange vegetables

Choose more dry beans
and peas

A friendly reminder from:

South East Produce, Ltd. (USA)
Maspeth, NY
(718) 417-8080

NEW ASIAN CUISINE

Where to shop for Asian ingredients? Visit www.newasiancuisine.com for a complete directory of markets and online stores.

Shopping for Ingredients

New York
141-40 Northern Blvd.
Flushing, NY 11354
718-358-0700

156-40 Northern Blvd.
Flushing, NY 11354
718-888-0005

29-02 Union St.
Flushing, NY 11354
718-445-5656

400 Hillside Ave.
Williston Park, NY 11596
516-699-0270

59-18 Woodside Ave.
Woodside, NY 11377
718-446-0759

New Jersey
1720 Marlton Pike
Cherry Hill, NJ 08003
856-489-4611

25 Lafayette Ave.
Englewood, NJ 07631
201-871-8822

260 Bergen Tpke.
Little Ferry, NJ 07643
201-814-0400

321 Broad Ave.
Ridgefield, NJ 07657
201-943-9600

518-14 Old Post Rd.
Edison, NJ 08817
732-248-8586

Pennsylvania
1138 Bristol Oxford Valley Rd.
Levittown, PA 19057
215-949-1003

7320 Old York Rd.
Elkins Park, PA 19027
215-782-1801

7050 Terminal Square
Upper Darby, PA 19082

Maryland
800 North Rolling Rd.
Catonsville, MD 21228
443-612-9020

12015 Georgia Ave.
Silver Spring, MD 20902
301-942-5071

Virginia
8103 Lee Highway
Falls Church, VA 22042
703-573-6300

10780 Fairfax Blvd.
Fairfax, VA 22030
800-427-9870

Georgia
2550 Pleasant Hill Rd.
Duluth, GA 30096
678-543-4000

Illinois
Niles, IL— coming soon

ONLINE SHOPPING www.HMart.com

For complete updated directory of over 1200 Asian grocery stores in all 50 states and over 40 online grocery stores please visit www.newasiancuisine.com

Thank You to All of Our Friends & Sponsors!

東南農產公司
South East Produce, Ltd. (USA)

BULL HEAD® Barbecue Sauce

GM printing
gm3343388@aol.com

W.Y. INTERNATIONAL INC.
華粵國際有限公司